To Jo

INSP■RATORS

Leading the way in leadership

PETE COHEN

Doris shut up

Pete@petecohen.com

Published by
Filament Publishing Ltd
16 Croydon Road, Beddington, Croydon,
Surrey, CR0 4PA, United Kingdom.
Telephone +44 (0)20 8688 2598
www.filamentpublishing.com
info@filamentpublishing.com

© 2019 Pete Cohen
ISBN 978-1-912635-81-8
Printed by 4edge Ltd.

The right of Pete Cohen to be recognised as the author of this work has been
asserted by him in accordance with the Designs and Copyright Act 1988.
This book may not be copied in any way without the
prior written permission of the publishers.

Creative support by Cate Caruth of Creative Words Ltd.
www.creativewords.cc

Cover design, book design and layout by Johan Siebke
www.kobolt.co.uk - design@kobolt.co.uk

Why should you read this book?

What if there was a book which had been written just for you? A book for you to read at this moment in time – because it is the pivotal moment in your life? You bought it because it was calling to you – because it was meant for you and only you. What if it could speak directly to you to lead you on your way to leadership? What if that book was able to bring out the best in you and create, in you, a great leader?

- A leader who works first and foremost on themselves?
- A leader who takes on challenges and seemingly overwhelming odds?
- A leader who believes in the people around them and seeks to bring out the best in them?
- A leader who never gives up, even when it seems hopeless?
- A leader who inspires everyone around them?

What if there was a new hope?

About Pete Cohen

Pete Cohen is one of the world's leading inspirational keynote speakers and business coaches. Hundreds of thousands of people from all over the world have been motivated and inspired by Pete's presentations.

He has been supporting organisations and the people within them to flourish for over 25 years. As a professional keynote speaker and coach, he knows exactly what holds people back and has dedicated himself to helping them find their true path.

Pete coaches business leaders, executives, corporate teams and sporting stars to achieve their best. He has worked with companies such as IBM, Boots, Pfizer, Bic, Barclaycard, M&S, Bupa, Dell, BAA, Royal Bank of Scotland, Boehringer Ingelheim and Thomas Cook.

Pete's interactive style is fun, thought-provoking and leaves a lasting impression. He is the author of 18 published books, several of which have been best-sellers across the world. He has also presented his own TV show, *The Coach*, and was the resident Life Coach on *GMTV* for 12 years.

Pete's background is in leadership, psychology and sports science. He specialises in taking leadership and personal development to the masses in a way that is easy for people to understand and apply. Working in sports performance coaching, Pete has helped world-class sporting stars and teams reach their peak performance, including Sally Gunnell, Ronnie O'Sullivan, Ellen MacArthur, Roger Black, the Kent Cricket team and the Arsenal Football team.

Also by Pete Cohen

Slimming With Pete: Taking the Weight Off
Feeling Good For No Reason: Proven Tools For Lifelong Happiness; Transform Your Life And Relationships, Work For Everyone, Every Time (Things That Really Matter)
Doing It With Pete: The Lighten Up Slimming Fun Book
Lighten Up: Feel-Good Slimming
Lighten Up: The Four-Week Weight Loss Plan
Habit Busting: A 10-Step Plan That Will Change Your Life
Fear Busting: A Proven Plan to Beat Fear and Change Your Life
Habit Busting: Stop Smoking
Habit Busting: Boost Your Self-Esteem
Life DIY: 12 Simple Steps to Transform Your Life
Ditch the Diet: 4 Steps to Reshaping Your Body
Body DIY
Sort Your Life Out: A 21-Day Programme to Help You Create the Life You Want
Sort Your Life Out – Slimming
Sort Your Life Out – Reshape Your Body and Mind
The Team Hannah Cookbook
Shut the Duck Up!
Why Am I Not Losing Weight?

The real inspirators

In the course of writing this book, I had the privilege to interview a number of inspiring leaders; some I have coached, some have been friends for many years and some I have met in the course of my work as a speaker and a leadership coach.

You will see their wisdom throughout the book. Their help and generosity in sharing their own journey is gratefully acknowledged. The Inspirators are:

- Alistair McAuley - Managing Director, AksoNobel N.U.
- Delphine Rive - Managing Director, Accenture UK
- Glyn House - Managing Director, Caffè Nero
- Richard Curen - Leadership Psychotherapist
- Chris Roebuck - Professor of Transformational Leadership
- Neal Stephens - Managing Director, Willmott Dixon South West
- Patti Dobrowolski - Visual Thinker and Change Activator
- Tony Taylor - Director, Leading International Bank
- Warren Rosenberg - Managing Director, Fusion Students Ltd
- Lucy Melling - Managing Director, Edelman UK
- Jon Sellins - Operations Director, The Football Association
- Simon Cook - Principal and CEO, Mid Kent College
- Drew Brown - Group Managing Director, nationally recognised hospitality business
- Chris Warburton - Expert in Innovating Processes

You will find the full interviews with these and other Inspirators at: www.inspirators.me

Here you will also be able to apply to become a part of my Inspirators Community, a place where like-minded leaders in business and in life can come together to share their journey and support one another.

You will find us at inspirators.me. To create a free account enter the promotional code: INSPIRATOR-FREE

Forewords

Alistair McAuley

Leadership is one of the most powerful commodities of the modern era.

Leading (and following) is something we all experience across many walks of life. We put our leadership skills to the test in many different ways – parenting; sport; business; religion; politics; schools; military and this has been the case for centuries. There is no pinnacle of leadership and as a result we all have the opportunity to improve. It's the curiosity behind great leadership that connected Pete and I and we've since become great friends as we've explored the breadth and depth of 'leadership.'

In *Inspirators* Pete brings this curiosity to life and on the back of many interviews Pete articulates what inspires people to grow as leaders. As authenticity sits at the heart of being a great leader, no two leaders are the same but many have similar attributes in their leadership DNA – character, composure, competence, compassion and confidence – and it's how we each adapt and flex each of these attributes that makes each individual leadership story so compelling.

A great leader truly excels at inspiring and enabling others to fulfil their dreams. They create the best possible environment for success and do this with humility and authenticity in their hunt for excellence.

The leadership journey never ends so let's all make the most of learning from each other to make a positive impact on society and become the inspirators Pete talks about.

Time to inspirate!

Alistair McAuley
Managing Director UK & Ireland,
Decorative Paints & UK Country Director at AkzoNobel

Forewords

Neal Stephens

A great question to start with is 'Why is Leadership so Important?'

Well, it is such a privilege to be a leader, to think that anybody would want to follow you in an organisation or even socially is such a fantastic honour. The thing is, how do we know if we are going to be a good leader or not. The fact is, we really don't until we've practised the art for some time and then sought feedback. It really is a journey and, speaking from experience, an exciting one at that. But it is incredibly important to realise is that if we want to be a remarkable leader, then we need to start off by getting the best advice we can get.

Leadership is personal. We can learn so much from our experience with our previous bosses. We already may have learnt an awful lot from our time in the workplace. This book, however, can really support you on the journey. It simplifies a significant amount of the key messages and the key directions that are needed to become a leader.

There is a lot in here about self-awareness and I believe that, without self-awareness, people cannot change and evolve and there must be a real curiosity and determination from within to drive you, to see how far you can go.

You also need to consider the understanding of others and what your role will be. It is about creating the right environment to allow your followers to flourish and achieve their potential.

Emotional intelligence is another key ingredient in leadership. It enables you to understand people all around you, understanding what their drivers are, understanding what part they can play in the game and, if they are playing your game, what position are you going to put them in?

Finally, it is about taking responsibility for making the big decisions. This book will help you plan your journey, reflect on progress and hopefully inspire you to drive to become the best leader you can possibly be. After all, what else would you want to achieve if it's not to be the best you can be?

So this book will ask lots and lots of questions and it is very thought provoking. Pete does it in such a fun way, referring to his research, with quotes from inspirational leaders from around the world and even referring back to films and key messages within them. I really enjoyed it and I reckon whether you are already on the leadership journey or whether you are just starting out, this book can be especially helpful and I'm sure it will inspire you to become the best you can be.

Neal Stephens
Managing Director
Willmott Dixon Construction for Wales and the South West of England
for the last 10 years

Willmott Dixon was placed 4th in the Sunday Times top 100 companies 2019
(1st place for Wales and the South West).

Dedication

This book is dedicated to my Dad, David Alan Cohen. He passed away on the 12th of May 2018, during the writing of this book.

Dad was a major positive influence in my life and always encouraged and inspired me to be the leader in my own life.

As well as helping others, my father was fascinated with the First World War. I didn't really understand his fascination until I was older, when he took me to the battlefields in Belgium and I was awestruck by the magnitude of what went on there.

What he loved about this period of history was the camaraderie of people. He would tell me the story of soldiers who were living in the most appalling conditions in the trenches. Yet they all supported each other as one big family. Many of the soldiers who were shot and taken to nearby hospitals, discharged themselves and returned to the front line because they needed to support their comrades.

I knew Dad was an inspiring person but it really hit home after he passed away. Mum received so many heartfelt letters from people who knew Dad. They all said similar things about how he always made people feel special and important. He had time for everyone and was genuinely interested in them.

Dad dedicated his life to inspiring others and was a true Inspirator. His legacy lives on in me.

INSPIRATORS

Leading the Way in Leadership

BY PETE COHEN

Contents:

A New Hope?

A long time ago in a galaxy far, far away...

THE INSPIRATORS

Episode IV –
A New Hope
"It is a period of organisational turmoil. Employees are uninspired and frustrated at the continuing 'carrot and stick' approach to leadership and are rebelling against the dark side of power. In their struggles, they seek autonomy, mastery and purpose and demand leaders to inspire them and show the way by being the example. Seeing the resistance from leaders to adopt the new way and become a force for good, Pete Cohen sets out on a mission to unlock the secrets of the Inspirators that can save people and bring freedom to the workplace..."

I was seven when the original *Star Wars* first came out. As a child I was transfixed by the film. Partly, of course by the story, but also by the concept of the force – of how there is a power which binds us all together and we have a choice of how to use it.

> *The Force is what gives a Jedi his power. It's an energy field created by all living things. It surrounds us and penetrates us, it binds the galaxy together.*
> **Obi-Wan Kenobi, *Star Wars IV – A New Hope***

This resonates now, as I think and work and coach in the field of leadership.

 Why does anyone follow anyone? What is it that makes others trust them and support them to achieve their goals?
Why would anyone follow you?

The problem with a lot of leaders is that, as soon as they get the title, they think they've made it and the power goes to their head. This is the dark side of leadership.

This 'them and us' style of leadership, where leaders use power to get what they want, is all too familiar. These leaders think it is all about them – and so miss the point entirely. We can all think of someone who acts this way. Sometimes it is us!

The result of this style of leadership is that those who follow do what is asked of them because they feel they have no choice. They feel oppressed and uninspired so they operate well below their full potential. They do the bare minimum to get by or resist at every turn.

There are – there always have been – great leaders out there too. They lead the way for others by leading themselves. They have been able to share their vision and unite others behind a cause, inspiring people to move – often beyond anything they had believed possible – to create something together and change the world. These are the *Jedi Masters* in the leadership world.

And, just as the first step in becoming a Jedi Master is to master the force in yourself, the first step in becoming an Inspirator is mastering your own inner power.

That power can then be used for good – to inspire others to be their best or become leaders in their own right – or it can lead to something else.

I will show you how to tap into your force so that you can bring out the best in others. To help them to have clarity of where they're going and then step back and let them get on with it. It may well be that the direction of travel is into uncharted waters and you will be asking a lot of people to embark on that journey, but if that is what you are asking of them – *to boldly go where no one has gone before* – then **you** have to boldly go there **first**.

This book – this journey you are about to embark upon – is the quest to become a great leader; to become the best leader you can be; to lead the way as a leader by taking the lead in your own life.

Jon Sellins

I think we can overcomplicate it. I do understand why there are management books and courses and videos, of course. ... But I personally believe so much of management and leadership is common sense and just thinking about basic stuff. Like 'how do you want to be treated?'

It doesn't take a genius to realise that a workforce that is communicated with, that is told what the vision and the objective is, that understands the restraints they work under, and is told when things don't quite go right what's gone wrong – you know, is kept in the picture – is going to be a bit more productive and useful to you than one that is kept in the dark and treated shabbily.

The Inspirators

I'm going to give you a different perspective on leadership – to show you what it takes. I'm going to make you an Inspirator.

Inspiration, looking at its Latin roots, means 'breathing life into something'. An **Inspirator**, then, is breathing life into their purpose and breathing life into others to bring them along on their journey. The Inspirators tap into their inner powers, their potential and their unique gifts and bring them to life.

Inspirators have a clear vision of what they are here to do and breathe life into that vision. They make that a reality by working on themselves every day. By doing so, they breathe life into other people.

When they do, their vision becomes a self-fulfilling prophecy.

Are you up for the challenge?

To be worthy of following isn't something you can learn on a two-week training course in leadership. You can't read a book and be a leader (that includes this book, by the way. If you were expecting that reading this would make you a leader, I'm afraid you will be disappointed).

The work to become an Inspirator is an ongoing process which never ends. It's something that is always changing and evolving.

What's more, leadership isn't confined to the workplace. To be an Inspirator requires you to look at leadership in a holistic way.

- Your health
- Your family
- Your personal ambitions
- Your relationships
- Your work

To become a true leader – an Inspirator, who inspires everyone around them to give their best and to be a leader in their own right – is incredibly challenging.

Challenging maybe, but also crucial. I believe that there has never been a more important time to inspire everyone to be their best and to show them how to be leaders in their own right. I believe that we need an army of Inspirators to be the example and show the way – taking on the world of the 'quick fix' and the 'this is how you should feel' and the 'you aren't good enough.'

Just imagine for a moment, the impact that these concepts could have on the world and how people are feeling.

The question is, do you have what it takes to stick with it, even when the going gets tough? Even when you make mistakes and suffer for it? Even when everyone around you is telling you to quit?

If you do, the reward will be to become a better you.

An Inspirator is on a hero's journey

This is not a quick fix. What I am asking of you is to embark upon a journey to create a clear sense of your own identity. And the journey you are on is one that has been recognised and identified since people first started telling stories.

Chris Roebuck

The criticality of this is not that it's culturally sensitive, not that it's complex, not that it's difficult, it's just that organisations are trapped in their own vicious circle.

What has to happen is to break that vicious circle, somebody has to say, "Actually, you don't need to think about leadership in a complicated way. You don't need to do complicated stuff, because you don't have time. You just have to do simple, practical stuff on a day-to-day basis, that you are already doing.

In 1949, American academic Joseph Campbell published a book, *The Hero with a Thousand Faces*, based on his studies of myth and religion across the ages. He had discovered that all heroic tales have the same 17 stages and this Hero's Journey, has been recognised ever since as the basic structure of all myth, legend and literature.

Since Campbell first published his book, there have been countless adaptations of the hero's journey as other academics and writers built upon his original idea.

Most notably, film executive Christopher Vogler published *The Writer's Journey: Mythic Structure for* Writers in 1992, giving a 12-step adaptation of the Hero's Journey for use in the film industry. Ever wondered why films always have that same pleasing structure to them that we all recognise? Now you know.

Be it Campbell's original, Vogler's movie-inspired version or any of the many others, the journey that is mapped out is the same one you are about to embark on.

You are on your own Hero's Journey – the Inspirator's Journey, with its own 12 stages:

1. The unwritten future – looking at where you are now in your life
2. The power to change – hearing the call to become an Inspirator
3. The coach – guiding you on your journey
4. Ignoring your power – do you have the courage to answer the call?
5. Stepping into the unknown – and facing your fear
6. Getting lost along the way – the challenges of change and that pesky duck!
7. Like-minded people – who you surround yourself with
8. The darkest hour – as you hit your greatest challenges
9. Ipseity – understanding your inner self
10. The plateau – when you feel that things have stopped moving forward
11. Flourishing – understanding who you are and what helps you to shine
12. Finding true purpose – which becomes the beacon for your life

Recognising that this is the journey you are on is crucial, even if you decide that being an Inspirator is not for you. We are *all* on a hero's journey. We all face the ups and downs of life and, every time we think we have come through a challenge, another one invariably comes along to test us further.

Answer the call

I'm inviting you on a journey – a heroic journey to learn what it is you stand for – with me as your coach. I'm like Gandalf in *The Lord of the Rings*. I'm calling you to come on an adventure.

We all have a desire to grow and develop. For you to do that you need to bring from within you everything that makes you the best possible leader you can be; and you need to let go of the things which have been holding you back from living up to your true potential. But as you go to work on yourself, you realise that you can't really see what is going on within you to unlock your full potential.

You need a coach to help you do that – to uncover the leader who is locked within you, piece by piece, like a sculptor who chips away at a block of marble to reveal the beauty inside – and develop your character as an Inspirator.

Everyone needs coaching. It doesn't matter who you are. If look at successful people, anywhere in the world and in any generation, you see that people have a coach – they have a mentor. It is one of the master-strokes of success.

In this book, I am your coach. Not only is it what I love to do, but I have also helped people get life changing results.

I was brought up believing there is an answer to everything and raised with the confidence and desire to find these answers. That is why, for the past three decades, I have been seeking solutions to the challenges people face in life and in business. By working with Olympic champions, business leaders and multi-national corporations across the globe, I have been able to amass a wealth of inside knowledge when it comes to developing leadership potential in others. Over the years I have honed, adapted and developed my technique and coaching skills to be the best that I can be. It's not all celebrity clients and senior executives, however. I have also worked with hundreds of thousands of ordinary people across the world, helping them to become better versions of themselves and, in the process, learning and growing to become a better version of me. I specialise in helping people become the leader in their own life.

Using this book to coach you

Is it okay if we spend a moment or two explaining how to make the most of this book? If you've never worked with a coach before, it can be helpful to understand their approach and method. That way you can prepare yourself and really get the benefit from the experience.

The book will distil my years of research into leadership theory and practice. It will also draw on my own experiences of seeing what it takes to really bring out the best in people.

In every chapter there will be one or two key concepts for you to explore. I'll give you a few tools you can use to develop yourself. I'll ask you coaching questions for you to consider and to help you take the next step. I'll provide ways for you to apply what you are learning to inspire others to become their best.

Here are the features to look out for.

Your personal adventure

We all love a good story. Right from early childhood, it is something we all latch on to and enjoy.

We love films because of the stories they tell and because we can identify with the characters. We see a story unfold in two hours or so and it can inspire us. We can get great ideas from films as well as using them to detach from our own lives for a short while.

I intend to make use of that to guide you through this book. Using both the Inspirator's Journey I outlined earlier – a format we all recognise – and popular films to illustrate the stages in that journey, I will help you explore the concepts in this book.

I've chosen films which are popular enough that you probably know the story even if you've never seen them. You don't need to watch every film – though it is great if you decide to do so.

So, look out for the movie time boxes, where I'll highlight how the film I'm using for each chapter relates to the topic.

 Movie Time

I'll also share experiences from myself and others in boxes marked:

 Story Time

Everyone is on a hero's journey and seeing how other people's stories have influenced them can be really powerful.

Take time to stop and think

You'll see a couple of icons pop up throughout the chapters:

 The 'Pause' button is an opportunity for you to reflect on how the concepts I'm exploring relate to you.

I'll ask some coaching questions or challenge your thinking. You may like to keep a notebook to hand, and jot down a few thoughts. Or just write notes in the margin of the book itself.

The awareness icon is here to remind you to become aware of how you operate in the world.

I will invite you to think about your own journey, experiences and history. It may be uncomfortable to reflect in this way but it is worth it. The more aware you become, the more you will be able to make better choices.

Biology and Chemistry and Physics – Oh My!

The coaching and ideas I'm sharing with you comes from 30 years of experience and learning. It is backed up by science and research.

What I have found is that the answers to most people's questions are really quite simple but, as humans, we like to over-complicate things. It is something I have tried time and time again to address, especially in my books where I've banished the jargon and psychobabble too often associated with my profession. I've replaced it with clear, straightforward, everyday advice, powerful tools and effective techniques which empower, invigorate and set you free.

This book, then, is not about the science. It is about the **application** of science: of biology, chemistry and physics.

Biology – Do you know how you are wired up? As animals we are driven to grow and make a difference at the most basic level. If we do this, we get a chemical reaction.

Chemistry – What needs to happen for you to be at your best? Within the human body there are a mass of chemicals which work to produce feelings and responses. The key is to maximise Oxytocin (the 'love drug') so you can enjoy the process.

Physics – What gets you moving and keeps you moving? When you love what you are doing, you build momentum. You learn to work on yourself instead of being caught up in yourself.

Ultimately, coaching is helping you make the most of who you are.

I'm not going to ignore the evidence and research though, so look out for

The 30-second science spot

boxes which will share some of the experiments and science which backs up the coaching.

Tapping into ancient wisdom

These days, we are all talking about Artificial Intelligence (AI) – the science of creating thinking machines. In this book I'm going to introduce you to a different type of AI – *Ancient Intelligence.* So much of what we know now has its roots in ancient history. Look for the black 'AI' boxes which give the origins of the concepts I'm sharing – the Ancient Intelligence which forms the foundation of being an Inspirator.

The word *leader* seems to originate in Old English when it referred to the 'one who leads, is first or most prominent.' The concept is far older – the qualities of leadership are described in Sanskrit literature and by Sun Tzu as "intelligence, trustworthiness, humaneness, courage, and discipline".

To be the one that others want to follow is a very old idea indeed.

Learn from others

How did you learn when you were small?

By copying. It is how we all learn as children. Then, at school, we are told "don't copy" and we feel that it is wrong to do what someone else is doing.

I'm asking you to think differently about copying. I invite you to be curious about how other people have achieved success and to ask yourself:

- What did they do to be great?
- How can I learn from them?
- How do I apply this to my own life?

I have also interviewed some of the top Inspirators in industry today. They have shared their individual philosophies on leadership and the journey they have been on to get to where they are today. From them you can learn and be inspired. You'll see quotes from some of them throughout the chapters and you'll be able to watch the full interviews with them in our online area (more on that below).

You will also see this box throughout the book:

The 30-second history spot

This will share how figures in history have also applied the concepts we are exploring. Just as you can learn from inspiring leaders of today, you can learn from leaders of the past.

Inspiring others

This is a book about leadership. I'm assuming that you are reading it because you want to be an inspiring leader.

Throughout the chapters, the main focus is on you. To be an inspiring leader, the first person you have to inspire is yourself. You have to go first.

If you are leading others, however, you may want to understand how to apply the concepts to others. In every chapter, therefore, there is a section which is about inspiring other people. I'll build on the ideas from the chapter so you can see how they apply.

Doing deep work

Knowledge is great but it only becomes useful if you apply it. At the end of every chapter is the opportunity for you to go to work on yourself with a mixture of practical tools and coaching questions, which you can use every day on your own journey.

More than just a book

As well as the pages of this book and your application of what is here, I have created a library of online content too. My interviews with the Inspirators who feature in this book are all here.

You'll also find more interviews, meditations, exercises and links to other experts. You can find it here:

All of this will give you the opportunity for you to create your own unique style of leadership. I will help you find out who you really are, what you stand for and how to be true to that every single day.

The first challenge

One of the fundamental truths of life, is that you can't change other people. However much you wish you could make other people be or say or do what you want, the only person you have control over is **yourself**.

If you want other people to change, *you have to go first*. This is critical and is an aspect of leadership which is missing from the vast majority of books and courses on the topic.

If you were to look in the mirror right now would you be able to say:

I'm inspired by this person. I like what this person stands for. I would follow this person – whatever the adversity. I'm being the example and going first.

Would you feel fired up and excited by the prospect of working with yourself? And prepared to take risks and make difficult decisions?

Probably not! What you would see would not be the finished article. There would be parts of you which you would want to change and improve and parts of you which you'd really like to let go of. What you can see is what no one else sees and that makes us doubt our abilities as a leader.

What I am seeking to create in you is a leader who is so fired up about the journey they are on, that those around them are inspired to follow. That requires you to accept who you are right now – imperfections and all. Treat your imperfections as a blessing. You see, while none of us is the finished article, we do all want to get better.

This isn't just a business book, then. It is a journey of self-discovery.

Leaving a legacy

Throughout this book we will be using movie heroes as a metaphor for leadership. But great leaders exist in all walks of life – in politics and business and sport. The New Zealand rugby team is a great example of Inspirator behaviour. Every member of the team is on a mission to leave the team in a better shape than when they arrived. The outcome of that is unrivalled success.

I want *you* to have unrivalled success. I want you to be able to look back at what you did and see the imprint you have left – to see your legacy. You know, deep down, that is what you want to do – it is what we **all** want to do.

I'm going to make you the best leader you can be. I'm going to do *more* than that because I'm going to inspire you and I'm going to teach *you* to inspire. I'm going to show you how to be the most inspired and inspirational leader in the world.

I'm going to make you an *Inspirator.*

So, let's do this. Let's go to work!

1: Your Future is Unwritten

If you always do what you've always done, you'll always get what you've always got.

Wind's in the east, mist coming in,
Like somethin' is brewin' and 'bout to begin.
Can't put me finger on what lies in store,
But I fear what's to happen all happened before.
                              Bert – Mary Poppins

In this chapter, we will explore
- why it matters to start by knowing where you are
- how the power of awareness is essential
- what challenges we face when 'being ourselves'
- ways to inspire others by understanding where they are right now
- the tool which will help you throughout your leader's journey – keeping a journal.

⚠ WARNING!
Questions, questions and more questions.

Take a moment to consider: Do you believe this is true?

Your future is unwritten and you have the power to change.

This is a fundamental question that I ask every leader I work with, because once you believe that your future is unwritten and you have power to change, the next question is:

What are you going to do about it?

> ### *Movie Time*
> Just as Disney's *Mary Poppins* starts with a sense of anticipation, this book too, sees you on the verge of something. It has happened before, as I pointed out in the Introduction. Becoming an Inspirator isn't about anything new. It is something which others have already achieved and now it is time to unlock that same potential in you.

So why would I use a film like *Mary Poppins*, of all things, to start you on this journey to become an inspiring leader? It is a great film, I grant you, but it is a children's film (and includes one of the greatest travesties of fake accents to boot!). Surely I should have chosen something rather more imposing and serious?

No. Every film I use in this book should be familiar and accessible to all. Even if you've never seen it, most of us know the story – via the book if not from the screen. Every film has been chosen for a reason.

> ### *Movie Time*
> Mary Poppins is the epitome of a disruptive influence. Starting with the children and eventually, the entire Banks family, she shows them how to think and act differently. She arrives in their lives and challenges the status quo.

What do you think my role is in this book? Why do you think I have arrived in your life? Have I arrived to disrupt your status quo?

I am here to challenge you to become the most inspirational leader you can become. This is a proven process. It isn't something I made up last week. It has been 30 years in the making.

Are you ready to begin?

Where the hell am I?

Before we go heading off on our leader's journey together we are going to need to spend a chapter or two getting a few fundamentals in place. The first of these to consider is where you are now? More crucially, *who* are you now? And how do you feel?

These might seem like strange questions and they aren't ones that people get asked all that often. What these questions are trying to get at is the culture in you

– just as I always seek to understand the culture in any organisation. I want the culture you work in – the one within you – to be as good as it can possibly be, so it can spread. When I ask *Who are you?* I want to know, what is the culture like in you? What does it feel like to be you? How are things done around here? What sort of experience is that?

That might seem like it's not important but actually it is the most important thing. Knowing where you are is crucial. Why do you suppose that is?

> ### Story Time
> Just imagine you wanted to sail to New York. You have the ship and supplies, you have the map, you have the compass. Ask yourself: do you have everything you need?
> Not quite.
> Which direction do you plan to take first?
> What's your current location?
> Without it, you don't know whether you need to sail North or South.

The chances are, you are impatient to set sail, but hold back for a little while. Don't be tempted to skip these first few chapters in order to get into the 'doing' topics.

Mind the gap

As you spend time understanding your current position, are you aware of the patterns and themes in your life? Through these, you will start to understand what you do and don't need for your journey.

What I have found with 99.9% of the people I've worked with is that there is a gap between where they are and where they want to be. Perhaps you picked up this book because you are aware of that. Through this book, we will go to work on closing that gap. First, though, you have to understand it.

This fundamental principle applies in every case – whether you are about to embark on a sailing trip, like the example above, whether you are looking to develop yourself and become an Inspirator, or whether you are considering a vast global business.

Even in business, big or small, there is always that gap – *this is where the business is, this is where the business needs to be* – and the same rules apply. The people within that business need to know where they are, so they know where they're going.

This is a journey – a quest – to recognise that gap, to understand it and then to find ways to close it.

Of course, even knowing the nature of the gap, you have the choice to do nothing about it. You can decide that the way you are leading right now is good enough; command and control works just fine, thank you very much! You can look in the mirror to brush your hair and never question if you would like to follow the person looking back at you.

But what do you think will happen if you don't try to close that gap – if you decline my invitation to come on this quest to become the person that you want to follow? Then you fall into the world of mediocrity.

> The word **mediocrity** comes from the Latin words *medius*, meaning 'middle', and *ocris*, which is a 'rugged mountain.'
> So, literally, mediocrity is 'caught in the middle of a rugged mountain.'

Mediocrity **is** the gap. You may already be here. Or, as we go on this journey together you might be inspired to move forward, *Yes, this is great! Charge!* and all of a sudden, things get difficult, and you fall into the gap. Either way, the question remains the same.

If you are in that place – what are you going to do about it?

So, assuming you want to close that gap – that you aren't prepared to settle for being mediocre – we have to start by understanding who you are: what's driving you and what is wildly important to you right now.

Underpants on the outside – here is your Super Power

My role as your coach is to help you become aware of what you are doing.

Part of the process of becoming an Inspirator is to become aware of the person you are right now and how to let go of what you don't need. Do you, for example, have any habits which you know are holding you back or get in your way?

Awareness is the tool by which you see how you move through the world, and question it. It is how you look at what is really going on and leave behind what no longer serves you.

By being aware, you start to see the potential in yourself. Seeing this, you can cultivate what works within you and move forwards in a way that is powerful. You can write the future that inspires you and then help others to do the same.

The Inspirators I have worked with over the years are remarkable. They are people who have been successful at achieving whatever they set out to do. They have transformed failing organisations, become leaders in their field, and competed and won at international level in sport.

On one level they all have things in common, but on another level they are as unique and as individual as they can be.

They are all **aware,** however.

These Inspirators have identified the

Chris Roebuck

[Effective leadership is] a combination of a) self-awareness, and b) awareness of other people. It's the ability to read what other people are doing ... Most people can read what other people are doing, but only if they're looking ... [If] you're not looking for the responses that the people have, ... you're not aware of what they are, and therefore you cannot respond to them. ... [And they] then come to the conclusion that you only care about the task and not them. Then from that point onwards, it's downhill all the way.

thread that links them to happiness and success. These are individuals who have managed to figure out their uniqueness – what makes them great – and then put that at the service of their goals. They know who they are. And they are committed to being that person, every single day.

Some people believe that every one of us carries one true message that we are destined to live out and deliver. Inspirators are the people who have gone to work on mastering themselves and figured out their message.

One exercise I get aspiring Inspirators to do is to imagine they have found a bottle, washed up on the shore. In it is a really important message – perhaps the most important message they will ever read. Maybe it says:

> *You are here to inspire*
> *You can make a difference*
> *Those around you need you to be the example*

If that was you, what might your one true message be?

When you are first faced with questions like these, it can be challenging, especially if you don't know what your message would be. It is essential to work it out at some point, though; either now or on this journey. Maybe finding your true message **is** your journey.

For now, just concentrate on being aware.

Perspectives and Aspects

What I have found is that people don't make lasting change when we tell them what to do. They change when their perspective changes. One of my goals in working with you is to help you look at yourself, help you look at leadership, help you look at others and help you look at the future, in a way that empowers you to make decisions that will move you forwards in the direction that you want to go. As you become aware, your perspective will change. As you take on new ways of looking at things you will start to think, act and decide differently and you will impact the world in more positive ways.

Movie Time

This is why I chose *Mary Poppins* for this chapter. The movie is all about finding the way through awareness and showing new perspectives. And, if you've never watched it, commit to watching it (you can fast-forward through the song and dance routines if you aren't into musicals).

Mr. Banks is beset by tradition. He doesn't communicate well with the rest of his family and he sees the 'perfect life' as the one dictated to him by those he follows at work. He is presented as the leader in the Banks household but, of course, it is Mary who is the real leader. As she shows him a new perspective, he starts to wake up.

Then, when his young son, Michael, won't let go of his own perspective on the value of two-pence and disrupts all order, causing mayhem at the bank, it awakens his father to what is really important. Finally, in his darkest hour – when he loses his job in disgrace – Mr. Banks finds a new way of moving through the world.

Are you a Mr. Banks? Have you shaped your life around the opinions of others and, in the process, missed seeing what is really important and who you really are?

I was very fortunate in the coach I had for 16 years of my life. This man helped me address many things that were going on, but most importantly he helped me to wake up and see the world with a fresh pair of eyes. His view on perspective is one I want to share with you now.

> *It's not about the two sides: the right and the wrong, the good and the bad, the up and the down, or the positive and the negative. It's more than that. There are seven perspectives: front, back, left, right, up, down and **you**.*

Together we are going to step back and look at things from multiple perspectives, so you can work out what fits, what works, where you need to go, and 'now what needs to be done?'

The first of these multiple perspectives which will guide you to becoming an Inspirator, is to become aware of the aspects of leadership you need to address.

I call them the **Big Three**:

• Health
• Relationships
• Work

To be a true Inspirator is to take the lead and work to be better in **all** of these three aspects.

I want you to think about that for a moment.
Leadership – Inspirator-ship (if you will) is not just about the workplace. These three aspects are the three pillars which form the foundations of being an Inspirator; the complete leader; the complete you.

And health comes first.

Don't believe me? Just imagine the alternative for a moment. Hopefully you won't ever come to it but what if your health gets so bad that you wished you'd done something about it sooner? As well as being an investment in your future, working on your health gives you energy and the vitality to move forwards in your life and powers you up for the journey ahead. Health has the additional advantage in that it is something **everyone** can do to set an example, so it's a great place to start.

Relationships are another key area of being an Inspirator. Whether it's a mother, father, sister, brother, lover, child or friend, seeing your role to inspire and be worthy of being followed is a vital part of the work we are going to do together.

Only then do we focus on work. I believe if you get your health and relationships right, you will automatically be a better leader to peers and teams at work.

I get it Pete. You're talking about work-life balance, aren't you?

Not in the way most organisations refer to it. Their definition tends to be about fitting the rest of your life around work. I don't believe that *work-life balance* actually exists because 'balance' isn't a place or a destination. We don't reach a balance between the different aspects of life and then rest on our laurels, ("Hooray for me – I made it!"). No; it is *work-life balanc**ing*** – a constant process of fine-tuning to keep the different aspects of life in balance with one another and a constant effort to improve them all.

Take a whole-life view – not just in the workplace or in one aspect of life – and consider fuelling the life you are living via these questions:

- What impact do you have on those around you?
- What is your vision for the future?
- How would you describe your current mental and physical wellbeing?

Questions like these are testing, if you approach them honestly and with 100% commitment. My advice is that you don't judge. Merely be curious about where you are in your life right now.

Isn't it true that we are who we are because of the choices we've made in the past? Haven't we subscribed to beliefs which are based on past history and experiences? Are they all still true? That is the past. Look back over it to learn – but not to regret or to judge.

I'm here to tell you that you can make different choices to change who you are and become more inspirational – aka an Inspirator.

How you do anything is how you do everything

Would it be okay if I am totally honest and upfront here?[1]

This book is about your growth. It is about you getting better, learning and developing as you become the leader and the person you have chosen to be. That's why such a massive part of this is becoming aware and waking up to what you do and how you do it.

For example, what happens when your alarm wakes you up in the morning? What do you do? Do you press snooze? Do you press it once? Do you press it twice? Or do you lie there, procrastinating and talking yourself in and out of getting up?

Just become aware of what is going on behind the scenes. There's no right, there's no wrong. So few people, in my experience, even consider how they are – until, that is, they are in pain or ill. That is the only time most people know they are alive.

What if you could take responsibility for what is going on in your internal world – the one that no one else sees and maybe you haven't had the time to look at? As we go on this journey, this adventure, this quest, we will work together to make you the best *you* you can possibly be.

That is where the change really happens.

---

[1] *I'm assuming you've said 'yes'. If you said 'no' then please proceed to use this book to prop up the leg of a wobbly table.*

People mess you up!

When we are little we are great at being ourselves. We don't know how to be anything else yet.

Story Time
I had a friend who was a teacher, who once told me how, when he asked his class of four-year-olds, "Who's the best person in the class?" every hand went up.
When he repeated this with his class of seven-year-olds, they thought for a moment and then pointed at someone else.

As we grow, our internal culture shifts. We become more self-conscious, hierarchies form and insecurities are created. We have been told, 'don't show off,' or heard those around us define us – 'he's just shy', 'she's a bit of a drama queen' – or we have been placed in circumstances which cause us to question ourselves.

The result, by default, is that we become less good at being ourselves.

Of course, for many of us, some of this reverses itself as we get older. We realise there are less sunsets ahead of us than behind us, and we aren't as willing to play roles in our lives or do the things we don't want to do. We begin to realise, once again, what is really important.

Are you prepared to wait until old age for this to happen?

The most important job as an Inspirator is to be as good at being you as possible.

I want to make sure you understand that this is not about changing who you are. I am not going to assimilate you into the Borg Collective from *Star Trek*. It is more that you are the *Six-Million Dollar Man*, and, through this book, we are going to rebuild you. I am going to help you reawaken the confidence you had when you were four.

Being you

How many times in your life has somebody offered you a well-meaning piece of advice and said, 'Just be yourself.'?

It sounds so simple but we all know it is more complex than that, because who 'yourself' is at any point in time is shaped by what you think of yourself – and that might be the biggest obstacle to you being a true Inspirator.

Most of us don't have a particularly high opinion of ourselves, especially as we live in a society that tends to make us think negatively. We think constantly that we're not

Tony Taylor

What you have to do as a leader, is to understand those individuals, to see whether they fit into the team, but more importantly where they fit into the team. You actually then join that team together, and it becomes one functioning outfit.

quite good enough and we don't have what it takes to succeed. This may not apply to you, of course, but it will apply to the vast majority of those you lead.

The overriding message that the world we live in delivers, is 'you are not good enough' (followed by 'now buy this car/ this watch/ this perfume/ this pill' to try and close that gap). We feel that the only chance we have is to fit in.

Have you, at any time, been any of the following?

1. What you've been told about who you are

Many of us have! I know I have been in my past. We are so keen to be liked and to fit in that we act on the feedback we receive rather than be ourselves. We act according to what others have said about us, 'Don't shout', 'You are such a confident person', 'Lunchtime is at 12:30', and act accordingly.

This is the most visible *you* that we see in the world – meeting the expectations of others. There are as many opinions of you as there are people, so we are constantly changing who we are. In its extremes, it manifests as approval addiction and is very debilitating.

2. What you think others want to see of who you are

This is subtler, but no less debilitating. You have a wishbone instead of a backbone as you quash your own personality, constantly trying to present the most favourable side of yourself.

Decisions in the first case are supported by 'What do people expect?', while in this case they are made via 'How will I look?' This is how I moved through the world for so many years.

This way of moving through the world is one where you are constantly changing. Who you wish to be changes all the time and that means how you present yourself has to change too. For those around you, what they see is inconsistency.

Becoming aware of it was one of the biggest steps I ever took in being my best self and genuinely helping people to do the same.

Richard Curen

We all wear different hats at different times, in different social situations and work situations. We all have to put on a bit of a façade. ... Being authentic 24/7 is actually almost impossible ... But I think someone who ... can ask the right questions, [can] know themselves really well. I think that's really key.

3. What you think of yourself

When people operate from here, they will have a superiority or inferiority complex, or both. If you have a superiority complex, you pretty much think you're the most important person. If you've got an inferiority complex, you suffer from an over-modest self-regard.

Both of those amount to the same thing; you have a fragile ego. It's either delusions of grandeur or delusions of insignificance or both.

For a superiority complex you need other people to be smaller and to fit around you.

> ### *Movie Time*
> Mr. Banks operates from here. He is convinced he is right in being who he is, even though he isn't happy. He leads with a 'my way or the highway' style of leadership – a dictatorship! Those around are, as a result, unhappy, unfulfilled or (like Mrs. Banks) following as they must but paying little regard when he isn't there. He wants order, calm and quiet, and yet, as we know, life is none of those things. Banks wants his children to change, his wife to change, the world to change.

Changing other people isn't possible and it is the last thing an Inspirator wants. They want to inspire other people to change **themselves**.

Living according to any version of yourself except the real one has consequences. For those of us who operate in this way, things don't really work out. We tend to have good days and bad days, experiencing extremes of mood; how that manifests depends on the way you have learned to be. So, as we move through the world trying to meet expectations of either ourselves or others, our days will shape up in one of two ways.

Some days we congratulate ourselves for having impressed others, looked good in the eyes of others or having 'got away with it' on some challenge we feared might not work out. On other days, we castigate ourselves for not being good enough or not measuring up to others, or not having received the level of attention we crave from a peer or mentor.

One way or another, life always comes up short and we constantly ask "what else can I do?" to meet the invented expectations of others.

Whose 'you' are you being?

When I work with leaders I ask them "whose *you* are you being?" and who they have been to those they lead. Many are being what they thought they needed to be or how they felt a leader should be.

> Let me give you a snapshot of a different world. Imagine how it would be to live this way:
> You don't need approval from other people and you don't take yourself too seriously. When you see the successes of others, you don't compare yourself in order to see how you fail to measure up, because you don't worry about not being them. You rejoice in their talents and want to learn how to develop your own. You see your role as bringing out the greatness in others and assisting them to find their best selves.
> Welcome to the world of the Inspirator.

Do you believe everyone has their own thing, their own uniqueness and special gifts? Do you believe that everyone has the potential within themselves to be an

Inspirator? As your coach, my mission is to support and guide you in how best you can be your greatest self, even if you don't currently believe it.

Will it be fun?

Not always. Sometimes it will be challenging as I ask you lots of questions you may never have been asked before to bring this about.

Will it be worth it?

You tell me. I know that when you figure this out it will be powerful and hugely impactful and incredibly liberating.

Understanding these ways of moving through the world is really important for you – not only for your own development as a leader, but also your awareness of how all of the people you influence and inspire move through the world.

 So, let me ask you – what is the unique experience of being you? What is it like? How does it feel? Who *are* you?
Too many difficult questions? Try this one:
How are you?

I love that question! The origins of *how are you?* are religious. In the middle ages, it meant, "How are you with God?"

Now, this is not a religious book and I'm not here to talk to you about God. The essence of the question was about your spirit and your essential self. "How are you with yourself?"

 ### *Story Time*
When I work with athletes, I always ask them, "How are you feeling?"
How they are feeling before a competition, how they are feeling when they are in the middle of a contest, how they are feeling afterwards...
I want them to connect with the feeling of winning, not with how they are feeling right now.

These questions are everything. I'm asking, 'What is the experience like of being you?' And, 'Whose you are you being?'

Knowing the answer to these questions is the foundation and the starting point of all achievement. It gives you your compass bearing and it shows you your gap. It matters whatever you want to achieve in your life.

One of the leaders I worked with had a massive realisation about this.

When you look at the answer to that question honestly, you realise that you're not what you have; you're not what you do; you're not even who you love, or who loves you. What's more, you come to realise that you're not your thoughts (because it's you who thinks them), and you can't be your feelings, (otherwise who's the you that feels them?); you are more than this.

To be able to say, "This is who I am, this is how I feel about where I am, this is why I want to lead, this is where I want to go, this is who I must become," is where it all starts.

So, start with who **you** are now.

Saving Mr. Banks

Movie Time
In *Mary Poppins*, Mr. Banks is comfortably uncomfortable, which is where most people are. He's not really happy; he's clinging to the security of the accepted order of things and doing what is expected of him. He's not uncomfortable enough to make a shift and do things differently. Then Mary arrives and challenges what's normal because she can see quite clearly that there is gap which needs closing.

Mr. Banks tries to defend the normal and rejects everything she presents to him. He rejects what she says, rejects what his children say and rejects what his wife says.

Sometimes the easiest thing any of us can do is to walk away from the things we need to do. We ignore what's wrong and carry on doing what we've always done before. But if you always do what you've always done, you'll always get what you've always got.

At this point, some of you may be thinking this book isn't for you. All this work on yourself, rather than some nice tangible theories of leadership and management wasn't what you bargained for at all!
Just give me the tools I need to change people, Pete. Enough with all the questions, already!
If that is you, you'll find an exercise at the end of this chapter to help you.

Just as Mary helps, guides and coaches the Banks family, through this book I am here to help, guide you and coach you. It might help you to see me as your Mary Poppins[2] or as Obi-Wan Kenobi or Gandalf. I will help you see, *I need to let go of the things that have held me back. I need to let go of the need for people to think I'm important. I need to let go of my frustration and doubt. I need to let go of my insecurities. I'm ready to become an Inspirator.*

Even though those frustrations, doubts and insecurities will always be there, when you let go and stop investing in them, you place your power somewhere else. An Inspirator uses powers to inspire him or herself and to inspire others.

---

[2] *Although I don't have the bottomless carpet bag or the talking umbrella!*

Rebirth

Make the decision to become an Inspirator and your journey can start.

Mary's departure at the end of the film isn't an ending. It is a beginning for the Banks family. They are about to set out on a new journey in which they are free to be themselves and to be authentic. Mr. Banks' darkest hour – when he is fired from the bank – is also his rebirth.

As we work together and embark on this leader's journey, there will be many questions along the way. This is a quest and by committing yourself to the quest and immersing yourself in this process, you have an opportunity to do something truly amazing.

Relationships – Inspire other people

The main focus of this book is in helping you to become the person you want to follow. But we can't ignore that leadership is about inspiring others as well. So how does everything we've been covering here, relate to those you lead?

Why do people follow people?

When one looks at followers one can put people into two different camps:

- People who follow because they feel they have no choice. This may be because the leader is a dictator, or because the culture is one of conformity or they may simply have learned from their own past, not to question those in authority. One way or another, they have learned to "do as they are told." These people are 'easy' to manage but they are not at their best.
- People who only follow someone who is inspiring. If they believe in their leader, in what he/she says and does, they will give their all to help achieve the goals of their leader. When they aren't inspired they can sometimes be seen as 'difficult' and challenging. That's not what is going on for them though. They need to get something else from you to inspire them.

Warren Rosenburg

... you meet the same people on the way up that you will do on the way down, and ... you need to treat everyone in the same way; with decency, honesty, integrity.

In the introduction I asked you to look in the mirror and ask if you would follow yourself. When you look at yourself and consider the relationships you have, would other people follow you? *Do* other people follow you?

And, for other people to follow you, what do they *want* from you. It would be easy to act as you expect they want you to act – 'whose you are you being' remember? – but the truth is, what others truly want of us is to be authentic.

To be an Inspirator is to be the example – how you lead yourself – but it is also about relationships for others to follow. There needs to be a connection – a reason for them to follow you. Those around you are all asking themselves why they should follow you – what is in it for them if they do.

Maybe you are asking why you should follow *me*. It is what we all do. And if there isn't a good enough answer, guess what will happen?

Movie Time

Look at Mr. Banks – his children are disconnected from him because he doesn't listen and he isn't being a whole person. He doesn't see things from their perspective.

So many leaders are a Mr Banks. This is why I am calling you to be an Inspirator. The world needs you more than ever.

Just as you become aware of yourself, become aware of those you lead

Through the pages of this book I want to coach you to a point where awareness is the super-power you use every day so you can apply it to others as well as to yourself.

When you interact with people, I dare you to listen – to really listen – to what people say. If you find that uncomfortable, then be aware of that too.

Look for the clues that tell you what is really going on. Be curious. Ask open questions to help them see where they are. Ask "How can I help?" and "Is there anything you need from me?"

What answers would you get if you asked the same question Drew Brown asked?

*What does it **feel** like to work in this business?*

Would people be surprised that you had asked it? Would they feel able to give an honest reply?

I challenge you to try it – and then to think about what answer you would like them to give. That, then, is your culture gap.

Simon Cook

[To] anybody who thinks they want to be a leader, I would always say, "Do you really know what that is? Do you know what the responsibility is and are you prepared to take the responsibility? Are you prepared to be true to yourself, no matter what that means? And who's that going to upset?" That's really important.

Drew Brown

My first two weeks I went around all of my businesses and asked everybody that I met one question, "What does it feel like to work in this business?" And ultimately the response to that determines the culture. I didn't get any good answers, to be honest.

So... in 12 months' time ... the first thing I want them to say is, "The business cares about me." Because if somebody's working for an organisation and they think the company cares for them, that's priceless.

Deep work

To help you on your journey, I will end each chapter by providing you with some tools and questions which I invite you to work on by yourself. Set some time aside for these – they will really help you make sense of what you are learning.

 Just for a moment, pause and ask yourself *What is my biggest takeaway from this chapter?* Consider what ideas have most resonated and sparked thoughts for you. Then think about what you now need to do as a result of what you have learnt.
I invite you to do this at the end of every chapter.

Invest in a journal

Let's start with something really simple for you to do.

Is this journey worth taking? Are you feeling excited (even if you are also feeling a bit daunted)? If 'yes' then do you think this journey might be worth recording?

Get yourself a journal. It can be as simple or as fancy as you like and, if you already journal, what I'm suggesting here can be incorporated into what you already use, as long as there is enough space.

Writing things down as you discover them and making notes of what you learn through the questions I ask along the way, will help you massively. By keeping a journal you'll be able to look back and see the progress you have made.

Use your journal to record any thoughts which come to you as you read each chapter. Throughout, you'll see that I ask you to reflect on things and ask you questions. Use your journal to make notes as you go through the book. Then write your answers to the exercises and coaching questions I set at the end or every chapter.

As you complete each chapter, ask yourself:

What's my biggest learning so far?
What am I going to do with what I've learned?

To pause, reflect and review is essential so that you take what you've learned from one chapter into the next.

What's your story?

Spend time on these questions and note them down in your journal. As you do this, notice how you respond to the questions as well as the answers. Are you looking objectively at them and seeing where there is potential for work? Or are you judging yourself and beating yourself up? Or are you doubting the method and questioning why you have to spend all this time on the here and now instead of getting on and changing things?

None of these reactions is right or wrong (and they are all perfectly normal!).

Coaching questions
1. If you were asked for a story of your life up to now, what are the key events which you would talk about to explain how you got here?
2. On a scale of 1 to 10, how do you feel about where you are right now?
3. Looking back over your life, what achievements are you most proud of?
4. Between health, relationship and work, what % do you invest in each?

If you are thinking of putting this book down

This chapter may have felt challenging – and the easiest thing to do would be to put it down and walk away.

This exercise will help you decide whether this book is for you. I am going to take you through a visualisation exercise. If you like what you see, then this book **isn't** for you and you can pass it on to someone who you feel would benefit from it.

Otherwise, you are going to want to keep reading.

Visualisation

Vividly imagine yourself in <u>six months'</u> time, if you choose to put this book down and carry on as you have been doing in the past. You carry on your life as before – leading as you have always done, with the same balance between your work, relationships and health. What kind of a leader will you be? What will your daily life be like? How is your health doing? Especially your mental health? How are your relationships? How do you feel in yourself? How do you feel **about** your-self? What are the emotions you experience most often – fear, worry, doubt?

Now imagine seeing <u>one year</u> into the future, still continuing with your current way of moving through the world. Is life looking good for you? Are you fulfilled? What's your health like? And your heart? And your energy? How much time have you spent with those you most love? How do you feel about that?

Now imagine yourself <u>five years</u> into the future. You've been moving through the world in this same way all that time. Are you an inspiring leader? How is your health now? And how do you feel when you look at yourself in the mirror?

The chances are, you are now feeling that you don't want this future. So, be thankful that none of this has come to pass and you have the opportunity to change.

Ready for the next chapter?

And finally...

> The biggest adventure you can ever take is to live the life of your dreams
> **Oprah Winfrey**

Oprah is an amazing example of confidence and inner courage. She has had massive challenges in her life but, when opportunity came her way, she grabbed it and followed the path.

To become an Inspirator, this book is your call to adventure – are you up for the challenge?

2:

You Have the Power to Change

Get comfortable with being uncomfortable.

This is your last chance. After this, there is no turning back. You take the blue pill – the story ends, you wake up in your bed and believe whatever you want to believe. You take the red pill – you stay in Wonderland and I show you how deep the rabbit-hole goes.

Morpheus – The Matrix

In this chapter, we will explore
• the decision to be an Inspirator and what to expect
• the power of *Why*
• ways to connect to your *Why* and use it to take you forwards
• a tool which will help you create a vision of where you want to go.

Awareness is your superpower – so we said in the previous chapter. But, as in any film, once a hero becomes aware of their potential, the next step is to decide what to do about it.

 Movie Time

The Matrix is a great example of this and that's why I've chosen it as the film to illustrate this chapter on your power to change. Throughout this book, I have tried to make it your choice whether to watch the films I've chosen. Everything I cover should make sense without it. Do watch this short sequence from _The Matrix_ however – it is a really powerful illustration of what we'll be covering in this chapter.

Neo has lived in the world created by others. On one level everything seems as it should be but at a deeper level he knows something is a bit 'off'. He has a good job but leads a second life – the life of a rebel. He is seeing signs and questions the conventional world. He is searching for The Matrix, but he isn't sure what it is – although he senses that it will show him the truth.

Then Morpheus (Neo's guide in the film) offers him the opportunity to see that truth. Once Neo takes the step into the unknown there will be no turning back however, and the truth is brutal.

Only Neo can decide.

The word **_decide_** comes from the Latin _decædere_ meaning 'to cut off.' Deciding means you cut off all other possibilities and commit to this one path.

 Take a moment to imagine yourself at a crossroads in your life. Now is the time to decide which path you want to go down as you develop as an Inspirator. Just like Neo, you have a choice to make. The 'red pill' sets you on the path to become an Inspirator. The 'blue pill' allows you to return to the life you've been living up until now.

Do you want to take the blue pill where you have lots of money and fast cars and recognition? Do you want to lead lots of sheep who just do exactly what you tell them to do? Or do you want take the red pill and bring forth the next generation of leaders – where you let go of your self-importance and you give selflessly to the development of others?

To be an Inspirator, the challenge is in doing things differently. Be warned, however, that every time you do something different, there's a part of your brain that will resist it. You are starting to break habits and that is uncomfortable.

If you want to try a little experiment, when you go to bed tonight, sleep on the other side of the bed. You probably won't sleep very well. You might hear a voice in your head, saying 'This doesn't feel quite right,' or you'd sense that the objects in the room weren't where they 'ought' to be and you'd feel uncomfortable. Your partner might not be very happy about it either – their habit is being broken too. We favour what is familiar and we favour what it is that we know.

From the work I do with organisations, I hear more and more people talking about 'growth mindset' and 'fixed mindset.' Let me give you my definition of what that is all about.

Acorns, cats and us

Put a person, a cat and an acorn together and there are visibly very different. What we all have in common, though – the acorns, the cats and us – is our desire to grow. Albert Szent-Györgyi, who won the Nobel Prize for Physiology in 1937, expressed this in his concept of *Syntropy*.

Syntropy describes how every single cell exists for one reason – to express itself to its greatest capacity. The oak tree outside, the robin singing on its branch, the cat stalking it from the ground, everything. Everything exists to express itself to its highest capability.

What is the biggest difference in us? It's what goes on inside out heads (our 'self-talk') and the decisions we make as a result. Nature relies on instinct and, while instinct plays a part in our lives, our instincts are shaped by our decisions.

The decisions we make determine whether we allow ourselves to grow and in what direction. If we allow ourselves to get better, then we really have an opportunity to leave the world in a better place. If we make our decisions based on the person that we want to become, then we can start to create this future that we want and tap into our potential.

 ### *Movie Time*

Neo is faced with the choice of two pills. Either he takes the blue pill to stay in the world that he's in, oblivious to the truth, or he takes the red pill to learn what is really going on behind the scenes and become the hero in his own life. He makes his decision and starts his hero's journey.
The decision this book is asking you to make, is to become an Inspirator. That is the 'red pill' I am offering you.

One thing to point out here is that, in common with most of the heroes in the films we feature, we see something called psychological reactance (which I'll cover in more detail in Chapter 3). Neo didn't want to go on this journey. He thought about staying where he was, he had doubts, he knew the journey would be uncomfortable and dangerous and there would be a price to pay. Then he did it anyway.

If you are feeling that way too, know that you are not alone. To help you, I would encourage you to read the words below, from the motivational speaker and entrepreneur, Jim Rohn, asking the first and most important of all questions: Why?

> *"I want you to ponder these four questions.*
> *The 1st question to ponder when you go home is WHY.*
> *Why go this far? Why try to learn this much? Why study? Why try to put yourself out? Why try to earn as much as you can earn? Share as much as you can share? Why become as much as you possibly can become? Why develop yourself to the full? Why try to do it all? Why try to take on this much responsibility? Develop every skill you possibly can? See every human you possibly can? Go to every class you possibly can? Touch everybody you possibly can? Why do that much? Why go that far? Why share that much? Why give that much away? Why try to see everything? Why try to do everything? Why try to become everything?*
> *The 1st question to ponder when you go home is WHY?*
> *Here is another good answer to 'Why?' It's the second question. WHY NOT?*
> *Why not see how much you can earn? Why not see how much you can learn? Why not see how many skills you can develop? Why not see what kind of person you can become? Why not see what kind of influence you can have? Why not see how many people you can rescue from oblivion? I want you to make that personal? Why not? Why not? You've got to stay here until you go. I mean what else are you going to do? Why not see how much you can do and how far you can go?*
> *Now here is number 3? WHY NOT YOU?*
> *You've got the brains. You can make decisions. You can study the plan. You can change your life. You can grow immensely in the next few years. You can make your dreams come true. You can build a financial wall around your family NOTHING can get through. You can become healthy. You can become powerful. Why NOT you?*
> *My very last question on the questions to ponder is WHY NOT NOW?*
> *There never was a better time. And what a time now for us to take this dream and not let it die. Take this dream and give it life. Take this dream and breathe into it your own personal spirit until finally it becomes a flame that burns around the whole world.*

As you start to heighten your awareness, taking what you've learned from the first chapter, I encourage you to open your eyes and face what is really going on.

> **Movie Time**
>
> In *The Matrix* we see Neo waking up to the world that he's living in and the realisation that the world is not the world that he thought it was. As he starts to become aware, he asks himself some fundamental questions about the meaning of his life and the world that he's living in.
>
> Just like Neo, there's a part of you that knows, deep down, that it's time for you to rise up and go to work on becoming the very best version of yourself.
>
> But as Morpheus says, "There is a difference between knowing your path and walking it."

Are you ready to walk the path?

It starts with Why

I am inviting you to come on this journey. We can do this together. It's not my first time. When I take leaders through this process it becomes clearer what they are here to do, and *why* they're going to do it. It will be the same for you. Once you know *Why*, you will start to see *How* you're going to get there.

> Don't be surprised if, at this point, your inner dialogue is questioning whether you can do this. That is fear and I will help you with this through this book (Chapter 5 is all about Fear). For now, just know that to feel this way is perfectly normal.

In Chapter 1 we discussed the 'gap' and, if you answered the coaching questions at the end of the chapter, that gap may be becoming apparent to you. It may not be clearly defined yet – you may know where you are but not yet be certain of exactly where you want to go (that is coming up!). For now, just remember, this journey is all about closing that gap and the easiest way to fill that gap, is to have a compelling *Why*.

> **30-second science spot**
>
> I have four nieces and, when they were small, they would often ask the question 'Why?'. *"Why is the sky blue?", "Why can't I eat the same food as the dog?", "Why do I have to go to bed?"* One of the theories in psychology is that children ask that question out of fear. They don't understand and they want to make sense of the world that they are in. They constantly ask the question and when they get the answer it makes them feel grounded. They feel secure. This lasts until they ask the next question. And they keep asking because, not only do they have a fear which needs easing, but they are also curious. They have a desire to learn and grow.

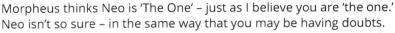

Movie Time

Morpheus thinks Neo is 'The One' – just as I believe you are 'the one.' Neo isn't so sure – in the same way that you may be having doubts. *I'm not good enough, What if I don't have what it takes? What will people think? This is too hard.*

The Oracle gives Neo a vague answer and tells him he is "waiting for something." In fact, Neo thinks he has heard her say that he **isn't** *The One* – because that is a safer answer than the truth. Being *The One* means the redemption of the world rests on his shoulders and that is too hard to grasp (remember this when we get to Chapter 4). He needs a *Why* to take the risks and do what needs to be done to become whom he must become. What he is waiting for is the reason to step into his power.

What are you waiting for to step into your power as an Inspirator? What is your *Why*?

Types of *Why?*

Before we get too deeply into this topic, I want to make it clear that simply having an answer to the question, is not what I'm talking about here.

Anyone one can come up with good reasons to do something (or to not do something). "I was told to do it", "I want to be a millionaire", "That's what is expected of me."

These are extrinsic reasons. There is nothing wrong with having extrinsic goals to motivate you – many businesses have these – but they don't tend to last and they seldom resonate with anyone else. They can be superficial or even artificial.

The *Why* we are seeking together here, however, is **intrinsic.** It is the reason within you which is a fundamental element of who you are and what you do. It is driven by something far more powerful and it drives you forward. Some people call it a *burning desire,* or *purpose* or *passion* or *ikigai*. The name doesn't matter. An intrinsic *Why* is an irresistible force. The recognition of your intrinsic *Why* is the difference it makes to you and the people around you.

The only difference between you and Inspirators is that they have a bigger W*hy*. I dare you – I challenge you – to have a *Why* so big it compels you to act. Often, when I challenge people in this way, and they've shared their *Why* some people laugh at them, while others tell them it is impossible. The kind of *Why* I'm talking about could be something like, "I want to create World Peace by making everybody healthy", "I want to motivate other people to be exceptional every single day", "I want to inspire 100 million people to be their best." Your *Why* should tell the world that you're prepared to

Alistair McAuley

I'm 80 years old and I'm rocking away in my chair. I've got my grandchildren jumping all over me and I'm reflecting on the highlights of my life; those moments that mean that I've actually achieved something. What's the impact that I've made?

create a new 'normal'. The world needs leaders with big *Whys*. The world needs new 'normals'.

One of the interviews I made with Inspirators was with Simon Cook. the Principal from Mid- Kent College who is a great example of this. Simon was a Michelin Star chef – which in the eyes of some, is the ultimate in the world of food. They saw him as a leader in his field. Yet now he is the leader to thousands of students and hundreds of staff. After the filming stopped, he told me that his *Why* was so big that he could hang his coat on it.

He can see what it is that he wants to create, something he must produce no matter what. He can deal with any *How* that comes along.

Find your why

In this chapter my goal is simple. To help you to create a *Why* and support you in it so that you can fall in love with it unconditionally every single day.

> The word **why** comes from multiple origins. In Greek it comes from *pei* meaning 'where.' In Latin *cui* is 'who.' Look into the Germanic languages and we see *hwi* which means 'what' and 'how'
> No wonder W*hy* is such a powerful word. To have a 'Why' is to know what and where and how and who.

This is what I'm calling on you to do. I'm challenging you to discover your *Why*. It might not be crystal clear to you now but over time perhaps your *Why* will become so big, that like Simon, you will be able to deal with any How.

A good way to discover your own *Why* is to listen to the *Why* of other people. One of the things I often do is to bring leaders together to share their *Why*. Hearing the *Whys* of others can help you strengthen your own. Be curious and ask questions of other people about why they do what they do and what drives them forward.

If you can't share your *Why* with other leaders at the moment, I invite you to look at some of the most famous leaders in history, from Mahatma Gandhi to Martin Luther King – people who have changed the course of the world in a dramatic and positive way. They had a big *Why* and that's often the difference that makes the difference.

But let us start with something more straightforward, but no less important: *Why are you reading this book?*

It is estimated that only 5% of people who buy a personal development or leadership book will read past the first chapter.
What is your *Why*? What was it that took you beyond Chapter 1 and got you to here? And what will keep you reading to the end?
Presumably you picked up this book because you want to be a leader. Why?
Why do you want people to follow you?
What will it give you, what will it get you?

Continued on next page

As you read this book, keep questioning yourself, as Jim Rohn suggests.

Why? Why go through this book? Why put yourself out there? Why develop yourself? Why take more responsibility? Why touch people's lives?

Why not? Why not learn new skills? Why not become a person of influence? Why not become an Inspirator? Why not go after you dreams? Why not chase something bigger than yourself?

Why not you? Why not you who is the example? Why not you to inspire? Why not you who makes the world a better place? Why not you who becomes financially independent? Why not you who is healthier?

Why not now? Why not now be someone different? Why not now follow your passion? Why not now be who you are meant to be? Why not now start on the journey to be an Inspirator?

This might seem full on – all these demands that you understand *Why* – but it is important. There has never been a better time, a more important time, to start on this journey.

Moving away

Let me ask you: when do most people have their strongest *Why*.

For many of us, myself included, our *Why* is often the biggest where we want to move away from something. We don't like how we look in the mirror; we feel the need to prove we are not the victim of our past; or we want to change the way others see us. This type of *Why* serves a purpose because there is a motivation to make change. When you have been driven to make change in this way – you don't like being overweight, or you hate your job, or someone in your circle of friends rubs you up the wrong way – what do you find happens in the long term?

What I've observed is that, usually, as you put distance between yourself and the source of the discomfort, your desire to change dwindles and you revert to old habits.

This is not a new concept. In fact, it is a very, very old one. **'Arambhashura'** is a Sanskrit word for being a 'hero in the beginning'. Even in the earliest of written languages, the idea of starting something full of energy and then losing interest was recognised.

How many times in your life have you been a *hero in the beginning*? How often have you started on a project, full of energy and excitement and then lost interest and fallen back?

Now, consider: When do we get to see the best in people?

There is greatness that exists within everyone which emerges during a crisis.

Cast your mind over recent world disasters and consider the stories surrounding it of people rising up and showing great courage to help others.

You have the power to change but is that power only accessed when difficult things happen? Is challenge a necessary ingredient for becoming a leader in your own life?

Think of times in your life when you have had a really big *Why*. With every big *Why*, how great was the challenge – be it physical or mental, relating to you or to others?

Story Time

A number of years ago my wife, Hannah, developed a very aggressive brain tumour and was given a terminal diagnosis. Hannah was in a terrible state, I was panicking inside and I didn't know what to do. So, I called my coach, Rafael.

He said, "Find people that are still alive and find out what they did." Then he asked, "What is she going to do when she gets better?"

I was dumbfounded. "She's only been given 18 months to live."

"So, what?" he replied. "People defy the odds all the time."

Rafael had given me my *Why*. It was probably my greatest ever *Why!*

A few years after Hannah had recovered I asked her about where we were going in our life together. I had no agenda in asking but, as I mentioned in the last chapter, you have to tend to every aspect of your life. I wanted to sit down and review our marriage, talk about what was going on, how we were feeling, what was working and not working, and so on.

If you think about it, it's all related to *Why*. To ask, "Where are we going?" is, in a way, asking, "Why are we married?"

Hannah started crying.

I was surprised and initially concerned. After all, when you ask your partner about your relationship and she starts to cry, it isn't the *best* start to the conversation, is it?

Then, as we spoke, I understood. Hannah was crying because she didn't have a *Where*. Her *Why*, after all she had been through, was that she didn't want to die. That's not a compelling reason. It doesn't bring out the best in people.

Connect with Why

To talk about *Why* and not mention Simon Sinek would be remiss of me, especially since his book *Start with Why* had a dramatic effect on my life and really started to open my eyes to why I'm doing what I'm doing. If you do nothing else, watch his TED talk *It Starts With Why?* which makes it so clear that people don't buy **what** you do or **how** you do what you do. They buy **why** you do what you do.

I believe that, fundamentally, people want to make a difference; they can see *How* they can make a difference when they connect with *Why*. If you can connect to your own *Why* and see how you are making a big difference, then you have an opportunity to make a massive impact.

Story Time

When I had called Rafael, faced with Hannah's terminal diagnosis, I thought my *Why* was already there, because I didn't want her to die. Survival of a loved one is a burning desire that I'm sure many of you can relate to, but the easiest thing would have been just to accept what we were being told. Just like Neo, I was tempted by the Red Pill – to walk away and pretend it wasn't going to happen. I was scared and I really didn't feel like facing up to the truth.

When Rafael told me that people defy the odds all the time, he gave me the connection I needed. He set me on a hero's journey and I believe that my wife is alive and well today because I had a coach that I could turn to.

Finding the treatment which saved Hannah's life was extremely challenging. We discovered a doctor in the US who would accept her on a trial but there were so many obstacles along the way, that I can't even remember them. There were days when I didn't feel like dealing with the obstacles and disappointments and challenges but that didn't alter the actions I took. How I felt didn't have anything to do with it. I had my *Why* and I was connected to it fully.

Being connected to that *Why* then becomes the support and motivation to keep going even when things get tough.

One of the classic examples to draw on for this is, of course, Nelson Mandela.

The 30-second history spot

The South African lawyer campaigned for civil rights and equality despite threats and disapproval because he knew *Why* it was a cause worth fighting for. It kept him going and he knew that *How* would become apparent. Even when he was imprisoned for nearly 30 years of his life, he never gave up on that cause. He had a big *Why* and in prison it did not go away. It would have been so easy to think, 'Well, there's no point anymore,' but he never did. There was **always** a point. From his *Why* he found the courage of his convictions even in the most difficult of circumstances.

Of course, I'm not suggesting that your *Why* needs to be equal rights, like Mandela, or throwing off a dystopian oppressor, like Neo. You don't need anyone else's *Why*. Your *Why* is yours. But if you connect to it, you will stand out. People will see it and they will also connect to it.

Connecting to your *Why* is about picking your star and going on the journey to get there. If you already know your *Why*, the journey we are going on together is going to strengthen it and make it more solid. And if your *Why* isn't immediately obvious, this journey will help you discover it. For now, keep asking yourself where you want to go and why you want to get there. Be curious about the *Why* of other people – especially those who inspire you.

> ## Delphine Rive
> What you get at work is who I am truly. And I think that's really important because I think people crave that authenticity ... I think some people look up to me because I'm just me. I've ... stayed who I am and not tried to pretend to be someone I'm not just because I'm in a work environment.

The biggest challenge is to find a *Why* which drives you forward, even when you *aren't* in a crisis. Going through that difficult time with Hannah has changed the *Why* I have for the way I live the rest of my life.

I will coach you to work out what your *Why* is and connect you to it. By doing that, you will wake up every day, and be able to move forward even on days with massive challenges. You keep going because you have a burning desire.

 What has been the strongest *Why* in your life so far? When did you do what was needed even when you didn't feel like it? How did that *Why* drive you forward?

I encourage you to write down *What is my Why? Why am I reading this book?*

Why work with me?

If I am to coach you, if you are to trust me as things start to get uncomfortable and I ask you to look at every aspect of your life, it is only fair that you understand why I do what I do. You deserve to connect to my *Why* as you embark on this journey.

My *Why* burns so brightly within me, that it doesn't really matter what's happening in the rest of my life. I'm going to continue to do what I do because my *Why* drives me forward every day.

I believe I was put on this earth to inspire people to look at things differently. I am here to empower others so they can confidently move forwards. As they are inspired, so others are inspired by them, and it changes the world.

I want to positively impact the lives of 100 million people around the world, to inspire them to do what they need to do; for them to feel fulfilled and happy and for them to leave the world in a better place than when they came. You can help me with my *Why*. If you are inspired by me and go on to inspire others, you are adding to the number of people I am impacting. Will you help me?

I believe human beings do the best that they can until they know better. Then when they know better, they do better.

One of those people is **you.**

That's what I want to show you how to do – to do better, to become an example to yourself first and foremost. I want to show you how to step into your power.

I don't think I've ever wanted to write a book as much as I've wanted to write this one. I want to inspire you to not want to put the book down. I want you to feel that I'm actually speaking to you.

Where are you going?

Why is a powerful force especially when you have a conviction of where you are going. When there is a destination, a place that you want to take your life, then your life is dedicated to moving in that direction, regardless of the obstacles that come your way.

 ### *The 30-second history spot*

A great example of this is British hurdler Sally Gunnell. In 1991 at the Tokyo World Championships, she had a big setback in her career. As she jumped the penultimate hurdle she thought for a second, 'Oh, I might just win this. I'd better not trip.' Of course, she hit the last hurdle with her foot and ended up coming second.

Sally was devastated but she used that setback to prompt her to get help. She started to work with former Olympic hurdler and sports psychologist, David Hemery.

As they trained, he asked her, 'Sally, do you ever think about the race? Do you ever picture yourself winning?' What her coach helped her to see was that she was frightened to visualise the race because she was frightened of losing.

It was the breakthrough she needed. In 1992 she won the Olympic Gold medal in Barcelona for 400-metre hurdles and then in 1993, she broke the world record. If you watch the video of that 1993 win, you can see the power of the visualisation she was doing, every single day. When she crossed the line, she didn't know that she'd won, not because the margin was too narrow, but because she'd spent so much time visualising it, she couldn't tell if this was real or a visualisation!

The only difference between you and Sally Gunnell is your destination. Hers was the finish line of a 52-second race. Yours may be something quite different. Maybe you have the idea of becoming an Inspirator, a leader who is inspired to follow themselves. Maybe, for you, it is about being out there and performing all the time, rather than aiming for a single event. Whatever the aim, the message is the same. Have a compelling vision of where you're going and dedicate your life to making that happen.

The greatest gift we have is our ability to create and manifest our ideas. And we all have goals, dreams and ambitions. What brings them to life are the pictures, images and feelings associated with where we're going. This isn't something that you just practice occasionally. It is something that, just like an athlete, you need to see, feel and connect with every day.

Athletes have to have an optimal performance state. I want you to have an optimal performance state in your life so you can develop emotional strength inside you and start to focus on where you're going in your life. I want you to see it so clearly, just as Sally saw herself winning, that you develop that belief and the conviction that what you're going after, **can** and **will** be achieved.

One of the tools I have provided with this book is a Priming audio, which is a type of meditation. I strongly encourage you to listen to the priming tool every day. This will help you to see your *Why* in action, just like an athlete going out to perform can see the competition ending in victory.

Lucy Mellins

... Understanding where [people's] strengths are, and ... where their interest lies, (because people usually put most of their passion into stuff they have a natural inclination for). That's why understanding who they are as people matters to me.

Seeing your destination

Story Time

When I realised that Hannah's ambition was entirely based on a wish not to die, I wanted to find a way to help her. So, I went online. I was looking for someone or somewhere or some tool, some tip, some technique to help people have a compelling vision of where they were going. I Googled "ways to help people think and draw their future." The first item on the list was a TED talk by Patti Dobrowolski who spoke about *your current reality and drawing your future*. I was fascinated!

Now, I'm no artist! I can't draw and, when I was at school, my art teacher told me that I didn't have the artistic gene. But everyone can create a picture, because we all think in pictures.

Continued on next page

If I asked you what you had for dinner last night, you would see, in your mind's eye, the food you had. If I asked you to think of your last holiday or to name someone you love or to describe your front door, you would visualise them. We all think in pictures.

Have you ever had a picture inside your mind that was so compelling that you had to move towards it? That was what Patti's TED Talk was all about. She was showing how, by considering where you are now – your current reality – and where you want to go – the desired new reality – and describing them in pictures, makes you more open to them. If you see these two realities as two islands, you can build a bridge between the two with bold steps.

Story Time

I showed this TED Talk to Hannah and she drew her picture of a future for us. She put it on the wall in her office and we looked at it together every day. We took steps towards that new reality in everything we did. Some of it, a house with a garden and her Dad living nearby, has come true.

That isn't the end of the story, however. I was so interested in the TED Talk Patti did, that I got in touch with her to see if she would be willing to do a Podcast with me. She said yes and even did it twice due to some technical challenges with the first attempt. We became friends and she is now supporting my goal to inspire 100 million people.

Not all vision is the same

At the start of this section, I said that we all see in pictures. Over the years, I have lost count of the number of people who, on hearing this, say to me, 'But Pete, I don't have a visual mind.'

We do all see in pictures – but not everyone sees in the same way.

Story Time

I really started to understand the power of this when I worked with the England Blind Cricket Team. Until then I didn't know how blind people thought because I didn't know many blind people. Perhaps I was too embarrassed to ask the question, "Exactly how do you move through the world?" of people with limited sight. Or maybe I had simply never thought about it.

What I learned from the team is that blind people 'see', they just don't see in the way that sighted people do.

When a blind person plays cricket, they are not simply holding the cricket bat and thinking to themselves, "I just hope I hit the ball today." No; the ball makes a sound and from that sound they're able to make a mental representation of what is going on. They use that to judge when to make their swing.

That is their way of 'seeing.' So, it may be that you don't conjure up vivid pictures in your mind – perhaps they are more abstract or are rich with sound as well as colour – but every one of us can manifest our desired destination and make it come alive. You just have to be prepared to do the work to make it happen.

Perhaps that's what Napoleon Hill was talking about, in *Think and Grow Rich*, when he claimed that only 2% of people have a burning desire. Perhaps only 2% of people take the time and effort and energy to manifest the vision of where – and why – they are going.

In doing so, you unlock your personal power – the power to change.

Connecting others to your *Why* – Inspire other people

I believe that the best approach to take with people is to be as honest and as upfront as possible. That can take courage as we are required to be our authentic selves, rather than who others expect us to be, or who we believe we ought to be.

To be an Inspirator, however, means you have the ability to look differently at your needs, your ideas around how business is done and where you are coming from. As you develop your *Why,* and have a clear mission of your destination, you are creating a context which empowers people to move forwards.

Why do people follow?

Have you ever considered that question: *Why should people follow me?*

In business most people will follow you if they feel they're a part of a team and feel they have a part to play.

What would they tell you if you asked them what they want? You'll probably get answers like "friendship", "to make a difference", "to learn and grow", and that's what you often see in organisations. You see groups of people forming tribes, working together on projects and learning from one another.

For years companies have operated in a way where they demand obedience and order. They have controlled people to align in a specific way. What I've seen from all the years I spent working with organisations, talking to leaders and studying the psychology of people in business, is that people's greatness is being stifled and squeezed out of them by this. We will never get the best out of people this way.

Richard Curen

If one can instil good followership, then one ... has ... been able to instil in them a sense that they're making a difference. So if people ... can see what the vision is of the organisation and of the leader, and that the leader embodies that vision, then you've got people who are going to go, "Yeah. I believe in this. I believe in what I'm doing and I can see where we're headed."

I think followership doesn't happen in organisations where the primary task isn't obvious, where there are things that aren't being addressed that are going on under the surface.

How, then, do we get the best out of people?

People want autonomy; they want mastery; they want purpose. They want to feel that they are making a difference. They want to connect to the *Why* of the company, the *Why* of their leaders and to their own *Why*.

The 30-second science spot

In 1944 psychologist Abraham Maslow developed his 'hierarchy of needs.' At the top of this pyramid he identified the 'self-actualised person'. Once we have satisfied our needs for survival, socialisation and self-esteem, the most important need of any human being is for them to feel great meaning and feel that they're contributing to the world. They need an intrinsic *Why*. That's what self-actualisation really means.

To give others this feeling, so they are inspired to follow you, you need to:
- Share your vision and explain why
- Use that as an anchor for what you do and say – and invite others to hold you accountable
- Invite others to think about their aims and to share goals and themes

Deep Work

There is no simple tool which you can use to discover your *Why* in a quick and easy way. Some of you will already know it, others will have an idea of it but have yet to manifest it clearly and others will have never even considered it before. Wherever you are, the tools below will help you connect to your *Why* as this journey progresses.

Daily Priming

The Priming tool is a guided meditation which starts to go into the workshop within your own mind.

This process starts with you filling yourself up with one of the most powerful human emotions – gratitude. Gratitude releases endorphins and serotonin and helps us feel lucky. Once you appreciate what you have, you start to think about things in your life that you want to manifest and to see them as completed.

The more you do this exercise, the better you become.

Snapshot of the Big Picture

Follow the link below which will take you a session Patti Dobrowolski did for my Mi365 coaching community, in which she guides you through the process of developing your own Snapshot of the Big Picture.

What's your story?

Here are your coaching questions to help you connect to your intrinsic *Why*. Spend time on these questions and note them down in your journal.

As before, notice how you respond to the questions and the answers and see what you can learn from this too. Remember that none of these reactions are right or wrong (and they are all perfectly normal!).

Coaching Questions
1. What would you do if you knew you couldn't fail?
2. Why would you do it?
3. And why is that important to you?
4. And why does that inspire you?
5. And why will your life be fulfilled in doing it?
6. And why does that make you an Inspirator?

And Finally...

> *Our deepest fear is not that we are inadequate. Our deepest fear is that we are powerful beyond measure. It is our light, not our darkness that most frightens us. We ask ourselves, 'Who am I to be brilliant, gorgeous, talented, fabulous?' Actually, who are you not to be?*
>
> **Marianne Williamson – Return to Love**

Note: This wonderful quote opens up the idea of the intrinsic *Why* better than anything else I know.

Nelson Mandela is constantly quoted as having used this in his inaugural speech as president. It isn't true. He never quoted it. Marianne Williamson is even quoted saying how she wished it was true but that it isn't. It is a nice story – we'd love it to be true. We want to hear these inspiring words spoken in the voice of an inspiring leader. It takes the power of the words and doubles, triples or even quadruples their impact.

Choose a leader who inspires you – alive or dead, famous or otherwise – and imagine them saying these words. Use it to power you up every day and to connect you to your *Why*.

3:

The Coach

Who says you have to go it alone?

All mentors have a way of seeing more of our faults than we would like. It's the only way we grow.

Padmé – Star Wars: Attack of the Clones

In this chapter, we will explore
- why you need coaching to become an Inspirator
- how to ask better questions
- ways to coach yourself
- ways to inspire others with coaching
- two tools to help you ask better questions of yourself and others.

Movie Time

Star Wars - it doesn't matter whether you love it, hate it, or you've never seen it. I believe there is no better sequence of films to express the role of the coach than the Star Wars series. In every film there is a key relationship between the hero and his coach.

Obi-Wan Kenobi is a student of Qui-Gon Jinn and then of Yoda. Obi-Wan goes on to coach first Anakin and then Luke. When Obi-Wan dies, it is Yoda who completes Luke's training. As Luke steps into his power, he begins to train Leia in the ways of the force as well. Then, the last Jedi coaches Rae as well.

So the journey continues – the hero is coached, becomes a leader and in turn becomes a coach to the next generation of leaders.

Leaders are coaches. Coaches are leaders. In every way and in every meaning of the word, to be an Inspirator means you must be a coach.

If you think you can be a leader – getting people from A to B – **without** coaching, then your only alternative would be dictatorship and, frankly, this isn't the book for you.

From the start of this book, we've defined an Inspirator as a person of influence and that the first person you need to lead is yourself. Influencing yourself is pretty tricky though. Seeing yourself objectively, separate from the default settings you've developed over time, is a massive challenge.

Inevitably, when someone becomes a leader, it can be a very lonely place. All of a sudden, you are put in a position where the responsibility is on you and people look to you.

So, whom does a leader look to?

We all know the saying, 'behind any great man, there is a great woman[1].' When you look at great and accomplished leaders in any field, you will always see that there are great people behind those people.

Great people have a coach behind them.

Chris Roebuck

That is fundamentally what a leader is. A leader takes you from one place to a better place. That's why it's so important.

Movie Time

Luke Skywalker is stuck as a farmer, seeing only the ideas given to him by his Uncle Owen. He does everything he can to make a farmer out of Luke, knowing what Anakin was and what he became. He is desperate to steer the youngster away from the path of the Jedi. He has the best of intentions, but the call of Luke's true purpose generates a sense of dissatisfaction in the young man and a need to get away. *Continued on next page*

---

[1] *This is a saying from a time when women weren't considered to be 'great' in their own right, of course. The gender may not be relevant but the principle is.*

It is Ben (Obi-Wan Kenobi) who opens Luke's eyes to his true purpose – giving him a different perspective on who he is and the power that he can tap into. The Jedi Master takes him to places he had never imagined possible. Luke steps out of the story he'd always believed and sees how he can become the best possible version of himself.

Ben is passing on what he has learned to bring forth the next Jedi.

The first challenge for Ben, of course, is to guide Luke to face the truth of who he really is.

 Look around you. How many Luke Skywalkers do you see around you – stuck as farmers when they could be Jedi Knights?

Have you ever considered how Luke's future would have unfolded had Ben Kenobi never come into his life?

Are you like Luke at the start of the film? Doing what is expected of you, following a path not of your own making? Frustrated and discontented?

And how many of those who you lead do you suppose are feeling that way?

That's what coaching is. Coaching has one fundamental purpose: to pass on wisdom, knowledge and perspective; to shine light on the truth; to ask, and keep asking, *how do you get better*?

What is a coach?

 The 30-second history spot

Coach emerged in the mid-16th century in Hungary. A '*kocsi'* was a wagon from Kocs – a village in Hungary which developed a new form of steel-sprung suspension.

A coach is a means of transport. It takes you from where you are to where you want to be.

The term first started being used in an improvement context the 1830s, as Oxford students started to get personal 'coaches' to help them in academic studies. Then, in 1861, it was first applied to competitive sport.

When the Yale-Harvard inter-collegiate football matches started in 1875, Yale was already using a coach on a regular basis. In the first 30 years of the matches, Harvard only won four times. They used a coach occasionally during that time but it took them 20 years to recognise the importance of having a regular coach for the team.

So, what **is** a coach in its modern form – in the way that I am your coach within this book?

There are many definitions, of course, and I'm sure you've come across plenty. I see a coach as someone who is there to help you in the face of obstacles. They are there to help, guide and support you.

What's in it for me?

One of my goals in assisting you through this journey is to help you get specific as to where you want to go, what specifically you need to do to achieve that. As I'm writing this, the question in my mind is *How do we add fuel to your power and help you to achieve your goals, dreams and ambitions?*

 If you could be the person of your dreams, who would you be?

When you work with a coach, you have the opportunity to take ideas, obstacles and complexities, and together find solutions for things. What is of particular importance is that you do it **objectively.**

If you seek guidance and opinion from the people around you be aware that they will have a vested interest in you – as a friend, a partner, a parent or a child. They may have their own opinions on who you should be and what is best for you. They care about you and may want to protect you or be kind. They may tell you what they think you need to hear or will act in what they consider are your 'best interests' in order to protect you (or themselves) from difficulty.

Lucy Melling

I'm not looking for praises or glory or anything else. I think the glory comes when I see people doing really well, ... I think that matters a great deal to me. I think I'm a facilitator and a leader.

 ### *Movie Time*

Ben Kenobi protects Luke from the ways of the Jedi, by instead allowing him to learn for himself. Ben's role is to open him up to new experiences and introduce him to new ideas. What the Jedi Master doesn't do is **tell** him. Had Ben introduced himself with, "Nice to meet you. You have unlimited power, your father is still alive and evil, and you need to track him down and kill him, to restore the Republic," Luke's reaction would have been very different! He would, no doubt, have resisted.

A great coach, for me, is someone who becomes your external eyes and ears, as you develop a more accurate picture of reality; they help you recognise the foundations you need to put in place and the actions needed; and then to help you build that better version of yourself.

This is why I encourage you to see me as your coach in this book – here for one simple reason: to guide you and support you as you go from being good to great, to truly being exceptional and to stand in front of the mirror and say 'I am proud of who I am and I want to follow me.' In short, being an Inspirator.

No one can tell you what to do

Remember what we said earlier? *People don't change when you tell them what to do. People change when their perspective changes.* This is what great coaching can do. The coach will help you step into your power and introduce you to new perspectives.

Alistair McAuley

The best leaders, I believe, see themselves in that light [not as a leader] ... they just naturally acquire people who follow them, who warm to them, ... who buy into what their values are, and the truth of those values, particularly around that authenticity piece. That's what brings people with them.

Movie Time

Ben gives Luke one area to explore at a time – to grow and discover things for himself. He allows him to make mistakes too. He isn't watching over him every step of the way. He knows, as any coach does, that we often get worse at something before we get better and that we learn from that experience. This is another reason why coaching should be a fundamental part of your process to become the best leader you can possibly be.

Imagine you are at the cinema about to watch a film. As the film starts, you look on the screen and you see a black mark in the middle of the image. You think to yourself, *I need to get that black mark off. It's annoying me and it's stopping me from enjoying the film.* You get up and head for the screen.

You rub at the black mark but it won't come off. You scratch at it, but it's still not coming off. You're scratching harder, and harder, and harder, and it starts to really frustrate you that the mark doesn't go away. You sit down again and try to ignore it but, after a few minutes, you realise that it is really in your way. So you go back to scratching at it. It is really driving you crazy by now!

That's when I arrive and ask, "What is going on?" You explain and I ask, "Why is this mark not coming off? What's *really* going on here?"

You ponder for a moment, and then I turn you around, and point at the projector. You look up and see a mark on the projector itself. That's the mark that needs to be removed.

Can you see how that mark is inside all of us? It is the darkness within us that we don't want to face. It is on the lens of how we see the world. The projector isn't broken – **you** are not broken – but as you travel through life, your lens has become affected by your experiences and inner voice.

When you think back over your past experiences, what marks have you picked up in how you see the world?

When have you had a challenge which has changed how you see a person or an experience or a way of moving through the world?

The mark represents what you have overcome.

Sometimes, you need help to become more aware of how you see the world through your own lens. You need someone to show you that it isn't the marks which define you – it is what you do about them.

Movie Time

At one point, Luke resists Ben's request to go with him because of the upcoming harvest. Ben replies, "That's your Uncle talking!"

He doesn't argue. He just gives a different perspective.

Getting out of the zone

Where do you think we grow?

When, in your life, have you learned the most, and achieved the most and made the best decisions for you and for those around you?

Answer: When we get uncomfortable.

Someone I am coaching at the moment shared an idea with me last year which I love so much I use it all the time: *Nothing grows in your comfort zone.* It is when we take risks and get uncomfortable and scare ourselves a little, that we make progress.

Story Time

When I used to spend time with my coach, I'd feel very uncomfortable in his presence, because I could really see myself. He was like a mirror to me. I could see things in myself, my frustration, my challenge at simply being in the moment, rather than always active. I wanted to act and he would give me a different perspective on that – to stop and think and be present.

A good coach will always encourage you to play at the edges of your comfort zone because that is where we learn and grow. Coaching and, indeed, your own exploration on this journey is not to consider how good you are **now**, it's the quest to get better. That is why the priming tool I gave you in Chapter 2 is such an incredible resource for you to use. With it, you will start developing the ability within your own brain to identify with the leader you are becoming. The more you think about and see this future-you - someone who is fitter, healthier, someone who is leading their way in the *Big Three* – the more you will be able to identify with them. This future-you is the 'you' who you are inspired to follow.

In order to be able to do this, the greatest influence you need to have is the influence you have over yourself. If you think about the relationship that I have with you, coaching you through this book, naturally I want to influence you and give you a new perspective. What I **can't** do is get you to **do** anything. I cannot make you change because it suits my *Why*. Even if I know it will help you, I cannot do the work for you.

People must do things for their own reasons – because they have a strong *Why* of their own. That means that following my instructions must be for your reasons, not mine – because **you** want to get better, you know *Why*, and you are prepared to trust the journey I am taking you on.

This is about holding yourself accountable and taking responsibility for your own journey.

Stop with all these questions, already!

> Judge a man by the quality of his question, not by the answer
> **Voltaire**

What questions have I been asking in this chapter?

What questions have you been asking **yourself** as you read this chapter?

How are you feeling as a result of the answers you've been giving yourself?

The quality of our life comes down to the quality of what we're saying to ourselves and to the quality of questions that we ask.

Questions are like heat-seeking missiles in your brain. If you ask a question of yourself, your brain will seek an answer which makes intellectual sense, based on the evidence it can find. The brain hasn't got a filter, however, and it won't be aware of what is helpful and what is not.

What questions do you ask? Most people ask questions such as:

- Why am I like this?
- Why does this keep happening to me?
- Why aren't I as good as that person?

And the brain looks for evidence. It trawls through your memories to find events and actions which, intellectually, could provide the answer. And presents them as **fact**.

You are like this because you didn't study hard enough at school. This keeps happening to you because you never apply yourself. You aren't as good as that person because, fundamentally, you aren't good enough.

Frankly, if anyone but you said these things, you wouldn't stick around, would you? Yet we buy into these messages every day. The whole topic of the *duck* – our inner voice – is something we will cover in Chapter 6 in much more detail.

What questions do you ask yourself on a regular basis?
How do they impact on how you act and the decisions you make?
How many of the people you lead do you think it applies to?
What does that mean for them and the way they move through the world?

Become Aware: I invite you to tune in to the questions you ask yourself and the feelings they provoke in you.

Anger and regret come from asking questions about the past: "Why me?" "Why didn't I...?"

Worry and doubt come from asking questions about the future: "What if..?"

Comparisons with others: "Why aren't I as good as..." will find all the reasons you aren't good enough and simply perpetuate the myth of your inadequacies.

None of these questions are powerful or helpful. They are seeking reinforcement of the failure so that's what you get. They are putting marks on your lens.

Story Time

A great example of a different way is through the career of 400m runner, Roger Black, who I worked with for a time. At the time Black competed in the Olympics, he was running against Michael Johnson, one of the greatest athletes of all time. Black knew that he wasn't able to run as fast as Johnson. Rather than focusing on Johnson's race, he focused on what *he* could do. Through the power of questioning, he was able to put himself into a space where he was able to transcend what someone else was going to do and was asking a better question, "How can I be my best here? What is it, exactly, that I need to do for me to be my very best?"

For him, the very best was Silver – which was what he achieved.

These are great questions that you can ask yourself. What will the brain do if you ask questions such as: *How can we do this? How can we make this better?* What evidence will it seek from your past?

It may take longer for the brain to come up with an answer, but it will be a good deal more helpful than providing you with a long list of reasons why you can't run as fast as Michael Johnson!

Richard Curen

... [by] knowing what the question is and knowing who to ask, you get buy in. You get people who feel empowered. They're not being told what to do. They're asked to come up with suggestions, come up with ideas, and then they feel part of the common purpose of the organisation.

As you have been reading this book, have you been asking, *How am I going to get the most out of this book?*
Think about that for a moment now.

Perhaps you'll get the most from it by going through it a few times and asking the questions, doing the exercises, doing exactly what your coach asks you to do. Or maybe you'll get the most from it by sharing it with those who follow you and working on it together. Or there might be some other way to make the most of it. The answer will come – what is important is that you ask the question and keep asking it.

Where do coaches come from, Mummy?

The vast majority of people who have been coached, go on to coach other people. Itzhak Perlman is a great example of this. Perlman was taught by Dorothy DeLay, the violin coach at the Julliard. Perlman had a prestigious career and he went on to coach other violinists too. With his wife, he co-founded a music school, (The Perlman Music Programme), and has been developing talent ever since. Throughout his career, he continued to improve and to work on himself. I remember reading an interview in *The New York Times* where he was asked if he ever used a coach. He said, 'Yes, absolutely. I've always had coaching. It was my wife.' His wife used to sit in the audience and take on that role of observing and then just ask questions.

Coaches create the next generation of coaches, just as leaders create the next generate of leaders. The roles are synonymous. Ultimately, an Inspirator is the coach of others.

Glyn House

I've got a team of 65 area managers, nine regional managers, the three ops directors. Some of those regional managers have got 100 stores each, like most retail businesses. They have to be fantastic coaches as well ...They want honest feedback, and they come to you and you spend a day with them, and they say, "What have you seen today?" and they're eager to learn as well.

What is the best way for you to bring out the best in other people?
How does the coaching I give you help you become an Inspirator?
How can you use that to inspire others?

There's never been a more important time for leaders to see themselves as coaches, there to bring out the best in other people. We live in a world where organisations see only a fraction of the potential of the people who work for them. As their coach, you can take them from where they are to where they want to be and, in doing so, take businesses from where they are to where they want to be too.

It was what my coach did for me. I am a better coach, a better person, because of what Rafael did.

And Rafael was a better coach because of *his* coach.

And what, *exactly*, did Rafael do?

Simply put, he would ask me a great question. Then he would listen to the answer and ask me another one. And another and another. By listening and asking, he guided me on my own journey.

Coaching DIY

A good coach will ask great questions to challenge you. Of course, not everyone can hire a coach to work with them one to one. You might not be able to afford it, or simply not have enough time. While being able to hire a coach like me would be great, that might not be possible. Or perhaps a coaching relationship has run its course. That happens too.

Chris Roebuck

There's something called 'discretionary effort'. What this is, is effort that an employee can give if they want to. Now, in most situations, an employee within a normal performance management system, can come up as performing satisfactorily, but still yet be withholding up to 30% effort. So ... they're not giving their best, but because they're doing the job and satisfactory, the organisation cannot tell that they're not giving that 30% extra effort.

Nor is it always necessary to have a coach. The most fundamental step that you can ever take to becoming a better leader and better at coaching yourself is to ask **yourself** better questions. The way to do that is to become curious.

But it kills cats!

Curiosity doesn't necessarily have to *kill the cat*. Curiosity can always make you ask, 'How do we make things better here?' Not just for you, but for every single person around you as you bring your best self to the party.

How can you use questions to take you forward?
What are the best questions you've been asked and which have been most helpful to you?
What do you learn about yourself when you are asked a great question?

Questions allow us to become more responsible. We become response-able. Able to deal with the situations that occur, when they occur: *That's interesting. Now what needs to be done?*

Ask questions every day such as: *What went well? What needs work?*

Asking these sorts of questions are what a good coach will always do. I ask them of all of my one-to-one clients; whenever we are working on something at each stage: *What went well? What needs work? Now what needs to be done?*

And then I **listen** to the answer.

So, be curious as to how things can be better. I want you to think very carefully about that question: *How do I get better?* And then listen for the answers you get.

Become Aware: When you ask a question of someone, how much of your mind is concentrating on hearing the answer?

Notice how much of your mind is thinking about the next question; or your own opinion on what is being said; or on what you are having for dinner tonight...

Asking great questions is only going to work if you make time to listen to the answers. You see, this book is not just about you becoming a better leader. It's not just about you becoming a better person. It's about you becoming a better listener and asking better questions.

The 30-second history spot

Success always leaves clues and, in this life, you don't have to reinvent the wheel. You can learn from other Inspirators through the ages. Perhaps one of the most curious people that's ever lived was Leonardo da Vinci. Da Vinci wasn't just an artist who painted *The Last Supper* and *Mona Lisa,* he was an inventor, a military engineer, a musician and a scientist. He was the ultimate polymath – he was even a great athlete and, apparently, a fantastic party planner!

Da Vinci kept copious notes on everything. In fact, Bill Gates paid $30.8 million for 180 pages of his journal. Why do you suppose he did that?

From those notes we know that da Vinci had a number of principles, and his number one principle was curiosity. Whatever he saw going on in the world, he wanted to know how and why, and how he could use it – and he wrote it down so he wouldn't forget it.

Use your curiosity on yourself – especially when you are facing challenges. Become aware of the questions you are asking of yourself. Observe how you are feeling at any point in time and ask, "What question did I ask myself to feel this way?" Contemplate what is going on to learn and understand – not to judge and criticise.

Becoming the coach – Inspire other people

How much are you applying the learning in this book, so far? Have you done everything I've asked you to do? Or have you promised that you'll 'do it later?' And will you?

How do you feel about the things you've not done, even if you know you should? In this book? And in life?

Think about the emotional impact of not doing things you know you ought to be doing, for your own good. Guilt, disappointment in yourself or irritation at me for pointing it out?

This is normal and it isn't just you. Everyone in your organisation will be feeling the same any time you tell them something they need to do and, for whatever reason, they don't do it.

30-second science spot

One challenge all leaders face is the law of **psychological reactance**. Simply put, people do not like to be told what to do. It's the bane of many leaders. They tell people to do things and they don't get done. The harder the leader tries to direct and instruct, the more resistance is built.

It is fascinating. Research shows that people are much **less** likely to do something once they've been told to do it.

In studies, people are given some problem-solving to do, and their levels of self-interest have been measured. Then, after a break, the process is repeated except, this time, they are told to focus on certain tasks and to avoid others. The subjects were much more likely to **avoid** the things that they were encouraged to do and much more likely to choose the things that they were told to avoid.

It's the rebel in all of us at work! We all recognise it from our own childhood: the rejection of authority and the refusal to do as we are told. Let's face it, however much you might have liked a tidy room, there was *no way* you were going to tidy it up when your parents told you to! Psychological reactance just comes to the fore.

Quite simply, the organisational approach, which is so common in business, of telling someone what to do and then selling them on the benefits will not work! It's primitive and it doesn't engage the part of the brain which motivates and inspires people to do what needs to be done and release the discretionary effort which rewards everyone.

Why, then, is asking questions so important?
Why have I been asking so many of them throughout this book?

Quite simply, by asking questions rather than telling you what to do, I am seeking to minimise psychological reactance. Can you see how powerful that can be?

In the same way, asking those you lead rather than telling them what to do has the same effect. By giving them adequate motive to want to do the task, they will feel good for having done it. Then they will want to do it again next time you need their help.

Compare these two:

A: I need you to write this report.
B: Would it be okay for you to help me with this report?

In turning you into an Inspirator I want to help you have more influence over others. In the first respect, it's about you having more influence over yourself. In Chapter 2 I spoke about you being a person of influence and how that would impact your life. Now take a moment to consider the impact you would have on the world if you were able to help others to influence themselves too.

This is about walking the walk and talking the talk. That means giving everyone else autonomy – giving people the same level of choice that you are starting to enjoy. Imagine having an organisation of people where everyone feels autonomy. They are self-inspired to be the best they can be and for the business to be the very best that it can be.

From all the interviews included in this book, there is a theme that runs through all the inspirational leaders I met. They all want those they inspire to have autonomy in everything they are doing.

When you think of many organisations today, they look like a triangle. You have leaders at the top and staff at the bottom. That is how organisations have functioned for years. When you listen to how Lucy Melling explained her role as a leader[2] however, she has flipped this on its head. She sees leadership as being the bottom of the triangle and supporting people to go up.

Ask better questions of others

One way you do this is by asking better questions of the people around you. Try saying, 'Listen, I'm really curious to understand, how can I get the best out of you? I want to inspire you and I want to support you. How do I get the best out of you?' A great question!

Just as long as you listen to the answers, of course!

If you start asking better questions of yourself and better questions of the people that you work with and lead, chances are they'll do the same. People learn by copying and mimicking and if you want people to get better, they need to copy and mimic what you're doing.

If you want to inspire others, act as you want them to act, so they have a good example to copy.

Deep work

The tool for this chapter has already been introduced: the questions you ask yourself. So here are a couple of exercises using questions which will help you develop this skill.

---

[2] *You can find her interview along with many others at Inspirators.me*

Question your way to action

If you need to take action, and perhaps you lack focus or motivation, this exercise will really help. It is great to use with other people too. It is great to help you to be consistent because it builds commitment. Doing this exercise will attach emotional feelings to change.

Start by picking a change that you want to put in place in your life. If nothing springs immediately to mind, choose something from the big three aspects of your goals - health, relationships, work. Then work your way through these six questions:

1. **Why might you want to change?**
   It's really important to emphasise the word "might," because "might" is non-confrontational, especially if you're doing this with other people. "But why **might** I want to change?" This is something you can journal. What is in it for you?

2. **How ready are you to change, on a scale of 1 to 10?**
   A measure of current commitment is always great to have. Ten means you're chomping at the bit and can't wait. One means psychological reactance is at maximum and you really don't want to do this.

3. **Why didn't you pick a lower number?**
   This question is really interesting, because it is so unexpected. Usually, people will ask "Why didn't you pick a higher number?" If you do that, you put pressure on yourself (it is another way of asking "Why aren't you good enough?") We want to fan the flame of your inspiration and we want to trigger you to think about the good reasons as to why you want to change.

4. **Imagine you have changed. What would the possible outcomes be?**
   This is helping you project the change into the future. What would your life look like? What would this do for you? What would it give you? What would it get you? This question is getting you to think about how the change will feel once it is made.

5. **Why is this important to you?**
   Now we reinforce the why. Remember, people don't buy what you do or how you do it. They buy **why** you do what you do. That includes you. Unless you have a strong *Why* for any change, it won't happen.

6. **What's the next step, if any?**
   It's important to emphasise that "if any." When you do, the immediate reaction is usually, "Oh, no, no, there is **something** I can do."

Now you have the next step to take, it is time to take action.

Have you been feeling some psychological reactance to this book so far? Are you aware that you are not releasing your own discretionary effort to get the most from it? Perhaps you could do this this exercise for *I want to get the most from this book.*

Develop your key question

Would you like to be a better leader?
Are you willing to get uncomfortable while you do it?
Are you prepared to invest the next 45–60 minutes of your time to do it right now?

If the answer to the latter of those questions is 'No' you might like to go back to the previous exercise and think about why you might want to spend the next 45 minutes on becoming a better leader even if you find it challenging.

Quick aside: Do you see what I did there?
I could very easily have said *This exercise will help you become a better leader. It will take between 45 - 60 minutes of your time, and it's going to challenge you!*

By telling you what to do, you might skip the exercise, or promise to do it later or find an excuse. That would generate psychological reactance.

And, if you do feel that reactance, I've given you a tool to use, to overcome it. Even if you *genuinely* can't do the exercise now – if you are on a train, or only have 5 minutes before a meeting, or don't have paper and pens right now – you have made a commitment to take action.
And now, back to the exercise...

Find some time where you will not be disturbed and write down 100 questions to ask yourself. They can be questions about absolutely anything. *Why is the sky blue? What is the meaning of life? Why am I reading this book? How do I fix the broken table leg?*

When you go through this process, the first few will just probably flow and then you'll get to a point where you feel that you can't think of any more. Keep going. You'll start to tune in to the questions you are asking yourself: *How do I improve my health? How do I become a better leader? What if I had my own TARDIS? How do I become a better partner to my spouse? What was the name of that cool app, Jerry showed me last night? What does a truly great day look like for me? When do I feel most alive? How can I take better care of myself? Why does a giraffe have a long neck? How can I manage my emotions more effectively?*

Once you have at least 100 questions, start looking for themes. Do not judge the questions – just group them around business, health, family, self-growth, money, general curiosity, fantastical ideas and so on.

Then, take the 10 questions that are most significant to you and within that top 10, rank them in order of importance. The one that you rank as most important is your **Key Question.**

Now write it down on a card or piece of paper where you can see it every day. Contemplate that question. Ask it of yourself every day, maybe several times a day, for a few days or a few weeks. Then maybe when you feel you have an answer that takes you forward, pick another question or repeat the whole exercise.

(Incidentally, whichever of those two options generates the most psychological reactance is probably the one you should do!)

This is an exercise that I did years ago and it fundamentally changed my life. The number one question many years ago was, "How do I get paid to do what I love doing?" I used to think about that question a lot.

What's your story?

I've been challenging you to ask better questions. So, try these as coaching questions for various situations to use on yourself and with others:

Coaching Questions
1. What can I learn?
2. What success have I had today?
3. Now what needs to be done?
4. How does this help me move forwards?
5. How can I be better today than I was yesterday?
6. Who am I inspired to become?

And finally...

> Be more concerned with your character than your reputation, because your character is what you really are, while your reputation is merely what others think you are.
>
> **John Wooden**

Considered to be the best coach in the world, John Wooden knew his role in bringing out the best in others. In particular, it wasn't about John Wooden – just as, as a coach to you, it isn't about me. It's about **you,** making change in your life. You did it.

And, for others, it is their actions that make the difference. All you can do is be the example.

4:

Ignoring Your Power

Changing your default setting.

Maria, these walls were not meant to shut out problems. You have to face them. You have to live the life you were born to live.

Mother Abbess – The Sound of Music

In this chapter, we will explore

- the truth
- the default settings you may have
- what it takes to get motivated
- how to inspire others by being the example
- two incredible tools to help you step into your power.

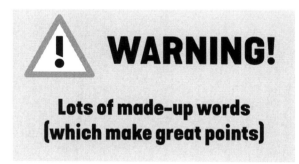

As if *Mary Poppins* wasn't enough, now we've got *The Sound of Music* as our film of choice for this chapter. *What's going on with all this Julie Andrews, Pete?*

Movie Time

I promise this is the last Julie Andrews film and the last musical I use but, for this topic, it provides exactly the examples I'm looking for. The whole essence of *The Sound of Music* is of people ignoring their true power and purpose. Maria, based on real-life Maria Kutschera, has entered the abbey in Salzburg. She has chosen to become a nun because she has fallen in love with the singing of the choir. Her inspiration is in music and she has followed the most obvious path towards it, but her true power isn't in the devotions of a convent. Unsurprisingly, she isn't a good fit and is sent instead to be governess to the Von Trapp family. She resists at first, clinging to the familiar, but is obliged to go, despite what she thinks she wants.

Do you believe that we all have a power – a purpose – which we must fulfil? I certainly do. What do you think happens when we ignore it? What are the consequences?

I have found that most people who are ignoring their calling – their desire to grow, to get better or to contribute – feel discontented and unfulfilled and question why their lives aren't as they feel they should be. In all aspects of their life they don't give their best. They pay lip service to their health, settle for unhappy relationships and simply mark time in their work.

So, if this is how we feel, why don't we take action and do what needs to be done? Why do we deny the truth of who we are meant to be?

The Truth

One of the things my coach used to say to me was:

> There is no such thing as the truth. Truth doesn't reside in books, in families, in religion. Truth resides in you. And as long as you're alive, and you're breathing, and you're causing problems in your life, **that's** the truth.
> Our role is to be our true self. Our desperation should be our inspiration for putting ourselves in difficult situations, so that we can do great things. There are no great things done without difficulty.

Truth is a difficult place to be and an even more challenging place to seek. If you are in any way nervous or frightened or scared by what this journey is calling you to do, that's quite normal. There can be uncertainty about exactly where we're going, right at this moment in time and uncertainty is uncomfortable.

Let us look at your truth. How do you feel about where you are right now? As I have said right from the outset, to be an Inspirator is to 'be the example' and that means being honest with how you think and feel and the impact that has on your life. What example do you set at the moment?

Consider how you act towards the big three aspects of leadership. What do you do to lead in your health, your relationships and your work? How consistent are you? How true to yourself? And how well do you balance between the three?

> ### *Movie Time*
> If that is too challenging, let's look at Captain Georg Von Trapp from *The Sound of Music* instead. He is lost in grief and the single parent to seven children in uncertain times. Unable to deal with his grief, he reverts to the way of acting which is most familiar to him – that of a naval captain. He runs his household as a tight ship – with fixed order and everything governed by whistles. His children are rebelling – though he cannot see it – and keeping a governess has been impossible.
>
> He may be the head of the household, but he isn't inspiring anyone to follow him.
>
> And yet, because rigid discipline and military precision are so familiar to him, he believes that this is the right way to operate and he is blind to how he is failing in his role as a father.

So what do you believe at the moment: about leadership? about yourself? about what is important? about the people you lead?

And who do you need to become to be the leader that you want to follow?

Whether you know the answer to that or if you are still trying to work it out, this chapter is to help you answer one single question.

What's stopping you?

Living in your comfort zone

In Chapter 2, I mentioned the concept of getting uncomfortable – that you need to be prepared for challenge in order to step into your power. I'm asking you to get comfortable with being uncomfortable.

Most of us think we are ready for change – we feel fired up and excited – but then, somehow, it doesn't happen. When you started this book, I expect you were full of enthusiasm for being an Inspirator: someone that people want to follow because you have a big *Why* and a cause. Perhaps you saw yourself being as inspiring as Winston Churchill or Martin Luther King or Joan of Arc. Then you started reading and I set you tasks and challenged your thinking. Have you done what I asked of you? Have you been looking in the mirror? Did you buy a journal? Have you been working on yourself?

No?

Okay. Before you read on, please do not give yourself a hard time if you haven't thrown yourself wholeheartedly into the process, just yet. You won't be the only one. This chapter is all about helping you understand why this happens – even for things that you believe you truly want.

And it all comes down to your superego, (that part of yourself which is there to guide you). It trips us up at every turn.

Do you remember the question I asked you in Chapter 1 about how you wake up in the morning? It is a simple example of how you live your life but if you are someone who hits snooze when the alarm goes off, or has to talk yourself up and out of comfort every morning, you are also the kind of person who will resist and be reluctant to take the steps necessary to become an Inspirator.

Story Time

My coach once asked me, "What is the nature of your mind?" I thought about it and gave him what I thought was a very clever answer about consciousness and feelings and self-awareness. He just smiled and said, "The nature of the mind is to *play tricks*. Most of these tricks are on you!"

He wasn't wrong. Our mind favours what is known, and it is made up from the information we are fed by others and will cunningly rationalise resistance. I've asked you to do exercises after each chapter of this book. Have you been doing that? Or did you resist? And did you say to yourself *I'll read the book all the way through first, then I'll go back and do them*? And will you?

Whenever you think about doing anything that's new, your superego will hold you back. When you are presented with anything that's

Richard Curen

There's a model [where you have] a superego and [an ego and an] id. ... The superego is one's critical voice ... that says, 'Oh, you're not good enough. You should have done this differently.' Or, 'You're always going to fail so don't bother.'

unfamiliar, difficult or dull, it tries to protect and generates a sense of "I don't feel like it" or "People will laugh at me" or "Oooh! Look! Kittens!!!" Disinclination, doubt and distraction are all ways your mind plays tricks.

We have formed habits. Why do you suppose we've done that? The reason we do this is so that we can do the action without thinking about it. We can forget about it. That way, we have room to learn something else. Unfortunately, the challenge this presents is that these habits over time, have created *default settings* and the mind doesn't know whether something is right or wrong. It just does what we've practiced doing.

Default settings

This is something I've seen in every person I've ever worked with and in myself as well. I have default settings in all areas of my life. In relationships, in the way I work, in how I move through the day and in how I live my life.

We all have so many default settings. What are some of yours that you are already familiar with? I invite you to start noticing others when they occur. Be curious about your default settings and how they serve you.

There are always a dozen excuses for not doing something that we can come up with. There is only one excuse for doing it.

It is what needs to be done.

We all make excuses and we all procrastinate.

Procrastination is defined as the combination of having an *intention* for action where there is a *needless or voluntary delay* and where the *delay is to our disadvantage*.
I believe that most of us put off being better than we are now.

Story Time

Someone once asked me, "What is most expensive land in the world?"

I thought about it and suggested a few places:
- Perhaps it was Palm Jumeirah – a man-made island off Abu Dhabi
- Or maybe Buckingham Palace in London
- Or it could be one of the plots of land in Monte Carlo

"No" my friend replied. "The most expensive land in the world is the graveyard. It is full of missed opportunities and unfulfilled dreams."

He was right. What value is being lost through procrastination in your life?

We all have that tendency to procrastinate, we all have that tendency to put things off, to stay where we're comfortable. We all 'just don't feel like it.'

Somewhere buried in our mind, we associate pain with an action. Have you ever considered why that might be?

In my experience, we procrastinate because we think the journey ahead will be hard. And, when we are faced with a choice or a challenge, where we don't do something to move us forward, we head back to the 'default settings' – the mindset, beliefs and attitudes we have always had.

This is where fear, worry, doubt and frustration sit because we know we're not doing what we really **could** be doing.

Patti Dobrowolski

There's a part of us in our innate cellular structure that wants to grow. And there's a part of our brain, the amygdala, that wants to keep us safe from harm. So, if you create too much strange or change in your basal ganglia, it's going to send out this warning, like 'Danger! Danger! Don't go any faster. This is terrible ...' I think that's built into our DNA ... When we had to protect yourself from the dinosaurs and that we've carried it over into our behaviour now.

Step up to the mic

Here is one of the exercises I love to do when I work with groups of leaders in an organisation. I'll ask if one of them wants to stand up and sing. It is rare that someone will stand up, because nobody wants to stand out. We all just want to fit in.

It is the superego at work again. In a room full of people, even the most amazing singer will hesitate to step up to the mic. The inner voice goes, "No, no, no, no, no. Don't do that. Let's stay put."

What we say to ourselves is key. I have spent many years training people in organisations how to deal with the interference in their head so they can become more at peace and to be more productive. This is something we'll go into in a lot more detail in Chapter 6.

For now, start to put your superpower of awareness to use in listening in to that inner voice and how it shows up. Become curious about what your own internal world is like and start to wonder about what is going on for other people.

Warren Rosenburg

For me, in order to be really successful in life, you have to fail, and you mustn't be scared of being wrong. That's very important... it's just natural isn't it? People get scared, people can generally feel suppressed and worried and anxious about decisions they make with the consequences that they make. And I just see it that, you know what, we need to be brave.

An end of *Should-ing* and *Must-erbating*

> When you are listening out for that inner voice, there are a couple of things to be particularly aware of. Look out for when you say to yourself either, "I *should* do this," or "I *must* do that."
> What happens when you do? Does the inner voice replies "You should, but you won't." or "You must? Who are you to tell me what to do?"

There is a rebel within us. We all dislike being told what to do; when that happens, even if we are telling ourselves, we resist.

So, stop *Should-ing* on yourself and stop *Must-erbating*. When you do either of these, distraction inevitable follows. The conversation usually goes something like this:

"I should do this; I really must. But I'll just do *this*" (some short task or check social media or reply to emails). "After all, it will only take a minute or two." Before we know it, that thing that we should do and must do has faded away into the background. We might have forgotten it or the reason for doing it is lost. And it never happens.

Take a moment to consider how many people all over the world are in that same situation. There is something they need to do to become a better version of themselves and reach their goals. All they're saying to themselves, however is, "I'll just do this first,'" or "I don't feel like it" or "I'll do it tomorrow."

Why don't we respond at once? Why aren't we taking action on all these important things which will change our lives?

It all comes down to who we are. In his book, *Straight Line Leadership,* Dusan Djukich calls it the 'inner stance' – where you are coming from right now.

Are you coming from a place of worry, fear or doubt? Are you looking at past failures and using them to shape your decisions? Or do come you from a place of optimism – looking at a possible future which will fulfil and excite you?

So many of us in this world act on how we **feel** rather than who we are.

Do you begin to understand why we spent two whole chapters on who you are right now and why you want to change?

You see, if you want to change your life and change the world around you, you have to understand how you operate now so you can decide how you need to change.

The motivation equation

So, what can we do to change this? How can I help you think differently about what needs to be done so that you can move from procrastination to procrastin**action**?

Even when you have a strong *Why* to give you personal power, there are other forces at work.

The 30-second science spot

One way to view this is to look at the Motivation Equation developed by eminent psychologist Dr. Piers Steel.

$$Motivation = \frac{E \times V}{I \times D}$$

Where E = Expectation, V= Value, I = Impulsivity and D = Delay

For your journey of becoming an Inspirator, the *value* is your *Why*. What will it give me? What will it get me? What difference will I make, if I go on this journey?

Expectation is to believe that the outcome is possible and to know what it will be like. To have a vision and faith in the future.

The aim is to maximise these. We have to drive up the value of who we will become and what we're doing and where we are going. And to believe in it and see the future where you have become an Inspirator.

Because, if we don't, then it is too easy to give in to *impulsivity* – in other words, all those distractions.

Continued on next page

I believe that the most squandered commodity in the Western world right now, for most people, is their attention. Our attention is massively drawn upon as we act on our impulses. In a world that's full of information, it's so easy to get distracted. It's so easy to decide to do something else and move away from the path. The tool for this chapter, '54321', is specifically designed to help you with this.

And, whatever, you may have heard or believe, multi-tasking is a myth. Our brains operate very much like any computer. We can only process one thing at a time. While we may be able to switch quickly from thought to thought, idea to idea and task to task, only one of them has our attention at a time. So if you are doing multiple things, you are flitting between them and not doing any of them as well as if you were just focusing on one thing.

When we give in to distractions and do something else, we are *delaying* our journey. And the longer it takes to get started, the harder it becomes to start at all.

I love Piers Steel's motivation equation because it helps you look objectively at the excuses you make and why you procrastinate. It is a way of putting a spotlight on yourself and raising your awareness. I invite you to use it next time you 'just don't feel like' doing something, to see what needs to be done to increase your expectation and value and reduce your impulsivity and delay. Just imagine for a moment what impact it would have if you used this technique consistently.

Know your default settings

Movie time

Default settings repeat constantly. In *The Sound of Music,* when Maria is challenged by her feelings for Georg Von Trapp, she runs back to the Abbey – returning to her default setting of wanting to be a nun, rather than facing the more difficult challenge of living in the real world.

What happens once we start to realise that we are made up of a series of habits and patterns and that we have a choice? When we see that leadership is constant growth and improvement?

We give ourselves the power to change. We become the leader who *goes first.*

What allows us to change is to approach similar situations with a heightened degree of awareness and use the opportunity to do things differently and get a different result. Think of it as being like the movie *Groundhog Day*, in which Bill Murray repeats the same day over and over again, always experimenting and trying different alternatives.

> So, over the next few weeks and months, start to become aware of the many default settings that you have. It's so easy to do what you've done in the past. It's so easy to go back to familiar patterns.
>
> See yourself as a detective, seeking out clues and looking for evidence. One of the greatest achievements you will have is to go into situations where in the past you might have reacted one way but now begin to realise that you can change the way you act.
>
> What would it be like to break that pattern? What would it be like if, the next time you face a situation which, in the past, has taken you to a default setting, you approached it with a heightened awareness and remembered that you have a choice?

This is a real journey of self-discovery. You will find out things about yourself that surprise you and you'll become more aware of where these things come from.

We have more power than we realise

An exercise I do with people is to ask them to put up their hand "as high as you can." Then, when I've seen how high they can lift it, I'll say "Okay, now put it up a bit higher." Everyone can go a little bit higher. It's another default setting! We unconsciously hold back and don't push ourselves to our limits.

Every single one of us has more power than we realise. Every single one of us can go that little bit further than we realise. Your decisions and actions are determined by the goals you set but, just as importantly, by your current mindset and attitude. If you identify strongly with who you are and who you want to become there is nothing you will not do to achieve it.

> ### *Movie Time*
> Consider Georg Von Trapp. While he reverted to his default setting of a military man after the loss of his first wife, he wasn't prepared to do the same when his core identity – that of an Austrian – was challenged. As the Anschluss loomed, he refused to welcome the idea of German supremacy or renounce his heritage.
>
> I'm sure he 'didn't feel like it' and he took huge risks, with his own life and with that of his wife and children, but he was prepared to leave everything behind rather than be anything but authentic.

One of the biggest transitions that you're going to make during the course of this leader's journey, is creating the identity of the leader that you are becoming. We'll cover this in more detail in Chapter 9 but here is where the journey really starts. You have a choice to embark on this journey, to form that new identity and to be that version of you every single day.

And it will be hard.

It is hard to be consistent and to be honest and to hear your superego whisper-ing, "What will people think?" or "You are going to fail – don't bother." You may even question that you are an Inspirator as you do things which are dull and ordinary and become commonplace: 'I'm not so special...' It can seem quite ordinary to be disciplined, but it is actually extraordinary. That's where great leaders are made.

This is a different form of expectation and is just as valuable on your journey as the expectation of a great outcome.

'Simon says' – Inspire other people

Did you ever play the party game *Simon Says* when you were a child? It is simple enough. You do what 'Simon Says' and ignore any other instructions. I used to play it and I absolutely loved it. I really focused on listening to what was said and, as a result, became something of a grand master!

To become a leader is to become 'Simon', not only to yourself, but also to others. Do what it takes and go the extra mile, because people follow those who go that little bit further than everybody else.

When something challenging needs doing, the traditionalist approach is to say, 'Look, just pull your socks up and get on with it. Stop making such a fuss.'

This is an example of one of the most damaging forms of 'institutional blind-ness'.

Institutional Blindness

Institutional Blindness, is a relatively new term referring to an organisation which is focusing on certain areas and failing to see the whole. They are either inward looking and failing to see how changes in the outside world affect them, or they are not looking at every part of their own business and only optimising on one front.

The institutional blindness I see most often is where people with influence and authority, fail to recognise what is actually going on for the people who work with them. They have no idea of how teams actually feel about who they are and what they're doing.

This is what exists in so many businesses.

The leadership fails to understand what is going on for people when they are being asked to embark on a new journey. People feel controlled and imposed upon. They have to change how they do things and move away from what is famil-iar, so they feel pressure. These external demands to achieve a specific outcome are something over which they had no say and have no control.

As a result, they will be operating from their own default settings. These may be a fear of not being good enough, or uncertainty about job prospects, or previous experiences of changes which were bad for them.

What would the impact be if we used a new approach? If we changed everything so that everything we do is to bring forward the next generation of leaders?

The best way to go about doing that is, of course, to go first. As you take the bold steps yourself, you'll empower the people around you to copy your lead.

What if you could create an environment where people are confident enough to take action? The world is full of people, especially in business, who don't want to take the action they know they should be taking. They just want to do what they've done before because they don't want to stand out. They don't want to make mistakes.

So how can we create the environment of people going from procrastinators to **procrastin-actors?**

You can do this by:
- Being open and honest when you catch yourself making excuses and encourage others to be aware of the excuses they make.
- Teasing out from your team what goals they are aiming for, and what potential might be within them.
- When they resist or delay, asking them (non-confrontationally) what is stopping them?
- Then asking, what actions could they take, today, to get started? And to unblock the obstacles?

The cure for institutional blindness comes with each individual curing their own blindness to what is going on. Ultimately, this is about people taking responsibility for what they think and feel and do. That's what Inspirators do.

As you are now starting to wake up and see things much more clearly around you, you will be able to lead the way for others.

Deep work

The tools in this chapter are designed to help you take action.

If you look over your life, can you see times where you failed to take action or follow through? Where your mind tricked you into not doing something which could have made a massive difference?

If you can start to do what needs to be done as quickly as possible without leaving time to hesitate, you'll be learning a very, very valuable skill of leaders.

The combination of these two tools is incredibly powerful and can change lives. Apply them as your read the rest of this book.

54321

This is one of the greatest tools I've ever come across. I use it *all* the time.

I first came across it in a TED Talk by Mel Robbins and it is a great way to start engaging in action. It works to get you started on something and also to cool impulses.

And it is as simple as it is effective.

What happened this morning when you woke up? Did you hit snooze, several times, lie there wishing for longer, waiting until your bladder insisted that you *had* to get up?

If there is something you need to do, or an impulse you want to control you have five seconds to act before your brain kicks in and turns on the default setting (be that fear and worry, to stay in bed a bit longer or to eat the bar of chocolate).

So, when the desire to act comes on you:

Five... Four... Three... Two... One.... And then, take action!

This is great for moving away from the impulsivity and delay which we discussed as the two denominators of the Piers Steel motivation equation. Just think of the difference it could make if you consistently used this technique. It's such a simple technique not only to move you forward, but to move you away from the destructive habits which so many of us have.

This is such a powerful tool to get yourself started.

- Five... Four... Three... Two... One.... Get out of bed
- Five... Four... Three... Two... One.... Don't snap at the kids
- Five... Four... Three... Two... One.... Give your team member your full attention
- Five... Four... Three... Two... One.... Go for a run
- Five... Four... Three... Two... One.... Turn off your mobile to avoid distractions
- Five... Four... Three... Two... One.... Close the fridge door

Always say it like you really mean it. I use the countdown from the *Thunderbirds* TV show 'Five, four, three, two, one. Thunderbirds are Go!'

Always count down. If you count up you could just carry on counting.

Never cheat on it. This is a tool which cannot be done casually. It has to be done with true conviction every time because if you don't do it that way, you will become a casualty of the exercise; Something else which adds to the evidence of, "you can't do this" and gives power to your default settings.

54321 will help you with the many exercises that will follow in this book. Look out for the symbol of the rocket ship to remind you. They have to be done with gusto and this will help you do that.

2-minute rule

This is another incredibly simple tool, for avoiding procrastination and this comes from David Allen's book, *Getting Things Done*.

If something takes less than two or three minutes to do, do it **now.** Don't write it on a task list or spend time delegating it – that would take longer than the two minutes it takes to complete the task. Get it done and out of the way and off your mind.

So, if I ask you to do something, especially if it's going to take less than two minutes to do, recognise the resistance and then go against that resistance by:

Five... Four... Three... Two... One.... And then, take action!

Coaching questions to ask yourself – what's your story?

In your journal, go through these questions to understand your default settings better. It should not take you any more than 2 minutes to do this (so there is no excuse to not do it, is there?)

1. What are the excuses you make to justify procrastination or to ignore the call to action?
2. What are you saying to yourself right now about the idea of being a different type of leader – an Inspirator?
3. When you are faced with a challenge or a call to action what are the default settings you have?
4. What one action could you take today to move forward (in other words, What's important now?)

And finally...

> *Fuck it – my final thought before making most decisions.*
> ### *Will Ferrell*

Will Ferrell is a great example of someone who took the call to action. When he was offered the movie *Elf,* he thought it could be the last movie he ever made – and it had the potential to be an absolute turkey! A grown man in tights? But he took the chance and it launched his career.

So the time has come for us to Five... Four... Three... Two... One.... and get on with our lives. It is time to take positive action every single day to drive yourself forwards as you continue to make waves, make improvements, become a better version of yourself and become a true Inspirator.

5: Stepping Into the Unknown

The point of no return.

Sam: This is it.
Frodo: This is what?
Sam: If I take one more step, it'll be the farthest away from home I've ever been.
Frodo: Come on, Sam. Remember what Bilbo used to say: 'It's a dangerous business, Frodo, going out your door. You step onto the road, and if you don't keep your feet, there's no knowing where you might be swept off to.'
The Lord of the Rings: The Fellowship of the Ring

In this chapter, we will explore
• fear – where it comes from and how you can harness it
• the small steps that make a big difference
• how to inspire others to see their own power
• two tools to help you step through your fear.

Movie Time

The Lord of the Rings is an epic adventure and, like Joseph Campbell, J.R.R.Tolkien was an academic who studied ancient stories and their patterns. Both *The Hobbit*, its predecessor, and *The Lord of the Rings* follow a classic hero's journey and it is easy to map it out against the plot. The quote I've chosen from *The Fellowship of the Ring* is, in some ways, minor and unimportant but not for Frodo or Sam. It is a huge step for them to take. They are moving into a new and uncertain world. They are leaving the Shire and entering into unfamiliar territory.

The adventure comes from stepping into the unknown. It's not just the excitement and uncertainty of the unknown that makes it worth the risk either. This is where our growth happens.

To move forward as an Inspirator means you must go into uncharted waters.

So, if this is what needs to be done and the benefits are so significant, what makes us hesitate from taking steps like this?

Fear!

We feel fear and it holds us back.

Have you ever considered the consequences of fear?

I've used the metaphor of leadership being like a sea voyage before. It is risky and you don't know what is going to happen. Surely staying in a safe harbour would be better? But ships were not made to be stuck in a yard or in a marina. In fact, that's where the ship will rust. Ships are made to go out and set sail and go somewhere.

So, let me ask you – what are **you** made to do? Are you made to stay in a safe harbour? Or to go on a voyage of discovery?

As you move forwards, you're always going to face obstacles, danger and crisis.

Tony Taylor

If you [are] someone who fears and lacks confidence ... then people [around you] say "My God, if he is afraid, what's going on? What don't we know? What's the problem?' So ... sometimes ... I will have a slightly less confident day, but you have to be very, very careful then how you interact with everybody.

Crisis arose from the Greek word *krinein* which means 'decision' or 'turning point.' The idea of a crisis being something to be avoided emerged far later. The idea remains. In modern Japanese, **crisis** has two pictograms, one meaning "opportunity" and one meaning "danger".

Do you remember what I said in Chapter 2, that you only get to see the best of people when they face some crisis? They feel they don't have a choice and are driven to move away from something and have to make a change. In doing so, they move forwards.

They are compelled to create something new. This journey to the new reality, this future, is a place where fear doesn't really have a place. Often, their fear becomes an energy that can excite them to move forwards.

I want to show you how you can use fear as a force which can take you forward. So, when you are faced with a crisis in your life, see it as a turning point.

The origins of fear

The 30-second science spot

We all experience fear. It is a basic instinct driven by the amygdala, one of the most primal areas of the brain – and common to most animals. Fear, as an emotional response, evolved to protect us. It occurs when we feel under attack or are faced with some other form of danger.

The amygdala generates a chemical reaction in the body (often known as 'fight or flight') preparing us to run away or defend ourselves. It is powerful and, in the right situations, amazing.

Someone once said that FEAR stands for *Forget Everything And Run* and that is pretty accurate in a lot of cases.

Some of those fears are of things in the external world – dogs or spiders or fire. Others will be internal fears – of failure, of not being good enough, of not being loved. These are not fears we are born with. In fact, we are born with only two fears: the fear of falling and the fear of loud noises. Everything else, we have learned: from what we have been told or seen or experienced as we grow up and explore the world.

Sadly, the brain isn't all that discerning. It knows that nothing nasty happens when you do what you've always done, (based on the evidence of your continued survival), so it tries to keep you there. What's more, it sees other people reacting with fear and decides (often on the basis of a single instant) that you should experience that fear as well.

Perhaps, once, when you were very small, you were told by your anxious parent, "Don't go near the fire." Maybe you were in real danger at that moment and they were alarmed and spoke sharply. You felt that alarm and became afraid of fire, even when it posed no threat.

Which means, more often that not, that fear is: **F**alse **E**vidence **A**ppearing **R**eal.

This is a subject that has always fascinated me. I spent years working with people with a range of different fears and wrote *Fear-Busting* to explore it further and help people deal with their own fears. It became an international best-seller and was translated into multiple languages which gives you some idea of how many people are struggling with fear and looking for answers.

As a psychologist and coach, the most interesting people I have worked with were often people that had fears that were the most unusual. I did, of course, work with people who were afraid of snakes, spiders or flying. Sometimes, though, clients would come to me with fear of, for example, a particular colour, or feathers, or buttons.

I would always work under the premise that their fear was real to them but was just an illusion that was created by their mind. We would work together and, just as they had learned to fear, they learned to respond in a different way.

In this chapter, that is what I want to show you. Anything you have learned in your past can be replaced by a different learning and tools like 54321 and some of the others I will share with you, will help you deal with this.

Delphine Rive

We all have fears. ... I have mine. You have yours. ... Finding a way to give people the confidence that they can themselves overturn the lack of confidence in themselves or these things they're worried about. I really admire the person who helped me to do that and I try and do it to others. It can be difficult, but I do try and do that to others.

Understand your fear

> Do you believe you can control your fear?
> Not always – and certainly not in the way most people use that word. If you are afraid of something you cannot simply **not** be afraid of it. Fear is automatic.
> Do you believe you can choose how fear affects you?

You learned to be afraid, which means that you can learn something different too. And the first step is to see fear for what it is.

Looking fear in the face

As with any change, the most important first step is to become more aware – to be curious about what you fear, why you fear, and how you fear and to see the impact that has on your life.

Why?

Simply because a curious mind is open to new ways of moving through the world. A curious mind becomes interested in what is on the other side of fear and what life would be like if you were no longer held back by a fear and, instead, could move through it.

What if you aren't prepared to examine and understand your fears? What is the alternative? What happens if you allow them to govern your life?

By putting fear in the driving seat, you nourish it and it continues to grow. Let me give you a simple example:

Story Time

I know someone who, when he was about six, was dunked in a swimming pool. It was a traumatic experience. When I first met him, in his twenties, he told me about it, saying, "I can't swim because I'm afraid of water."

Over the years, he continued to say this to himself and to everyone around him: "I'm afraid of water." By the time he was in his forties he couldn't take a bath and, in his fifties, even a shower became a place of fear.

In all that time, he had no other traumatic experience in water. He'd never been out of control or been in danger. But the fear had grown, simply on the strength of one experience and what he had continued to say to himself.

This may seem like it doesn't relate to you but, every time we say to ourselves or to others, "I can't because I'm afraid," we are feeding the fear and making it stronger. Even the internal fears, such as, "What will people think?" will grow if you continue to nourish them.

The most powerful thing we can ever do is to realise that it is okay to be afraid; to be more curious about where we are and what we are going to do about it rather than running away or suffering unnecessarily.

Movie Time

Think of Sam and Frodo. The easiest thing for them to do would have been to turn back but then, of course, nothing would have changed and the outcomes for the world would have been very different. And we wouldn't have watched the film!

By being curious, by asking the right questions, we gain an understanding of what is really going on.

It could be as simple as asking yourself a question like, "What is this fear here to teach me?"

Or even, "How would I teach someone else my fear?"

One effective method I've found when working with people who experience fear, is to ask them to teach me how to feel their fear the way they do.

You can do it too. If there is a specific fear you experience, just imagine you are the world's expert in that fear and you now need to teach your expertise to someone else.

As you do this, you will probably start to see that your fear follows a certain process. Perhaps it starts with thinking about it, then picturing something in a certain way, which then produces a feeling and then a dialogue inside your mind starts which tends to repeat itself over and over and over again.

As I've mentioned before, the mind is an extremely powerful tool. When you tune into it in this way, you can see your imagination getting to work. *You see a button, you make an inner association with a previous trauma and then imagine a whole world of disaster.* How creative is that?

It is this creativity and imagination which leads the mind to play tricks on us but it has advantages too.

The mind is also a channel and, if you put it in a particular place, it will continue to follow the path you have set it on.

Be mindful of your fear

Do you multitask? Are you good at it? Our minds can only do one thing at a time effectively. Multitasking doesn't work. The flip-side of that, however, is that, if you give your mind something to do, it tends to keep doing it unless given an alternative. It will follow a particular pathway and, through practice it starts to do it automatically.

Have you realised that this is how you learn to fear in the first place? Someone or something tells you to feel fear in a circumstance. Next time that circumstance arises, the brain remembers and repeats the pattern and, over time, creates an automatic response. Fear is just a habit!

That habit will continue until you develop a new way of directing your mind.

One of the simplest ways to deal with fear is to be grounded in the present moment. Some people call this 'mindfulness', some people call this 'meditation.' Whatever you call it, one of the reasons to practice something like this is for you to be more able to direct the focus of your mind.

Take a moment to think about your inner dialogue when you are talking about mindfulness. How do you feel about the idea of stopping and 'doing nothing' instead of taking action? How you feel about things affects your thoughts and your thoughts affect your actions.

Right now, try this (using 54321 if you are feeling resistance). As you breathe in say, "Now I'm breathing in," and as you breathe out, say, "Now I'm breathing out." This simple instruction just brings your body and mind together. If you do this for 10 or 20 seconds, you're starting to meditate. As you do it, you'll start to notice how your mind wanders. As your mind wanders, just bring it back and start again.

And again.

And again.

And again.

By practicing like this every day, even if for just a few seconds each time, you start to connect to the present moment.

If you do this when you feel fear, your mind will stop running the familiar fear processes. The mind plays tricks, remember? This is one of the tricks it plays.

You may well be asking, *Why are you talking so much about fear, Pete?*

I'm doing this to help you face your fear of becoming an Inspirator.

Harness your fear and put it to use

What separates an Inspirator from the rest?

The true greats among us have learnt to act **despite** their fears or to use their fears as a powerful energy. They know that their infinite potential exists in them moving past the things that scare them. They know that they'll never be a champion in the things that matter to them in life if they don't use fear to step through the fear and get stronger.

Whenever you step into the unknown, fear is bound to appear. You will have doubts or you'll ask yourself 'what if..?' or you'll recall a previous, similar situation where things didn't work out. It is natural and something we all experience.

Fear, however, is actually a very powerful energy, and if you can harness it, you can become incredibly strong. You become the fearless leader who people want to follow.

 A quick aside about being fearless.

Think for a moment about your favourite inspiring leader. Do you believe they were without fear? Do you suppose they never had doubts about the path they were on?

When I talk about a *fearless leader,* I don't mean that you feel no fear. That isn't realistic – nor is it desirable.

The only people who experience no fear are people who have experienced damage to the amygdala and, because they do not fear, they have no sense of self-preservation. They have to be prevented from stepping out into traffic or walking into fires or jumping into shark-infested waters. Trust me – you don't want that.

 When I use the expression *fearless leader* I am referring to someone who does not allow their fears to hold them back. They step up and step out and, even when it seems really hard to get started, they: "five, four, three, two, one," and do it anyway. They use the activation energy that is needed not once, not twice, but over and over and over again. Once you start to do this, your life will transform.

So, how can you harness your fear and put it to good use? Let me answer that with a true-life case story. Let me tell you about Thomas Edison.

Oh no – not ANOTHER story about Edison!!!!

The 30-second history spot

Thomas Edison is remembered as a prolific inventor and was one of the pioneers of the electric light bulb. He was the first man to produce one which was viable for production. As he was working on ways to get previous versions to glow brightly, not burn out the filament and not need more power to run than was readily available, he failed over and over again.

At one stage, someone asked him, "How do you feel to have failed so many times?"

His reply was, "I have not failed. I have just found 10,000 ways that won't work." He saw those failures as opportunities; as ways to learn and grow stronger. He flipped his fear into excitement for the new possibilities.

And do you want to know the best bit?

Thomas Edison committed himself to working on the electric light bulb because... *he was afraid of the dark!*

It is often said that *necessity is the mother of invention* and it was certainly true here. Sometimes fear can drive us forward and encourage us to seek out new opportunities.

Own your fears

When you experience fear do you believe you have a choice of how to react?

Often our instincts make us want to fight our fears. We want to struggle, suppress our feelings, or back away.

The more aware you become, however, the more you notice it, so take a momentary step back and acknowledge the fear. The more you are mindful in the moment, the more you are able to choose a different option. You'll start to spot the patterns and processes you usually go through and nip them in the bud before the fear overtakes you.

You'll start to notice what you are saying to yourself and decide if it is based on truth or illusion.

Simon Cook

I've been through [challenges] so many times in my career ... where actually you go in thinking the worst is going to happen and you come out knowing the best happened, but you never think that at the beginning.

> *Never let your feelings get you down*
> *Open up your eyes and look around*
> *It's just an illusion.*
> **Lyric from 'Illusion' by Imagination**

When facing fear, can you ask better questions? Here's one: *If I was excited about this thing I'm afraid of, how would I feel right now?*

The 30-second science spot

That is a particularly powerful question because fear and excitement are very similar emotions. In fact, the body chemistry is the same in both cases. The only difference is our perspective on how we feel and where we focus our attention.

Instead of fixing your mind on the past – when you've had a previous bad experience – focus on the future. How will you feel when you take action **despite** your fear? How will the world be a better place as a result of you doing this? What does the future look like if you don't listen to your fear?

We've mentioned the technique of visualising your future on a couple of occasions already but seeing it when you feel fear is particularly powerful. When you see your future and know that fear won't stop you, you have hope.

The science of hope

Hope originated in 13ᵗʰ century German and its meaning has never really altered. **Hope** is where you see a better future than what you have today, you believe you have what it takes, and you're prepared to take multiple pathways to get to where it is that you want to go.

To develop hope in yourself and the people around you is to become a true Inspirator.

Story Time

My own story has been a journey towards fearlessness. I lived in fear for many years: a deep fear that I wasn't good enough, and a desire to move away from my past, seeking affirmation as external proof that I was worthy. Then I learned to focus on the future and became very driven to move forwards.

Over the last five or six years, however, I've learnt through working with others, just how important it is to dream of the future, and to be grounded in the moment and to be excited about what I can learn along the way. I know that the obstacles that I'm going to face are just signposts for me to get stronger, to learn, to get better and to be the person I'm truly capable of being.

I've seen this same pattern in thousands of people I've worked with in the last 30 years. Are you ready to be one of them?

Most people fear stepping into 'the unknown', but if you have hope and you see a future worth fighting for, then it's not unknown. We are going to talk more about hope later in the book.

Acting in the face of fear

At the very start of this book, I told you that leadership is not a destination. Being an Inspirator means to be constantly pushing the boundaries of what we've done before.

You have great goals, yes. You have vision and mission and purpose and you know *Why*.

But you can't wait to be inspired to attain these ambitions. You have to go and find that inspiration yourself.

Inspiration comes from taking action. Power, your **real** power, comes in taking action. It moves you forwards in the direction that you want to go rather than sitting and waiting. This is the best way for you to get in the game of becoming a true Inspirator.

And this is one of the biggest changes that you will make in your life.

If you take action you move away from fear and move towards being a fearless leader.

Nothing in life is more important than action.

This is another key aspect of success. I want you to start to focus more on the **process**. If you execute the process, the outcomes take care of themselves. You must recognise that it's the little things done over a sustained period of time, being incredibly consistent, which brings about massive change in yourself, the people around you, and organisations.

John Sellins

He showed how important clarity of vision was because recruiting them was one thing, keeping them all on the same path all the way through [was another] ... We did that by regular and constant briefings. ... And he was brilliant at it. And he would say, 'Today the message is this. We're going to do that. And we're going to do that.' And he'd say it again and then he'd say it again.

As an Inspirator that means you need to do deep work around your health, your relationships, and your work and to do it in a consistent way. Turn off distractions. Be truly present.

In his autobiography, Nigel Mansell mentions something similar. He would be so focused on driving each lap as perfectly as the last that sometimes, the pit team would need to talk to him to prevent him going to sleep. Can you image falling asleep while driving at over 100 miles an hour?!

In order to do this, whether you want to win a Formula 1 championship, or be an Inspirator, you must forgo validation, approval, selfishness, being self-absorbed, self-promotion, and impulses. Instead, you are looking for *kaizen*.

> ***Kaizen*** is a Japanese word which means, *'change for better'* with an inherent meaning of *'continuous'* or *'philosophy.'* It has come to mean *'continuous improvement'* and is used widely as a method for improving processes via incremental changes. To me it means taking the small steps every single day which add up to huge change.

Kaizen is how you can break fear down into small, incremental steps every day.

Application

Another way to look at these small steps and daily actions is to have *rituals*. Daily routines and actions which ground you in what you are aiming for and, at the same time, lift you up and give you a sense of achievement.

There is another point to taking action – even when fear holds us back. This book, like any book, is of course, about knowledge. More importantly, (unlike many books) it's about the **application** of knowledge.

Knowledge only has value if you apply it. My coach used to say to me, 'Pete, you have read enough books. Go and use the knowledge to **do** something.'

The best way to apply knowledge is to take action. The greatest achievement is the consistency you show when you take action, even when you don't feel like it. It's a way of moving through fear. It allows you to prove to yourself that the world won't end, you won't die and no one will hate you for doing what you were previously afraid to do.

This is a key part of growing your confidence, by becoming a person who does what you say you are going to do, when you say you're going to do it.

So, how do you get yourself to take action when your default settings are doubt, fear, worry and procrastination?

What does Nike know?

This challenge is something that one of the biggest companies in the world recognises. Nike is one of the most recognised global brands for sportswear. They know that, however good it is for us, many of us don't want to take exercise. So, they made their strap line *Just do it*.

It is a great saying and a great piece of marketing. They recognise that, like it or not, you just have to get on with it. Even the name, *Nike,* comes from the Greek goddess of victory. Putting on your running shoes to go for a run is a victory but you have to 'just do it' – it's up to you.

What their advertising doesn't recognise is that, while you can 'just do it', you can also, 'just **not** do it.'

'Just do it' might work for a 30-minute gym session but when it comes to thinking about some of the things in life which are on a larger scale, the brain resists. Just imagine if your mission was world peace, for example. When you say to yourself, "Just do it," your inner voice replies, "It's too big to *just do*, so I'm just not going to do anything."

The answer is to break it down, get the brain focusing only on the first step and to get rid of the debate.

Would it be okay if I offer you an alternative? Instead of *Just Do It*, how about *Just Get Started*?

 That example of world peace may seem ludicrous but, just for a moment, imagine that it *was* your mission. What one thing could you do to make a start on that mission?

Is it possible that, to have peace in the world, the way to get started is to have peace within yourself? And then to show everyone around you how to have that same inner peace within themselves?

The hardest thing to do in life is just to start. Literally!

Childbirth is incredibly challenging for the mother and the baby (it's pretty tough on the father too!). Once that new life has arrived in the world, matters get considerably easier.

Just think about it. Think about the energy that it takes to launch something, whether it's a car or a plane or a rocket.

It was the same with this book. When I decided to write it, the hardest thing to do was to get started. With every chapter, the hardest thing to do was to get started. When you bought it, I'm sure that the hardest thing to do was to start reading it – instead of putting it on the shelf with all the other books you 'should read' and 'must read'.

But the most productive people out there consistently take action and just get started. So much of that launch energy comes from being an Inspirator. It's what 54321 is all about.

Power Boost – Inspire other people

Do you remember what I said my goal was for you? How I want to show you how to be an inspiring leader – an Inspirator – so you can bring forward the next generation and lead them to unlock their fullest potential?

Is that your goal? How committed are you, on a scale of 1 (not interested) to 10 (all in)? Why didn't you give yourself a lower number? (Did you see what I did there? This is one of the tools from Chapter 3.)

Is it possible that your fear is holding you back so you aren't as committed? Or is it possible that you don't believe you have what it takes?

The first challenge for many of us is that we aren't even aware of our full potential. We don't see it, we don't know it is there – all we are aware of is the fear. Most organisations are blind to the fact that the vast majority of the people who work for them live in fear.

They go to work every day, carrying with them the two biggest fears of them all: fear that they're not good enough; and fear that they won't be loved.

No one wants to show their fear; they want to keep it buried inside; they don't want people to see a weakness within them.

By the way, that's why public speaking is one of the biggest fears in the western world (most people would rather die than speak at their own funeral!). If you get up on stage and invite people to look at you, you risk showing who you really are and being exposed as imperfect and disliked as a result.

An Inspirator is a leader who sees fear for what it is and recognises instead, their incredible ability to tap into the power that exists, not just inside themselves, but inside every single person around them.

Tap into your power

That then is the challenge when leading others – to make people aware of the power they have within themselves. And, as in all other leadership challenges, it is about showing the way by giving people the permission to be powerful.

Power is so frequently seen as a means to gain the energy, cooperation and efforts of other people. They are obliged to 'do as I say' because you hold the power. And yes, if your leadership style is authoritarian, power is all about **taking**.

Here's the key to it all, though. Power, when used correctly, has an amplification effect (by which I mean, it becomes more than the sum of its parts).

True leadership is where you recognise the power that you have and understand you can best use it by **giving**. Give your power to others, allow them to use it and learn from it and grow within it so that they can unlock their own power. When you do, they will return your power to you and also give of their own, newly unlocked power. The result is an unstoppable force.

The result is an organisation of Inspirators.

For your team to face their own fears, as always, you need to go first. You must first face your own fear. As leader, that will include the same fears as everyone else on the planet:

- What if I'm not good enough?
- What if people don't love me?

To face this and lead the way, you have to open up and be honest and authentic. When you are challenged and don't know what to do, admit it to your team.

This is a huge, frightening step to take. Absolute honesty when you are expected to have all the answers is very exposing but also immensely liberating. Whether you do this with your team right now is a judgement call. They might not be ready. Many Inspirators, however, have found that it helps to create an environment to share fears.

If you say you don't have the answers, you can ask for their help and their views. You can hand them your power and unlock theirs. You can show them that it is okay to be weak, it's okay to be insecure, it's okay to be imperfect.

What isn't okay is **not** to tap into the true essence of who you are. That is why leadership is a gift, and that is why it's the most valuable commodity in the world right now.

Being the fearless leader is to become a person who others want to follow when they see you acting despite your fears. For you to truly get the best out of other people, you have to get the best out of yourself and you do that by overcoming the fears that have held you back.

Deep work

Overcoming fear isn't a quick and easy process. My coach, Rafael, used to tell me that we have a choice: Love or Fear. You can either decide to love your fear or to resist and back away. This is easier if you have a big *Why*.

It takes time and application. There are, however, things you can do to work on it every day.

Bring it on

This is a tool I often invite people to use to manage fear – inspired by the work of Barry Michels and Phil Stutz.

Take a moment to make a list of all of the things that you're frightened of. Write them all down – both the external, (things like spiders or fire), and the internal, (perhaps you fear that someone will find out you don't have all the answers). No one but you will see this list, so you can be 100% honest in writing everything down.

Now look at the list and ask yourself what have you learned to fear? How has each fear affected you in your life? What has been the consequence of not dealing with these fears? What if you had learned to love moving through the fear instead?

For some, the consequence will be small (if you fear sharks, but live in the UK, the consequence will be nothing worse than not being able to enjoy *Shark Week* on TV). Others will have major impact; I know of people who have remained in abusive relationships, for example, because they feared being alone. Don't judge or get caught up in regret. You are where you are and you can't control the past. This exercise is about taking control of the future.

From this list pick something you fear. Right now, I want you to work with something which isn't a major, debilitating fear but, at the same time, isn't trivial. It should be something which, if you overcome it, you'll feel better for having done so.

Think of the thing that you're frightened of. Stand up when you think about this, feet flat on the floor, back nice and straight, and picture it. See it in front of you as if it was a cloud a few feet above your head.

On the other side of it, know that's where your potential exists.

Say to yourself, 'Bring it on,' and imagine stepping through the cloud, doing what frightened you, and then stepping into your potential.

Imagine doing this over and over again, and feel the excitement, the pleasure and the joy and the strength from stepping into the unknown and doing something that frightened you.

There will always be a part of you that tries to hold you back and make you stay put. By developing the mental strength and the capacity to see where it is that you want to go, you have an opportunity to become a true Inspirator. To *bring it on*.

Practise this technique. It's so simple and so profound and so easy to do.

Note: *Bring it on, 54321 and Just Get Started are all similar types of tools – all are about tapping in to activation energy. Play with them and see which ones work best for you in which situations.*

What's your story?

I love this exercise. It is great for helping you see who you want to become and what that would mean for you but it also motivates you by facing the consequences of inactivity.

Give this exercise some thought and revisit it regularly as you continue on your journey. You may also find it helpful to discuss it with your greatest ally.

Coaching Questions

Start by writing a description of your ideal self – the self who is fearless and takes action towards goals.

Think about the impact you would have if you were this ideal version of yourself:

- How do you look, feel, move through the world?
- What would your life be like?
- What would you be able to achieve?
- How would you influence those around you?

Now consider the consequences if you **don't** become this person and you continue to allow fear to hold you back:

- How do you look, feel, move through the world?
- What would your life be like?
- What would you have achieved?
- How would you influence those around you?

And finally...

> *I have learned over the years that when one's mind is made up, this diminishes fear; knowing what must be done does away with fear.*
> **Rosa Parks**

When Rosa Parks made her 'stand' on a bus, by refusing to give up her seat for a white person, she must have been full of fear. She, like all black people in Alabama at that time, was raised in fear. The consequences of defying the laws of segregation could be frightful.

She did it anyway.

Through her courage and the indignation of her arrest, a movement was born. Martin Luther King was inspired to lead that movement and, eventually, racial equality was enshrined in American law.

One small act taken, despite fear, can change the world.

6: Getting Lost Along the Way

Shut the Duck up!

Hannibal Lecter: You still wake up sometimes, don't you? You wake up in the dark and hear the screaming of the lambs.
Clarice Starling: Yes.
Hannibal Lecter: And you think if you save poor Catherine, you could make them stop, don't you? You think if Catherine lives, you won't wake up in the dark ever again to that awful screaming of the lambs.
Clarice Starling: I don't know. I don't know.

The Silence of the Lambs

In this chapter, we will explore

- the victim mindset and how it shows up in us
- how what we say to ourselves (aka the duck) impacts us
- how to inspire others with love
- the tool that everyone loves – which is as simple as it is effective.

Movie Time

While few of us will encounter someone as disturbing and twisted as Hannibal Lecter, most, like Clarice Starling, will be led off the right path from time to time.

Like her, some of the things which divert us come from stories in our past and how these have shaped our lives – just as the screaming of the lambs being slaughtered stays with Clarice into adulthood.

Others come from the encounters we have. Lecter is determined to play mind games to manipulate every situation.

Still more come from the rush to achieve future dreams and ambitions. Clarice gets lost – so eager to work with Jack Crawford that she is prepared to falsify an offer to get co-operation from Lecter.

Have there been times in your life when you have 'lost the plot?' Have you realised that you aren't being who you are capable of becoming?

The more we think about this as a heroic journey, just like the heroes of films and books who have gone before, we come to realise that it is the same for us. The only difference, in fact, is that the script is already written for them.

In the plot of any film, just as there is in real life, there is adversity and challenge and distraction. All in all, it's difficult.

And, when we are lost, overthinking and second guessing distract us even more.

Story Time

It happened to me when I was writing this book. It was all mapped out – a 12 step journey to becoming an Inspirator and half the book was written. Then I took the time to go back over what had been written so far – I wanted to get one chapter into good shape as a model for everything going forward.

In doing so, I started to realise that chapters were too long, the ideas needed reorganising and there were some ideas I'd missed out completely. What we really needed was a 16-step journey.

I had to dismantle the whole structure and, in short, felt a bit lost. There were 'bits' of book all over the place and, for a little while, I couldn't focus. My mind was full of questions about how it was supposed to work out and how was I going to hit the submission deadline.

Now what?

When something like this happens – when you are second guessing and feel lost – you have a choice of how to react and whom you listen to. This is your opportunity to write your own script.

You can use the confusion and fear to your advantage, or you can continue to allow it to lead you astray, allow it to limit your potential and shape the choices that you make.

Easy to say – not so easy to do because of what is going on for most of us, most of the time.

Rescue me, Rescue me!

Who is your worst enemy?

Dare I suggest that it is probably you? Most people are 'in their own way' and most people have a victim mentality.

> **Victim** comes from the Latin *Victima* meaning a 'sacrificial animal.' The first references to it meaning 'a person hurt or tortured by others' comes in the late 17th century and not long after this (1718) it was first used to mean 'person oppressed by some power or situation.' Towards the end of the 18th century it started to mean 'person taken advantage of.'
>
> Today, many companies operate in the space of victim and oppressor – taking advantage of the people around them, using and abusing power to get what they want or simply using the talents of others without giving anything in return.

A victim doesn't have a vision and doesn't focus on the ultimate outcome or goal. They are living in the 'wrong kind of now'.

To become the Inspirator, especially if you are leading people and want them to follow you, now is when your need to be the fearless leader we discussed in Chapter 5. Using fear and moving through it will make sure everyone around you doesn't end up feeling the same confusion. You must be prepared to break free of where you are, and what is going on, and step into the unknown once more.

> ### Movie Time
> We see the victim mindset showing up in many of the films we feature. Clarice is victim to her early childhood and she drives herself hard to try and escape that. Hannibal preys on that – you can see him preying on her victim mindset.

Of course, in real life, a victim mindset shows up in much more subtle ways, as people seek the quick fix promised to us by TV and social media and, especially, advertising.

> Have you ever wanted to get healthy, be fit, feel better or lose weight? What did you do?
>
> Most of us look to see what the most successful or popular diet or fitness programme is – or the one that one of our friends has been successful with. This is a victim mindset at work.
>
> I'm not as fit and healthy as I want to be. Come on diet – FIX ME!!
>
> A diet is a way for you to be rescued and you simply become the victim of the rules of that diet.
>
> If you want to be healthy, you can't put it in the hands of anyone else. You have to take ownership and break free of the diet trap.

I believe that's why a lot of people suffer, because deep down they know they're not being who they're truly capable of being. They are gifting their capability and power to others and expecting to be 'fixed.'

How do most people feel most of the time?

Most people feel *not quite good enough*. Most people feel vulnerable. Most people are frightened to stand in the light and just be the very best that they can be.

Do you know anyone like that? Do you see it in yourself?

In many organisations, the response to this is, 'Well, we're not interested in that. We pay people to do a job. Why should we worry about how they feel?' This is where the victim mindset comes from. If you put pressure on people to do things without giving them adequate motives such as appreciation, support, understanding and the space to overcome their own inner challenges, they feel oppressed. They feel the victim.

They just do the work and, as long as they are paid enough, it stops them from leaving out of fear. Fear of unemployment and uncertainty.

And if someone has that sense of powerlessness, then it's not conducive to good ideas, creativity, or well-being.

 I invite all of you to think about what type of environment you want to create and what type of environment already exists within you and within the business where you're working.

If you're really interested in people being more engaged, being more resilient, being more productive, being happier and being healthier, then it's only through helping people change their relationship with themselves that they might change their relationship with you and the company. That is when you get the best out of them.

Inspirators are the ones who make the difference. I invite you to take a look at the interviews I've made of people I've coached and Inspirators I've worked with to learn from them.

Now this might sound complicated but, ultimately, what does this all mean? It means being the change you want to see in others; in other words, being the example so you can help other people bring about change in themselves.

Here we go again....

'Change' is one of those words which is bandied about in organisations as if it is a finite and tangible object. Bam! There you go. We've **done** change.

Glyn House

If I say to you, 'I'm going to send you to France. If you go to France, you'll have a much better time if you learn French. [Therefore] we're going to teach you French. You okay with that?' ...

When you're leading change or managing change, you have to get people to [learn French].

I can't teach you French. I can point you in the right direction, but *you've* got to put the work in to learn it. It's a strange analogy, but it helps me understand that that's why people would start to develop and learn themselves.

There is a mindset of 'once and done' but change is a continuous state of transition. Even its origins (from the Latin and emerging from commerce – exchange of one thing for another) suggest it as being a word of movement and continuous improvement.

In my experience, people see change as a process or a system, rather than recognising that all that does is apply pressure.

People don't like change, especially if they see themselves as a victim in their life, because of its inherent state of uncertainty. They recognise that they don't have all the answers, feel oppressed by the idea of being imperfect and an expectation that they need to have it all figured out. They think, "I'll get found out."

Because of the short-term view of many leaders who link change to specific projects, it leads to the cynical voice within people crying out, "Here we go again. You want me to act and be different but you're just paying a lip service to the idea of involving me to get what you want. Nothing really is going to change because you don't really care about me."

Add in a healthy dose of psychological reactance (Chapter 3) and countless cases of Arambhashura (Chapter 2) and you can see how an organisation which announces a change programme is faced with a barrel-load of resistance.

Of course, that sense of victim, or 'nobody loves me' often comes from a combination of things and people have developed many limiting beliefs about themselves. They are killing parts of themselves and don't move forward and grow because they feel oppressed, often even just oppressing themselves.

> ## Chris Roebuck
>
> One of the questions I repeatedly ask ... leaders ... is, '... what percentage of initiatives have you seen launched got anywhere close to full and successful implementation?' ...
>
> The consistent answer is ... that only somewhere between 20 and 30% of initiatives ... ever got anywhere near full and successful completion. ... What organisations are not addressing is the simple fact that of all the initiatives they launch, probably 70% don't work properly.

Does this sound familiar? What are you feeling right now about the changes I'm asking you to make to become an Inspirator?
Can you see how this might relate to the organisation you work in?

The victim mindset isn't a permanent state, but it does come to us all at some point. Have you have had days when, however fired up you are about your life, you have a wallow in self-pity? Maybe a day where it all feels too hard? Or did someone you felt you could rely on let you down? Or have you ever just felt glum because it has rained for three days straight? You wouldn't be human if you didn't think 'Poor me' from time to time.

This is why every one of us need to work on ourselves. We need to have a vision, and to support it with mastermind groups (which we'll cover in Chapter 7), otherwise people fall back into the default setting of a victim mindset.

And this has to be much more than just an initiative. This has to be a way of operating. It's just who we are and what we do.

Duck!

The quality of our life and the story that we create has a huge amount to do with the communication that goes on between our ears.

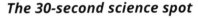

> ### The 30-second science spot
> How many thoughts do you have in a typical day?
> It's estimated that human beings have between 12,000 and 60,000 thoughts in one day. There's a lot of thinking going on and some of that thinking is monotonous – we think the same things today as we thought yesterday.

For many people there's a constant stream of thought; a chitter-chatter that is constantly playing, 'I'm not quite right the way I am. I'm not good enough.' It may not be you, but it will be the case for a lot of the people around you. Think about how this affects the quality of their lives and their happiness.

It is like a duck, quacking away continuously. It doesn't matter whether you feed it or ignore it – eventually it just starts quacking again.

Everyone has a duck, whether it's Usain Bolt – who every year asks himself, "Can I run as fast as I used to?" or you saying, "Don't get out of bed this morning" or "Don't make that extra phone call" or, "Don't bother to exercise."

We always have thoughts and our thoughts can either move us forward or move us back. It's as simple as that. In our thoughts, we're moving forward into growth or back into safety.

> Spend a minute or two just writing down your thoughts, as they occur to you. Jot them down as fast as you can; it won't be fast enough, even if you know shorthand, but grab as many as you can.

It all starts with thinking. And many people's thinking is... well... stinking.

Stinking Thinking.

> You are probably talking to yourself right now as you're reading this book. You'll be reading the words inside your head and, at the same time you may be hearing an inner-critic ('what does he know?') or your own duck ('I haven't got what it takes to be an Inspirator. Might as well give up'). The more you have been working to become aware, the more you'll be hearing it.

There is darkness – a thief in your mind – trying to steal your light. I call it the duck, others call it the chimp or 'Part X.' The name doesn't matter. What matters is that you recognise that it is there.

In organisations, when people start to work on the internal chatter it can be very challenging. They are held back by fear. They don't want to show what is going on behind the scenes.

There is always going to be a part of us that wants to limit our moving forward. At the start of this book I used the analogy of leadership being like 'The Force' in *Star Wars*. This is the dark side (the duck-side even!) that exists within every human being.

Story Time

As a coach, one of the great questions is, "Where do you see yourself in five years' time?" I was often asking people that question when I was coaching them and asking executives about where they wanted to be and where they wanted the company to be.

When I was being coached, however, I used to resent being asked that question. I was, like many of us, lost and victim to a voice that was constantly asking, "What's wrong with me?' So, I was desperate to prove to the world that I was somebody. That last thing I wanted to do was think about where I was going.

If someone asked, then, "Pete, where do you see yourself in five years?" I could feel this anguish inside me and that voice in my head saying, "You are asking this question of others and you haven't got a clue of the answer for yourself." But I wasn't about to admit that to anyone else.

What was driving me, then, was a massive desire to move away from where I was, rather than seeing a vision of where I was going.

This is where I believe that 98% of people exist in the world today – something which Napoleon Hill first claimed in the 1930s.

And yet, humans have a desire to grow and improve and to be a cause for good. Why then, would anyone learn to say all these terrible things to themselves?

The history of your duck

The 30-second science spot

Let's go back to when you were born.

Did you talk to yourself? No. Did you know what tomorrow was? No. Did you know what yesterday was? No.

You knew nothing. You came into this world and you weren't ready. You formed dependencies and you couldn't do anything on your own. You needed people.

The only way you could communicate was to cry. You made noises when you wanted something – food, love, comfort, a nappy change...

Over time, the noises you made developed and you learned to speak. Your first words were probably 'Mummy! Daddy! No! Mine!' You were the centre of

Continued on next page

your own world. You were selfish. You didn't care about anybody else. You just wanted everyone to take care of you and if you saw something, you wanted it and would find any way possible to let the world know. Most of the things you wanted were still the same – food, love, comfort, a nappy change...

As you struggled for the things you wanted, you learned to walk so you weren't dependent on others. You saw things you wanted, so you moved towards them. Even though it was difficult and you fell over, you kept going.

You learned to play as a way to explore the world. You wanted to grow and learn.

As you started to play you would talk out loud. You chatted to your toys and imagined the toys talking to each other. But something started to happen from the age of around four. You became self-conscious. You started to realise that there was a world outside of you and that world was full of 'big people.' Those big people would often tell you what you should and shouldn't do and you realised that they didn't talk out loud when they were playing. In fact, many of them didn't play.

So the playing and talking out loud became quieter and quieter until it went inside, and you started trying to make sense of the world inside your head.

That's where most people's life problems start. Because you're not vocalising what you're thinking and feeling, you bottle things up. You may think, "I'm not good enough", and there is no one to hear that and tell you different. So you believe it.

Many children bottle these ideas up for years. They struggle even more when they become teenagers and the questions they ask include, "Who am I? What do I do? Who do I hang out with? What music do I like?" because they are trying to fit into the world being presented to them.

This is where the duck inside your head really starts to quack away. "You can't do this; You're not good enough."

That's how it starts and, because no one shows how to think differently, it dominates your life.

Even if, in reading this, you feel that it doesn't apply to you, as an Inspirator, it is vital that you recognise that this is what is going on for the vast majority of people.

Self-talk comes in different forms. I like to think of it as...

The four levels of quackery

Level 1 – Duck-talk

We've already discussed this. This is where you are telling yourself, "I can't do this. I'm not good enough." Duck-talk will always be there. We may want to get rid of it, but it will never completely go away. It holds you back and fills you with doubt about whether to take action. You hesitate and, usually, stay where you are; in safety but without achieving what you want to achieve. The duck rules.

How often do you listen to your duck-talk?

Level 2 – Battling the Duck

This is where you go up against yourself. When you hear the duck-talk you tell yourself, "No, I'm going to make that call/ go to the gym/ resist that doughnut. I can do this." You take on the Duck. Your self-talk becomes a battle of wills. You take action despite the duck but, as with any battle, there is a winner and a loser. Sometimes it is you, sometimes it is the duck.

Can you think of times when you've been battling your duck?

Level 1 and 2 are where most people live but there is another level.

Level 3 – Self-coaching

We covered this in Chapter 3. One of my main roles as a coach, is to teach and guide people so they can coach themselves. When you coach yourself, you become more aware of duck-talk and what you're saying to yourself and you realise, "Hey, I actually have a choice here."

It is all about catching yourself and being really aware that what is going on is **just the duck**.

Are you learning to question your duck and accept it and then move on to make other choices?

Level 4 – Genius-talk

In life we have become adept at hearing duck-talk – but there is another voice, which has been drowned out by the duck. As we go through this journey together you'll become aware of the other side of your inner power.

There is the negative duck who quacks and holds us back and there is your inner-genius inside you that we all have. We are going to discuss this more fully in the next chapter so, for now, know that you can learn to unlock your genius and move confidently in the direction that you want to go.

Become aware of the moments in your life when you are in a place of true inspiration – when there is nothing going on inside you but the voice of success.

Are you a genius?

Think about that question for a moment – and be aware of what your duck is saying as you do.

Did it immediately say 'No.'? Or did you feel uncomfortable at the question? Or did you start to find all the reasons why you might *not* be a genius?

A ***Genius*** as we view it today, as 'an exceptional ability', isn't how it originated – that only emerged in the 17th century. The word itself is Latin, evolving out of '*gignere*' (meaning 'beget'). It came to mean 'attendant spirit present from one's birth, innate ability or inclination.'

Not, then, the preserve of a fortune few, but the inner light within every one of us. When you hear the duck quacking at the idea of you being a genius, just remind it not to argue with the Romans!

What's really going on?

Story Time

A number of years ago I was a director of a golf school. We had over 50 students each year who came and did two years of golf education. One of the things I noticed was just how hard many of these students were being on themselves when things didn't work out the way they wanted.

So, one day, I gave them an exercise in awareness. I said to them, "I want you to imagine you have a journalist following you around for 18 holes of golf. He's got access to everything you think, everything you feel, everything you hear and he's going to write an article about the experience of having access to everything you were thinking."

Of course, some of the students didn't take it seriously but the vast majority of them were very honest about how they approached the exercise. As they walked off the 18th tee, they handed me what they'd written down.

I couldn't believe what I was reading. The mental torture and anguish people had put themselves through, as they played this round of golf, was incredible. Conversations would run like this:

"Oh, I hope I don't miss."

"I hit it over there last time."

"I could make a mistake."

"Oh my God, I'm terrible."

"I'm rubbish."

"Everyone is going to think I am useless."

"Oh my God, I have to make this putt. I have to make this putt."

"Oh, I didn't make it!"

"I'm getting so angry and agitated."

"What will people think of me?"

"I feel like throwing my club."

"I threw my club."

"What do I do when they find out I'm not as good as they think I am?"

There was very little joy or happiness. That round of golf was full of frustration, fear, anger, sadness and depression.

The exercise made them all aware of the self-talk going on inside them but, when I first saw all those notes, do you know what my first reaction was?

"Oh my God! It's not just me that thinks like that!" Then I began to wonder why it is so hard to talk openly about this dialogue going on all the time.

These messages are automatic scripts which run and are instinctive. That's why people need help. Only once we have learned to tune in and listen to what is going on can we start to do something different.

How aware are you of what goes on under the surface? When you wake up and become fully aware, you start to realise that some of the ways you think and feel aren't productive. Some of them aren't even authentic because the duck-talk is an echo of what others have led you to believe. It's not the real you.

Take a moment to imagine stepping outside of yourself and look at the way that you're performing. I've done this with many top performing athletes. As you do, you see your whole person and how best to move through the world. You become more aware of what you're thinking, what you're feeling, and what you're doing.

This total and objective view of self is a way for you to take responsibility for yourself and to learn to respond to the ability ('respondability' – get it?) that you have within you.

This is where confidence comes from.

Confidence

The word **confidence** comes from the Latin word '*confidere*' meaning trust within yourself. In other words, self-belief.

As we work together you will realise that trust is something that you will build when you do what you say you're going to do. You become a person of your word, you start to live your own truth, you start to live where you're going every single day. As you do this, your confidence grows.

Confidence is in the stories you tell yourself and how you relate to your duck. You'll need confidence at every stage of your journey and many of the things we have already covered come together in building your self-belief so you can pass that on to others.

Would it be okay if I asked you to think of confidence as a garden? That may sound strange but confidence needs to be cultivated. Right now, your mental garden may be full of weeds in the form of negative messages: "I'm not good enough", "I can't do this", "People will laugh at me." So, if a garden is full of weeds what do you do? You do some weeding!

Weed out the negative messages – by being aware and seeing them for what they are – and feed your garden with nourishing positive messages instead.

The 30-second history spot

A great example of this in history is Eleanor Roosevelt, wife of FD Roosevelt and First Lady from 1933 to 1945, when her husband died in his 4th term as President of the USA. She grew up extremely insecure, having lost both her parents at a very young age and yet she had the confidence to work tirelessly for the betterment of others.

During the Great Depression she was able to convey to her husband some of the real issues that the average American was experiencing. She said, "We must do what we think we cannot." Even when her husband died, she continued to do this for others, when she was elected the first Chair of the United Nations Commission on Human Rights.

When we have confidence, we are able to make progress and to achieve in all aspects of our life.

It's not you, it's me – Inspire other people

What do you think the biggest shift in leadership might be? Is it possible that it is the point when you realise that it is all about you?

In order for you to be the example for others, you have to focus primarily on yourself. This, however, is one of the easiest ways to get lost on your journey.

'All about me' can, so easily, become a selfish and narcissistic exercise when, to be an Inspirator, you need to do the exact opposite.

Having an unhealthy belief in your own importance can really divert you from working on your own and mastering your craft. It takes you away from creating insights and working well with others and building relationships, loyalty and support. Basically, it's a magnet for errors.

Richard Curen

...When we talk about people being egotistical, actually what we're talking about is probably someone being narcissistic. ... really desperately feeling that they can't quite find it within themselves to love themselves and need other people to do it for them.

Movie Time
Dr Chilton – Hannibal's psychiatrist – is the best example of this: so keen to further his own career that he is lost to the higher purpose. He uses his research with the patients in his institution to place himself in the limelight. He wants to be the man who identifies Buffalo Bill more than he wants the serial killer to be caught.
He prevents the subterfuge Clarice and Jack Crawford put in place and, as a result, is fooled by Lecter to chase the wrong person.

One of the things that I have seen from many of the Inspirators who I have interviewed for this book is that they know there is a much bigger picture here. They have to be themselves but they have to be the change. They have to be the example for others to follow.

Mirror, mirror
I dare you to go and find a mirror, take a look in it and ask yourself:
Do I want to follow myself? What do I need to do to inspire other people to follow me? How can I be the example? How can I align myself to everything I want to inspire others to achieve?

All you need is love!

The ultimate challenge of an Inspirator is not only being someone who wants to follow themselves, but someone who loves themselves. They love who they are and what they're doing and who they are becoming.

This is not just the type of love that we think about when a man and woman love each other, or love their parents or their children – though it is partly that. It's also about something called *positivity resonance*.

Positivity Resonance is a concept described by Dr Barbara Frederickson as part of her research into positive emotions and, especially, love. To her, love is an essential nutrient for every human.

She describes Positivity Resonance as "the idea that when two people share a positive emotion, it is unfurling across their two brains and bodies at the same time." She goes on to describe it as a form of 'mind-meld.'

It is, then, a state where people are connected and feel important and valued and truly a **part** of the journey.

 Take a moment to think about how you feel when I say, "I love you."
Who? Me?
"Yes, you."
"I love you for buying this book."
"I love you for working on yourself."
"I love you because you have the courage to do this."
People are afraid to love – to show it and to accept it.

If the exercise above is too tough, then try this instead:

Say to yourself "I love my job." Start saying it every day and, as you get comfortable with it, add to it:

"I love the people I work with."
"I love our customers."
"I love the challenging days."
"I love achieving."

Never shy away from giving love and expressing the love that you have for your purpose, the journey, and those who are on it with you. If you do, then change is going to happen.

Deep work

Buy a duck

The metaphor of the duck is one that many people I've worked with find very helpful. I give them out when I speak.

What I invite you to do, as I have for so many people, is that you go out and buy a duck. It can be a simple plastic duck, or one of the many duck personas that are now available – anything that you feel you can relate to[1].

Give your duck a name and, when you spot the negative self-talk, pick up your duck and tell it to calm down.

Oh, and the final aspect of this tool? Notice what your duck is saying to you right now at the idea of going out and buying a duck!

What's your story?

Your self-coaching for this chapter will help you become more aware of your victim mindset and, most crucially, the duck. The questions here will help you tune into the negative voices in your head and start to think about what is going on behind them.

It can really help to carry a small notebook around with you and make notes throughout the day. Get negative thoughts out of your head and reflect on them once they have passed.

Coaching questions
1. What is your duck saying to you right now?
2. What evidence is the duck using to create that thought?
3. What action can you take to calm the duck?

Your *Why* is your greatest ally in seeing the duck and changing the script. With a clear *Why* you can see what you are doing to yourself and, maybe, even laugh at the things you say to yourself.

That's what Usain Bolt does when his duck strikes. He has found a way to see through the doubt by having the vision of what he is here to do.

And finally...

> *Anytime I feel lost, I pull out a map and stare. I stare until I have reminded myself that life is a giant adventure, so much to do, to see.*
>
> **Angelina Jolie**

This is such a great idea. Sometimes you may feel lost on your journey or worried that you are 'winging it' and making things up. We all do!

Remember that you are a hero on a journey – and explorer out to discover new lands and find exciting treasures. So, in being lost, who knows what you may find?!

That was how Columbus discovered San Salvador, after all. He was looking for India!

---

[1] *If the duck isn't working for you then pick a character which does: a troll, a monkey, a snake. It isn't the duck that is important – it is the ability to personify the voice within you.*

7: Like-minded People

The Mastermind Alliance.

Jimmy Dugan: Sneaking out like this, quitting, you'll regret it for the rest of your life. Baseball is what gets inside you. It's what lights you up, you can't deny that.
Dottie Hinson: It just got too hard.
Jimmy Dugan: It's supposed to be hard. If it wasn't hard, everyone would do it. The hard... is what makes it great.

A League of Their Own

In this chapter, we will explore
- the importance of a Mastermind Alliance
- the different types of alliances for different purposes
- how to inspire others to form an alliance around you
- how to seek out the mastermind alliance which you need.

There are a wealth of films themed around the creation of teams from a diverse group of people: *Star Trek, The Magnificent Seven* and *Ocean's 11* to name but a few.

Instead, I picked *A League of Their Own* because it is about women. Women, in general, form bonds differently from men so the film gives different perspectives and other things to learn compared to some of the 'classic' buddy movies.

When we look at our primal roots, women would form communities in order to protect themselves and their children, while men would compete. You can still see these patterns in communities today.

That does not mean that women are not competitive or that men don't form strong friendships, just that there are differences in attitudes to be aware of. Men relate differently to men than to women. Women relate differently to women than to men[1].

We've been focusing most of our attention so far on being aware of how you move through the world. Now we are going to look at how others move through the world as well.

Jim Rohn once said, "You are the average of the five people you spend most time with" and I've seen it again and again when I have been coaching people.

In my experience, people fall into a number of categories (or 'archetypes' as Joseph Campbell called them):

- **Inspirator** – who is working to become their best self, and to be the example.
- **Coach** – who is looking to bring out the best in others via a range of methods: challenging, questioning, listening, encouraging and reflecting.
- **Master-minder** – who is there to support and to provide skills and abilities within a team and work towards a common goal.
- **Nay-sayer** – who sees the negative in a situation. They don't have evil intent but will always give the reason why *not* to take action.
- **Victim** – who sees the actions of others as having evil intent and that 'if only' circumstances, (the diet, the job, the car, the money), other people, and the universe were on their side, everything would be great.
- **Rebel** – who wants something different in life and to play by their own rules.
- **Nemesis** – who has a different agenda and will make every effort to divert you away from your goal to achieve theirs.

People can fall into many of these categories – an Inspirator will also be a coach to others, and may act as master-minder to another Inspirator's goals. Equally they can be a rebel, a nay-sayer or a nemesis to the goals of other Inspirators. None of these archetypes is 'good' or 'bad' (although movies might like to set them out that way). In fact, it can be powerful to try the different roles in some circumstances to get different results.

---

[1] *This is, of course, a generalisation. We are all unique and different. What I'm describing here are patterns which have been observed in the majority, not hard and fast rules for everyone.*

Can you think of times in your life when you have played one of these roles? And times where you have played more than one of these roles at the same time? And times where, by playing a different role you may have got a better outcome?

 Movie Time

You can see it in *A League of Their Own*. Dottie is clearly an Inspirator to the rest of the team, Kit is a victim, Mae is the rebel, Rosie the nay-sayer, Jimmy the nemesis. Over the course of the film, those roles change. Jimmy lets go of the past and starts to step into the coach role and the team comes together as a mastermind. What's more, every one of these archetypes has a part to play.

As the characters develop they are looking to see *How can I help you? What can I learn from you?* and this helps each of them in their own personal journey.

How we interact with others is a key aspect of being an Inspirator.

Mastermind Alliance

There is a saying: *TEAM = Together Everyone Achieves More*. When you bring people together and everyone is focused on the same goals, you are able to do more, faster. Your role is to create that team – to tune in to how everyone is feeling, and help them feel better.

The concept of **Mastermind Alliance** is not new. Humans are tribal animals and all the great people in history had others around them to help them achieve their goals.

The term, though, first emerged in the 1930s in Napoleon Hill's book *Think and Grow Rich*. The mastermind group, in his words, consists of *'an alliance of two or more minds working in perfect harmony for the attainment of a common, definite objective.'*

In outlining his 17 principles, the Mastermind Alliance was Hill's second principle. I must admit, I was quite shocked when I read that he'd put it so high up the list of principles. *Really? Is it that important?* Yet, when I thought about it I realised he was right. No man can become a permanent success without the support of others and without taking others along with him.

For example, people like Henry Ford, Thomas Edison and Andrew Carnegie, (all interviewed by Hill for the book), could see that they couldn't succeed on their own. They were constantly asking *How can I learn from other people?* And *How can I help you?* The best modern day equivalent I can think of is a Formula 1 team. They are all focused on one mission – driver, engineers, pit crew, personal trainers…. And they look to help and support one another to make a winning combination.

Every Inspirator I have interviewed for this book has mentioned those who supported them and helped them achieve their goals – some were coaches and mentors, others formed part of mastermind alliances.

As a leader, when you're influencing people and dealing with lots of challenges, it can be a lonely place. The quality of the support you get directly affects the quality of your leadership and your ability to inspire.

That is not to say you can't be great on your own. I just want you to imagine what you could become if surrounded by the right people.

Warren Rosenberg

So the light bulb moment was, I came into a group, I suddenly realised that I had all these people in different types of business, whether it was selling bags to stores, or cleaning stadiums ... and hotels. It just showed me that everyone had the same sort of issues within their business but each person had a different way of looking at it.

Story Time

I personally worked for years in isolation, and one of the things that my coach said to me on many occasions was, "You need a support group. You need a group of people around you who can support you in what it is that you are doing." Finding the right people, however, was massively challenging. How did I find those who were capable and able to support me in the way that I needed to be supported?

At the time, I thought it was *them* – that no one else could think as I did and there was nobody who was prepared to 'show up' like I was.

Now, of course, I realise that it was me. I wasn't ready. I hadn't done the work needed to be enough of an Inspirator to allow others to help me in my purpose.

Once I was ready, I took the steps to create an environment for Inspirators to come together. Together we are helping leaders across organisations create mastermind alliances so they can learn, grow and be supported to make better decisions and be even more inspiring.

How do you find your Mastermind Alliance?

When he spoke about what you need in your Mastermind Alliance, Napoleon Hill said what you are looking for is for people who are:

- **dependable** – Hill's view was that having people you can rely on was the most important characteristic of an alliance. You need people who do what they say they are going to do, when they say they will do it.
- **loyal –** the people around you need to be loyal to you, loyal to the company, loyal to the organisation and loyal to your goal.
- **able** – the ability of those in the alliance comes third. You need capable people, of course, but it isn't the top priority.

- **positive** – the people around you need to have a positive mental attitude about what is to be achieved and the journey you are on together. A positive group will generate energy – and if any one person feels down or hits a tough spot, the alliance will support them through it.
- **willing to go the extra mile** – there are going to be challenges along the way and times when things don't go to plan. Your alliance needs to be made up of those who are willing to dig in and do what it takes at times like this.
- **faithful** – your Mastermind Alliance needs the ability to see where you are going and see their part in it, to have faith in the goal, in the group and in you. Just as importantly, they need faith in themselves.

Alistair McAuley

Harvard's ethos is to create leaders who will make a positive impact on the world. Listening to my classmates unique stories and how they articulate problem solving opened my eyes to new ways of learning. We had an astronaut, talking to us about his story and his ambition to be an astronaut since childhood. We had many global CEO's sharing their stories and I'm now in a WhatsApp group with 139 people from all over the world who are driven to make a positive impact as leaders.

When you read that list, you can see how forming an effective Mastermind Alliance can be massively challenging. Where would you find people who have mastered all of these characteristics?

Of course, this isn't about only allying yourself with those who have perfected all of these things – none of us is perfect, after all. What Hill's gives you is a *blueprint* of the characteristics you need to develop in yourself and in others. As you work to build these six characteristics in your teams, your friends, your family and your community, you are showing them how they can be the best they can possibly be.

It is about finding people who recognise their own power and potential and, even if they waver sometimes, are willing to work on growing into being a masterminder.

The aim is to bring together a group of people within your mastermind who are working to be their very best, to overcome obstacles, and to march forward, regardless of the circumstances. When you're surrounded by people who are all marching to the same rhythm, they can help you move steadily forward and keep the pace going. And, with every beat of the drum, the group powers you up.

This is vital in business but is just as important in the other aspects of your life because you may find yourself in need of more than one mastermind, just as you have more than one goal in your life.

Different types of Mastermind Alliance

Have you ever been a part of a Mastermind Alliance? What was its purpose? What roles did those within it play?

I want to explore different types of mastermind groups with you because it is important to recognise that different people can support you towards different goals in your life – health, relationships and work.

Leadership tends to focus on your role within an organisation. Yet, the most powerful alliances are outside your work and business.

Social alliances

Family and friends are vitally important in the life of an Inspirator. We are social animals and we want and need the support of those around us. Life partners, friends and others within our community, all contribute to the alliances we need to meet our relationship goals and also for our other goals in life.

Story Time

We are all searching for a sense of belonging – to fit in. I am no exception. From an early age, I was filled with a sense of "What's wrong with me," and was desperate to fit in and be like everyone else. In my teens this became even more marked and I fell in with a crowd where 'fitting in' meant drinking, smoking and acting the fool. I did what everyone else did.

Eventually, I saw that this urge to 'be like the rest' wasn't nourishing for me and I sought out another group. I talked my way into University and found a different 'in-crowd.'

This is also where we may well spend least time in managing the alliance. Marriages can struggle or grow stale from lack of care and attention or the goals can change and diverge over time. Similarly, we can form a friendship and then maintain it long after it ceases to serve a useful purpose.

Supporters become nay-sayers or rebels or, in their own life, they play the victim and look to us to rescue them.

Specific goals outside work

Sometimes we take on a challenge outside of work – to run a marathon or take part in a pageant or festival or to perform in a concert or go on a trip.

A mastermind alliance here can help you prepare and provide the range of experiences you need to complete the challenge.

Movie Time

The classic example, is, of course, a sporting team. You can see them form in *A League of Their Own* as the common goal of winning the World Series brings the diverse group of women together.

One of the most powerful and extraordinary Mastermind Alliance is football supporters. Vast groups of strangers come together and do all they can for a single purpose – to see their team win. Then, they all go home at the end of the match and resume everyday life – until the next match.

This form of Mastermind Alliance is finite but that doesn't mean you should take less care in its formation and maintenance. Your ability to meet the goal depends on the effectiveness of the Mastermind Alliance supporting you.

Extra-business alliances

One of the most powerful of the Mastermind Alliances in the working world is the one made up of people in similar situations to you, but not in the same organisation.

It may include people you have worked with previously or from a ready-made organisation formed to bring like-minded people together or it may just be people you have met in other contexts.

Jon Sellins

I think, as a good leader, [my mentor] saw in me traits that he didn't have and skills he didn't have. And that's a real lesson, isn't it?

Who do you surround yourself with?

People who can do stuff that you can't do.

Specific goals within your business

We are all familiar with the formation of project teams in work. Bringing together groups of people from different parts of the organisation to meet a specific goal is common in business.

For example, if the business is installing a new IT system, a multi-skilled team may be made up from all across the business.

The Mastermind Alliance you form in these cases is not necessarily the same as the project team (although it might be). You want people to support you in leading that team and leading yourself within that team in order to complete the project. It may be a subset of the project team or be made up of people not on the project who can give you the support and guidance you need.

Ongoing within your business

Finally, you have the Mastermind Alliance you form to help you in the day-to-day as a leader and an Inspirator.

In this alliance, the focus is all about why the company exists, what the alliance is here to do, and what is it that you are going to master together through practice.

This alliance is about building a bond that becomes unshakable that is simply working towards the betterment of the organisation, the betterment of the people within the organisation and to do things perhaps that have never been done before.

In the past, which of these types of Mastermind have you been in? Think of one which you remember being really powerful. What was great about it? How did it make a difference? What impact did it have? What impact is it still having – on you or on others?

Which mastermind groups do you participate in?

Of course, you may be invited to join Mastermind Alliances, instigated by others and the benefit they bring you could easily be different from the benefit for the person who set it up.

For example, I have set up Mastermind Alliances in a couple of my business ventures. I run two online coaching groups, one for people seeking to lose weight and another for people looking to be their best selves.

For me, that is an alliance within work – for them it is outside their own work but is helping them become better leaders in their own organisations.

We have also set up an Inspirators' Mastermind Alliance and, if you choose to apply to join, it is a way for you can get yourself around like-minded people who support you as you are. This is something which all leaders and aspiring leaders are welcome to join and gives you access to all the interviews I did for the book plus many other resources.

Glyn House

I think you need to recruit like-minded people, but you don't need to recruit clones. When I'm putting a team together, I like people that are going to get on with each other and they're going to fit in and identify with the values of Caffè Nero, but if you recruit everybody the same, then that doesn't work.

There are plenty of ways you can form alliances to help you but how can you tell those who are going to be a good fit?

Forming your alliance – Inspire other people

Story Time

There's no question that the coach that I had for 16 years of my life was not your everyday coach. He did things that I've never seen anybody do before or since.

When we used to put on events and workshops, we would look to create a mastermind group. When we did, he would often ask people to complete a handwritten questionnaire. He wanted them to answer four questions: how they felt about where they were in their life, what they were doing that was important, how they felt about their future and; what were the biggest obstacles they faced. Then he would ask them to sign at the bottom of the page.

When he looked at the responses, he was able to see where people were coming from just by looking at their signatures. He'd learned this during his childhood in the Philippines.

As Rafael once said, "Someone's signature is the most unique thing that anyone can do. No one has the same signature as anybody else." He had learned to read, from this unique expression of self, what might not be on show in the everyday.

Continued on next page

I'm sure with the way we think and react in society today, many of you are saying to yourself, "Well, that's just nonsense." And yet, it worked.

On one occasion, having looked at responses, he picked one out and said to me, "Who is this person?"

I explained who it was, and he asked, "Why did you invite him to this event?"

I replied, "Well, I don't know him too well, but I thought he could be someone who could help and support me in what I'm doing."

He said, "Listen, this guy is really disruptive, and he will be disruptive during the day."

Of course, the sceptical part of my brain was going, "Yeah, Yeah, Yeah," and I went ahead, including this fellow anyway. And, no surprise, he was very, very difficult and challenging through the day. He argued with everything that was being said.

Why am I telling you this story? Not because I advocate the use of graphology to form your Mastermind Alliance but just as a reminder that there is more going on for people than what you see at face value.

People want something real and something true to who they are. They want to know what they will gain from any situation and to trust that it will happen for them. If someone is looking to you as a potential leader, what answer would they get back if they asked, "What's in it for me?"

When forming your Mastermind Alliances, it's important to understand that nobody does anything for nothing. There has to be a reason for them to work with you, to be reliable and loyal and to give of their abilities. Personal growth is almost always a driver.

When you include people in a Mastermind Alliance you are giving them the opportunity to grow. Remember *syntropy* from Chapter 2? We all have that innate desire to express ourselves to our fullest potential – to learn, to grow and to be the best person we can possibly be.

There is something else people are looking for – everyone wants to be a part of something. There are many studies which prove that money doesn't drive people or motivate them. They want inclusion.

Now, before you argue that, in the workplace, there are plenty of people who come to work simply because of the money, let me ask you how many of them are motivated, excited and inspired by what they are doing?

What fires people up is, *I'm a part of something, I make a difference, I'm important, I matter.*

That's why people don't buy what you *do*. They buy *why* you do it. They are looking for an alignment of what is important to you, with what is important to them. An alignment of values, if you will.

In your organisation to inspire people you must ask the people who work around you to buy your *Why*, your vision, your goal. When you do, you build a culture of growth and inspiration.

Deep work

Find a Mastermind Alliance

The main mission for you from this chapter is to identify those who can form a Mastermind Alliance with you. This could be for any one of the goals you have set yourself and could be within work or in a social setting.

With that goal in mind, ask yourself:

- What skills, knowledge and talents do I need which I don't possess in myself?
- Who do I know who is reliable, loyal and has the abilities I need?
- What can they gain from being a part of the alliance?
- What can I learn from others?
- What support can I give them to grow and develop?

Remember that *Just Like Me* isn't always what you are looking for or what you need. Never be afraid to get the help of someone who knows more than you or who will challenge you. A Mastermind Alliance is not there to validate you. They are there to help you get better and hold you to account.

The people you identify may well not be those you are most intimate with right now. They may not be ready to be a part of your Mastermind Alliance because they need your help to grow and develop.

There will be others, too, who will want to be a part of what you do who don't possess what you need. They may resent not being included and may seek to disrupt what you do. You have a role to play here too – what can you do to help them become worthy of inclusion in your mastermind group? What can you help them to achieve in order to get ready for the next time you need to form an alliance? Do they have talents needed in someone else's alliance?

What's your story?

It can be really powerful to stop and take stock of those who are around you and are part of Mastermind Alliances which have formed 'by default.' They may not be serving you or they may have potential which you haven't recognised before.

Coaching questions
1. Who are the five people you currently spend most time with?
2. What do they say when you share your goals, dreams and ambitions?
3. How do those around you react when you hit an obstacle – do they look to blame or seek rescue? Do they look at what they can learn?
4. In your life, who has influenced and inspired you?
5. Who has held you back?

And finally...

> *I wish to have as my epitaph: Here lies a man who was wise enough to bring into his service men who knew more than he.*
>
> **Andrew Carnegie**

I'm a huge fan of Andrew Carnegie and all he accomplished. This quote sums up what it takes to be an Inspirator. It takes courage and strength of character to know what we can and cannot achieve and to ask for help. In doing so, we come to know our own true self.

The Darkest Hour

Facing failure and your own inner demons.

You have the full weight of the world on your shoulders. But these inner battles have actually trained you for this very moment. You are strong because you are imperfect. You are wise because you have doubts.

The Darkest Hour

In this chapter, we will explore
• a different perspective on failure
• the darkest hours in my life and how each has influenced me
• what it really means to be a hero
• the tool to help you learn from past failures.

Movie Time

In *The Darkest Hour,* Winston Churchill is faced with pressure after pressure. It is early 1940, Europe is being over-run by the Nazi forces, the British are stranded in France with no hope of getting them out, and his own cabinet is turning on him. Disaster seems to follow disaster and millions of lives are his hands.

A dark place indeed and it feels like a place with no hope and no way out. It feels like he has already failed.

Can I be completely honest with you here?

Things are going to get tough. There will be times on this journey, times in your life, when you feel you have reached rock bottom.

What will make those times easier is to have a different perspective. So, may I offer you one?

It is said that, in life, we are either heading towards a crisis, in a crisis or coming out of one. It is going to happen to you and it will happen in one (or maybe more) of the three big aspects of life. Maybe you will have a major health challenge, or someone you love has one, or something in the world of work goes really badly wrong.

I'm not telling you this to depress you or to make you want to give up. I'm telling you to prepare you. I'm telling you because I have been preparing you. Everything we have been doing together has been preparing you for this moment. Remember how, in Chapter 5 I told you that the Japanese have two words for crisis: *Danger* and *Opportunity*. Your darkest hour is your opportunity to put into practice all the deep work you've been doing to create habits you can rely on.

Sometimes an ordeal is short-lived – like the confrontation Ben Kenobi has with Darth Vader in *Star Wars IV* ('*If you strike me down, I shall become more powerful than you can possibly imagine'* says Ben) – but, more often, it is a longer struggle with both internal and external factors weighing down on you.

Have you ever failed at something? Have you ever wondered if you are on the right path and whether you shouldn't just give up and be a traffic warden instead[1]?

We all have. We all fail. We all feel like giving up.

But let me share something with you – something so simple and yet so profound, it will change how you look at dark times forever.

There is only **one** failure and that is giving up.

Changing direction isn't failure. Deciding to do something different isn't failure. Having a plan that didn't work out isn't failure.

It is all just part of the journey.

---

[1] *With apologies to any traffic wardens who are reading this. I mean no disrespect to your worthy profession.*

Movie Time

We, of course, know the final outcome in *The Darkest Hour*, for the Nazis did over-run Europe but didn't invade mainland Britain and the British Expeditionary Force was successfully rescued from the beaches at Dunkirk by thousands of small boats.

Churchill doesn't have the advantage of hindsight, however, when he has to make the decision to fight. All around him is a War Cabinet (an 'Inner Cabinet' if you will) which is hostile and seeking capitulation. He is alone and he seems broken.

So, he seeks solitude – locking himself away to find the quiet space he needs to think and then he takes the time to reach out to the very people he is there to lead and protect. He seeks their views and then musters the support of the Outer Cabinet – creating an alliance of people who thinks as he thinks.

You cannot prepare or plan for life-changing events whether they come upon you gradually, like the conquest of Europe in the 1930s, or more suddenly, like the death of a loved one. But it is in crisis that we find greatness.

Life is a series of ups and downs (and round-and-rounds and getting-nowheres). We all have 'success' and 'failure' but none of it makes any difference if we look at it in the right way.

What does success mean to you? How do you know when you have it?

Failure is a topic which fascinates me and I have come to see that most people define 'success' in very narrow and specific terms and consider it to be 'good' while 'failing' (anything but 'success') is very wide ranging in its definition and 'bad'. What I believe, however, is that failure is a weapon we use to destroy confidence and as an excuse to stop us moving forwards.

What if that were true? What if every 'failure' you've had has been a 'failure' because of how you chose to look at it.

Think about the hero in any film. They fail and that failure is there for a reason. It isn't just padding to make the film long enough. There is something for our hero to learn. In the same way, any failure you experience brings with it something for *you* to learn. I believe that *everything happens for a reason*. It is your choice how you look at the failures in your life and what you take from them.

30-second history spot

Have you ever wondered how many leadership books have been written that have mentioned Winston Churchill? Hundreds, probably thousands. I consider him to be one of the greatest leaders ever and we are using the recent film *The Darkest Hour* to frame this chapter. But I wanted

Continued on next page

to make sure you understand the difference between this fictionalised account and the true leader at that time. The real Churchill was just as disliked and opposed when he came into power in 1940 but, while Gary Oldman's portrayal shows a man who was unsure and who hesitated, the real man had a definiteness of purpose and a clear *Why*. His memoirs show that he already knew Hitler could not be trusted and that peace talks would be futile. His decision to lie to the people in order to keep up morale, which we might see as reprehensible, was a calculated action to avoid panic. So too, was the harnessing of the support of the 'Outer Cabinet' when the War Cabinet was divided.[2]

It is without doubt that Winston Churchill was a truly inspirational leader and he took Great Britain from the brink of almost certain invasion in 1940 to victory in 1945.

In the writing of this book and especially this chapter, I wanted to learn more about great leaders and how they came to be so great. This is where I came across the book by Harvard professor, Nancy Koehn and her book *Forged in Crisis*. In it she focuses on the stories of some great leaders: the explorer Ernest Shackleton, Abraham Lincoln, and the former slave and author Frederick Douglass, to name three. If you decide to look in depth at people like this, you may come to realise, as I did, that their greatness really emerged under extreme pressure.

If you were going to take a bet that a farm boy with no formal education would have become the President of the United States, or that the leader of an expedition which had become immovably trapped in Antarctic ice would bring every one of his people home alive, what odds would you give?

For both Lincoln and Shackleton the odds were against them, but when you find people with great causes, odds pale into insignificance because they have a burning desire.

Plenty of books on leadership talk about great leaders throughout history and we can think "what a great story!" I invite you to do more than enjoy the story. Ask yourself what you can learn from them. Choose a leader who inspires you and imagine they were in front of you right now. What would they say to you? What would you want to know? What could they show you?

There's something about great leaders who are forged in a crisis. For me, Churchill is a shining example of an inspirational leader. He stood up for something greater than himself – repeatedly. He breathed life into what he was doing, and breathed life into others, showing them how to reach a better place.

He was every inch the Inspirator.

---

[2] *And, while we are comparing history with fiction, while Churchill was prone to wander off and show up somewhere in London in amongst ordinary people, there is no record that he ever took the Underground!*

Everyone has dark times and disasters

Failure is a unique and individual experience for everyone, so to address it in the abstract of theory may not be helpful. Instead, would it be okay if I share with you aspects of three dark times in my life, to illustrate how they can affect us?

These incidents shaped my life and, looking back, I learned from them.

Fear comes in our darkest hours to keep us there

Story Time

The first major incident that shaped my life was a physical challenge that occurred when I was about nine years old. I noticed that one of my testicles was getting bigger. I didn't tell anyone, even though I was concerned. I kept it to myself and became more and more self-conscious.

Nine, of course, is a time in life where many people are learning to be self-conscious. They are asking themselves, "Who am I? Who do I hang out with? What type of person should I be?"

For me, then, I began to also question myself. *What's wrong with me? Why is this happening?* I became consumed with self-consciousness and wouldn't take my clothes off in front of my friends.

I made numerous appointments with the doctor but cancelled them because of fear. There was a battle that was raging inside me and every day and every week and every month, it became more intense. I remember one day, seeing a photograph of myself when I could quite clearly see the lump. Yet fear and self-consciousness stopped me seeking help for seven years.

Eventually the testicle got so big that I had to go to the doctor and, unsurprisingly, he warned me, "I think you might have cancer."

I did then what many of us do at times of deep trouble. I called my Mum! She took charge, came with me for an Ultrasound – which showed a non-malignant cyst – and supported me when the lump was removed.

There was some physical scarring of course, but the mental scars were far more significant. The fact that the lump had been removed didn't remove the insecurity and self-doubt that I had created over the years.

Looking back on this, I've learned so much from it; mainly how powerful fear is and how paralysing it can be. Can you see how my insecurities became habits?

So why am I telling you this story? I believe everyone is often consumed by fear: fear of not being good enough, fear of not being loved, fear of not being quite right...

We live in a world that is full of messages that tell us we're not good enough the way that we are and that anything which is different or makes us stand out, is to be hidden and ignored.

This is where courage comes in – the courage to be able to openly express ourselves and to speak up when things are difficult or we are worried about things.

And this is where an Inspirator can lead the way. In sharing their own vulnerabilities, they can show others that it is okay to admit to not being perfect and to ask for help.

Story Time

From a very early age I've always had huge amounts of energy. People often used to say to me, "Do you ever shut up? Do you ever turn off?" And the answer to that was, "Very rarely!"

School was not a good experience for me and I left with only one O-level (in History). What I did learn was a sense of not being good enough. I learned how to feel insecure and to be afraid that "the world is going to find me out."

I desperately wanted approval; I desperately wanted to fit in; I desperately wanted to show the world that I was good enough.

I developed a dislike of doing nothing and just being still. It wasn't that I didn't enjoy my life. It was just I was so self-conscious that I really couldn't sit still and appreciate what was going on around me. In fact, it's probably one of my biggest regrets in my life that I was so busy *doing* that I didn't really stop and make the most of what I had achieved.

I know that during my teenage years and all the way up to the age of about 25, I lived my life in such a way that it really wasn't healthy.

I talked my way into university and got a degree in Sports Science and then worked in health clubs. I worked ridiculously long hours with no regard to the healthy rhythms of life. I worked up to 90 hours a week and, by the age of 25, I started to burn out. My energy levels dropped and it was a struggle to keep going.

I was diagnosed with chronic fatigue syndrome (CFS) and ME (Myalgic Encephalomyelitis). At the time, the conditions weren't well understood, (CFS was charmingly termed 'yuppie flu'), and I didn't know what to do. To the outside world, I looked fine but inside, I felt terrible.

There were days when I was so exhausted that I didn't want to get out of bed but somehow I would push myself to keep going.

This was my life for 10 years. To the outside world I was full of energy and always on the go. I was making regular TV appearances, writing best-selling books and having the kind of success in my life that many people only dream of. But when no one was looking, I was a wreck. It got so bad at one point that I remember saying to my Mum, "Look, I just want to close my eyes and I don't want to wake up tomorrow."

I'd been brought up to believe there is an answer for everything so, all the time I was sick, I was looking for answers.

I tried all sorts of regimes. I did a 10-day juice detox; I took a salt bath which made me catatonic; I was wrapped in ice sheets; I had garlic tied to my feet to draw out toxins. I even saw one specialist who looked at how my cells responded to the resonance created when I sang.

Continued on next page

> It's really hard to convey in words exactly what I was going through but, at the time, I was desperate. It was my darkest hour but, in my darkest hour, I kept looking for answers and trying things to help me.
>
> The only problem was that I wasn't looking in the one place that would make a real and lasting difference.

We go looking for answers outside

Here in the western world, when we are ill, what are we told to do? Where do we go? What do we expect?

We go to a doctor or other expert and we expect them to fix us. We want a pill or an operation or even a replacement for a part of our body. We are looking outside ourselves.

Story Time

That was what I was doing. I was looking for people to make me better. I was looking for pills and potions and things that I could do. I knew I was unwell but I was looking for a solution outside of myself, when the real the problem was me.

One of those places I went in desperation to be 'fixed' was Tai Chi. Someone said to me, "This could really help you relax and improve your health and improve your well-being," so I went along ('Maybe Tai Chi will make me better'), and started to learn. After a few lessons, the Tai Chi teacher suggested I come with him to meet his teacher, who was from the Philippines now living in Dallas and over in London for a visit.

I went to meet his teacher, Rafael, and as you will have guessed, this was the man who went on to have a massive impact on my life. He became my coach for 16 years and he was the man who not only shaped me and helped me get better, but he also saved my wife's life.

It takes inner strength to make the change

> *Progress is impossible without change and those who cannot change their minds cannot change anything....*
>
> **George Bernard Shaw**

One of the reasons I wanted to use *The Darkest Hour* for this chapter is because of one of the stories behind the film. Gary Oldman was offered the part of Churchill and turned it down. He didn't think he could do it. But he went home and thought about it and found the strength inside himself to take on the role which he then won an Oscar for!

Story Time

In my own journey it was only when I met Rafael and he showed me how to work on myself and manage my own energy that I began to recover my health. Change is within us, not in the outside world and to look within ourselves and do the hard work it takes requires courage. We need help to make that change.

I needed help when I met Rafael. I needed mentorship and a new perspective. While that time in my life was incredibly challenging, it was also important in making me who I am today.

I look back now and realise that this experience eventually brought out the best in me. I believe if I hadn't been so unwell, I wouldn't have developed a massive appreciation for my health and well-being. I wouldn't have met the man who inspired me and totally changed the way I moved through the world.

I didn't realise at the time that my character was being forged under intense pressure.

It was only by adopting the fundamentals of my own health (which I will explain more later) and properly managing my energy, that allowed me to recover.

The superhuman hero

If I ask you to name a few people who you think of as a hero, who come to mind? I'm sure you can think of several in your own life, as well as famous leaders and fictional characters.

Hero comes from the Greek word *heros*, meaning 'protector.'
Thus anyone can be a hero if they step up to protect themselves and others from the darkest hours when they come. That is what Winston Churchill was – a protector.

Do you see yourself as a hero? As an Inspirator, who seeks to be the example and inspires others to be their best? Can you protect yourself and them from the challenges of the outside world?

What you may well find is the heroes often only show up at the darkest time and they aren't always where you expect to find them.

This was something I learned in the third of the major incidents that affected my life, which happened just over eight years ago.

Story Time

I have already told you some of what happened to my wife, Hannah, when she was diagnosed with a brain tumour but, as with any story, there is always more to be told.

Continued on next page

Hannah, who I'd known for a few months at the time, was staying with me at my parents' house one night. She'd been feeling unwell for a few weeks, but nothing in that prepared us for what happened next. At about 4:00 in the morning, Hannah had a massive epileptic fit – a 'grand mal' seizure.

I didn't know what was happening. I tried to wake her up, thinking she was having a nightmare, but she wasn't waking up. I started to panic and shouted for help. All I wanted to do was to run away. I really didn't want to have to deal with what was happening.

Then my Mum arrived.

Up until that moment, if you'd asked me to describe my mother, I'd have told you she was something of a worrier – always wondering 'what if' and a bit anxious as a result.

That night, I saw a side of my mum that I had never seen before in my life. She just took charge. In this crisis, her true greatness came to the surface and she managed the situation until the ambulance came and we went to the hospital.

I have to be honest at this point. I'd known Hannah for about 10 months when she was rushed to hospital and, while we were getting along well enough, she wasn't someone I was planning to spend the rest of my life with. I really didn't expect the relationship to go that way.

When she was rushed to hospital, however, Hannah needed a hero and I was cast in the role. She needed someone and, because her Mum was ill and her Dad was caring for her Mum full time, there wasn't anyone else who could be there for Hannah.

Much of what happened over the next few weeks was a complete blur, but it didn't take long for me to realise just how serious the situation was. The tests on Hannah showed an aggressive brain tumour and, within a few weeks, she was in surgery.

She had an eight-and-a-half-hour operation on her brain but they couldn't remove all of the tumour without causing permanent brain damage. After the surgery, we sat down with the surgeon and the specialist nurse and they told us, "It's not good. These cells that you have are very aggressive and the prognosis is not good."

I'll never forget leaving the hospital that day and thinking to myself, "What is the point? What is the point of all of this?" Hannah was 27 and I was being told she'd never see 30.

It was a hot sunny day and both Hannah and I were extremely upset so we sat down on a bench before going back to my parents and thought, "We're going to have to do something." I had to take the lead. There was no alternative – failure was not an option.

Hannah was given a course of radiotherapy which caused all of her hair to fall out but it wasn't slowing down the growth of the tumour. She was given 18 months to live – and it was me (not Hannah) that they told.

I was in a situation that I didn't want to be in and it tested every single ounce of my being.

Continued on next page

So what did I do? I phoned my coach, Rafael. I called him and his advice changed the world, my life – and saved Hannah's life.

He told me to "Find people that are still alive who have the same condition and find out what they did."

My Dad, who was the greatest influence of my life, had always told me "It's not what you know it's who you know." As a Rotarian for over 50 years, he knew hundreds of people. He was a master networker and he'd taught me to do the same.

Added to that, my Mum has always said to me, "There's an answer to every-thing[3]," and that is something that I have been raised to believe.

So I started to look.

Taking the challenge to find people that were still alive wasn't an easy task, although it was a lot easier than it might have been, had it not been for the internet. I began to connect with people from all over the world.

I found people that were still alive and one doctor's name kept coming up, a doctor in Texas called Dr. Stanislaw Burzinsky.

Dr Burzinsky's treatment, still in clinical trial, was extremely controversial. For every positive thing I could find, I could find 20 negative things. Feel free to Google him. You will find the same. When I spoke to people in the medical profession, they either said, "We've not heard of this," or, "Don't go anywhere near him. He is a charlatan."

When I contacted people who'd had Dr Burzinsky's treatment for the same brain tumour as Hannah had, I got to speak to people who were still alive after years. I really didn't know what to do for the best. One of our family friends, a specialist in the type of tumour Hannah had, urged us not to go. She phoned me at one point and begged me, "You must not do this. Please don't go."

I contacted someone I'd worked with when I had been on television – a doctor friend. He looked into it and, in the end, said, "If it was me, I would go because there's quite clearly nothing for her here."

Taking the decision to go was one thing, actually getting there was quite another.

Burzinsky's clinic was in Houston, Texas and that meant that, when we came back to the UK, there had to be a doctor here who would oversee her treat-ment. I must have consulted with 30 or 40 general practitioners, all of whom said no, until eventually, I came across one who looked at the situation and said, "Well, what's the worst thing that can happen? If it helps, it's amazing."

To pay for the treatment we had to find over £200,000 and the FDA in the US had to approve Hannah's case so that she could be accepted on Burzinsky's trial. Every day, there was at least one major incident or obstacle that happened on our road to get us out to Houston. Hannah had constant headaches, we were both living in fear all the time and, when Hannah was finally accepted, she didn't want to go.

Continued on next page

---

[3] *Actually, in my youth she often said, 'You've got an answer for everything.' I was a bit of a smart alec!*

All I could do was give her the time to eventually decide it was something she wanted to do and, once she had made the decision, she put all of her energy into going to Houston and getting better.

I recorded Hannah's time in Houston and you can watch it here:

We were in Houston for seven weeks in total and then we came back to the UK and Hannah's treatment continued here for another 18 months. I became her nurse. I had to take her blood, manage the medications and take care of her full time. I stopped work and devoted myself 100% to what we were doing.

Of course, the odds were stacked against us, but eight years on, Hannah is cancer-free and alive and well.

During that immensely challenging time, the most incredible thing happened. Together we dealt with this difficult situation, mainly through humour and by enjoying each other's company and by finding some hope and joy in the crisis that we found ourselves in. And that is how I really fell in love with my wife.

Coming out the other side

It was never my intention in writing this book to share with you so deeply some of the major incidents that have occurred in my life but I believe it will make a difference to at least one person reading. Who knows? Maybe more.

I want people, when faced with a crisis, to remember, *If Pete went through all that and came out the other side, maybe I can too.* I want them to ask for help and to keep seeking answers and to find others who have been there too and find out what they did.

In reading my story, what do you see as the greatest learning? Perhaps you now realise that there is an answer to everything, as my mother taught me. Maybe you have noticed how my Mum has been a golden thread throughout my life – a hero and an Inspirator to me. Or it could be that you are starting to see the importance of the three aspects of life – health, relationships and work – and how they inter-relate and come together to support us in our darkest hours.

For me, the greatest learning of them all is simple – we are strong; much, much stronger than we think we are. Whatever the challenges life throws at you, you can survive them, learn from them and come back stronger.

> Think back over your life. Where have you experienced crises and dark times? They may not have been like mine but we all have them. Reflect on yours now. What did you achieve in coming through each crisis? What do you learn from your darkest hour? What good has come of failures in your life?

We were all forged in the crisis – the crisis of being born and, in doing so, we became stronger. *Opportunity* and *Danger* remember? The danger creates the opportunity and, to be open to opportunity you must also be open to danger.

There is no greater lesson to be learned than going through something that is difficult, that is testing and that questions our ability. The way I see it, the greatest quality in an Inspirator is to be able to face their darkest hour, to become the hero, protecting those they lead and to inspire them to continue to be their best.

Be the lighthouse – Inspire other people

Would it be okay if I use another analogy to explain what it is to be an Inspirator? Just imagine I had a light bulb in my hand and I said, "Right, are you the light or are you the bulb?" In fact, you are both. The bulb is your body and your mind. The light inside the bulb is what makes you come alive, what makes you shine bright. As a leader, you can see yourself as a beacon, shining light on to other people until they too are shining, especially in times of darkness.

> ### The 30-second history spot
> Beacons are one of the oldest forms of communication. The simplest forms were lighthouses, to tell ships to keep off the rocks. The Romans used them to create a 'line of sight' when building roads in a straight line. Famously, a continuous line of beacons ran from Portsmouth to London and across every high point in England in 1588, to warn of the attack of the Spanish Armada.
> They are still used today in the UK to celebrate royal events.

People are full of insecurities and doubt and you need to be an example – not only to inspire people to follow you, but for them to start illuminating the way for others too. Leadership is the most valuable commodity in the world today, and we need people to become great examples to light up the whole world.

Churchill was a great leader during a global war. Do you see yourself as any different? I don't. There is a war going on right now. A war inside people as they battle against fear, worry and doubt – as they struggle to understand what is asked of them and seek ways that they can achieve. Inspirators are the heroes who can protect people, show them the way and liberate them from themselves.

And it starts with vision – shining light on the aims and goals of the organisation, showing what it is that, together, you can create. Vision expands and lights up parts of our brain.

Deep work

Send in the auditors

I invite you to look at your life – to conduct an audit and, just as I have done, look at the major incidents in your own life with fresh eyes. Some of those past failures may be painful to look at but do not underestimate the importance of doing this. Ask yourself great questions as you reflect and recall how you have coped during your darkest hours.

How have these crises shaped your life? How did you get better as a result of each one? How did they make you stronger? What did you learn? How did these challenging times forge your character? How have they shaped who you have become?

This way of looking at your past, with a curious mind, can change your life and can also help you understand others better – particularly those you lead and influence.

Asking questions like this may become quite emotional and challenging. These are deep questions which may test you. Don't rush the exercise, though. Really open up to the experiences which have shaped you. It matters because of what is coming. Just as Jim Rohn said, the future is opportunity mixed with difficulty and you need to get stronger. You need to be a better version of yourself because obstacles and crises are coming.

What's your story?

We've spent a little time dwelling on past challenges – not always a comfortable place to be, so now I want to ask you a few questions to prepare you for the next time (because there will be a next time, whether we like it or not).

Coaching questions
1. What ordeals and challenges might I face in the future?
2. When the dark times come, whom can I ask for help?
3. From my past challenges, what have I learned which I can draw on to carry me through the next one?
4. What skills and talents can I bring to the fore in future ordeals?

143

And finally...

> *Success is not final, failure is not fatal. It is the courage to continue that counts*
> **Winston Churchill**

This is a quote from the great man himself – not the movie version. We so often associate him with victory – making the 'V' sign in public photos and leading Great Britain through the war – but he was not a paragon and both before and after the war, he made mistakes. Some of his greatest quotes are on the topic of failure and showing resolve in difficult times.

If you are inspired by Churchill, be inspired by his heroism in dark times as much as for his great successes.

9:

Ipseity

Who are you at your core?

If you're so smart, how come you went to MIT to become a cable repair man?

Julius Levinson – Independence Day

In this chapter, we will explore

• the genius that is within every one of us
• the importance of an authentic *Why*
• the meaning of ipseity and how to love your imperfections
• how to inspire others by being authentic
• what you stand for and how to stand for it every day.

Movie Time

Independence Day was a massive blockbuster from 1996 using an age-old theme of invaders from another land (outer space in this case), seeking to eradicate the locals.

What is interesting about it from my perspective, though, is the number of characters who are struggling with their identity and what they stand for. As a theme of the film – deliberate or not – it comes up again and again. And, at different times and in different ways, each of these characters takes the role of the Inspirator during the course of the film.

Do you remember me saying, at the start of this book, that anyone can be a leader? There is no one type. Think back over history: can you think of some great Inspirators who have been modest and quietly spoken or even invisible?

Think of Harper Lee for example. She wrote *To Kill a Mocking Bird* which challenged the thinking about attitudes to race and which became almost a mandatory text in schools and yet she, herself, was barely visible. She spoke through the characters in the book.

Movie Time

In *Independence Day,* David Levinson is hiding from his true self. He is still clinging to a failed marriage, working in a job far below his capabilities and living in fear of environmental disaster. He is quiet, retiring, and unassuming.

Leadership isn't all about being loud and energetic and charismatic.

Do you believe that every one of us has a desire to make an impression on the world in some way – to be the Inspirator in some shape or form? Do we all have an inbuilt desire to grow and improve? Do you? Do you know how you want to make your mark on the world?

If that is what we all want, we know there is a gap between where we are now and the Inspirator we want to follow.

The single most fundamental step across that gap is to have a clear sense of who you are and what you stand for – and to be that 'self' in every aspect of life.

Movie Time

David Levinson wants to save the planet. It is David who first recognises the threat from the visiting aliens and, faced with a challenge that is of more importance than his own inner turmoil, he steps into his own light for the first time. He puts his talents to work when it would be so much easier for him to run away and hide. This, however, is something which he can't ignore.

It is often when we are faced with our greatest challenges in life that our true selves come to light – that is why, on Campbell's hero's journey (and on our Leader's Journey), the stage of *Inner Self* comes so close to the *Ordeal*.

It takes courage and power and resolve to take the bold steps to finding our true character.

Often it is only in our darkest hour that we learn who we really are.

Once you know **who** you are and **what** you stand for and then stand for it every single day, it makes every other part of your journey easier. It makes it so much easier for everyone who follows you too. This is the work I do with leaders that has the most positive impact. Once they understand their *Why* and what they stand for, they can withstand any obstacle.

 How often, in your daily life are you absolutely consistent with your inner values and true to yourself?
80% of the time? 50%? 20%?
And how satisfied are you with that state of affairs?
Do you, like so many of us, find yourself saying, 'I just wish I could be myself'?

In my experience, most people fall into that category. They put on a persona to the world and hide their true self – to expose their true self makes them vulnerable. In doing so, we are making the gap wider in our move to becoming an Inspirator.

That true self – the inner-you – needs to come out. You need to express it in everything you do. The Greeks called it *Arete* while the Romans gave it another word.

The Genius that you are

Are you a Genius?

You would probably say not because most of us use a very narrow definition of the word.

If you look at its true meaning, **Genius** is another word for inner self. The Romans embraced the idea of *Genius* as being 'that within us which makes us unique and great.' The Greeks also had the same concept – which they called the *Diamon*. As is often the case, the meaning has been distorted until it seems to relate only to measures of IQ and those who are uniquely gifted or innovative.

We are all geniuses.

You are a genius and you need to show it to the world.

You have an inner light within you which needs to get out.

To show your Genius, then, you need to first know your own value and principles (your *virtues* if you will) and you need to live by them every single day.

Our virtues are how we express our individuality. We draw on these from within ourselves to lead and know who we are. Our virtues are how we connect to our inner self and are true to that in everything we do.

These are the building blocks which form our character.

It can be a challenging process. Think of yourself as a marble statue, trapped in the rock; as you chip away at all the debris and things you don't want or no longer need, your true self emerges.

> I saw the angel in the stone and set him free
> **Michelangelo – talking about his sculpture of 'David'**

So, it is time to look at who you really are and what is the essence of you.

Authenticity

In Chapter 2 I shared with you the importance of having a strong and powerful *Why*. This burning desire is the first step in becoming an Inspirator but it isn't the whole of it.

Through this book I am coaching you to live according to that *Why* in everything you do – even when it isn't easy. I want your *Why* to define who you are as a person.

I'm coaching you to **be** that person.

I'm coaching you to be authentic.

> The word **authentic** comes from the Greek *authentikos* meaning 'genuine.'
> To be authentic is to act on one's own inner authority to be really and truly yourself. **Author** as a word probably grew out of 'authentic.'
> This is your opportunity to be the author in your life and to create a new story.

Authenticity is essential if you want people to follow you. Today more than ever, people are being mis-sold to, misread and misunderstood. They are desperate for someone to be a genuine light in their lives, someone who they can follow, someone they can believe in.

Can you see how leadership, then, is about authenticity?

I'm asking you to become real and to let go of some of the things that held you back in the past.

I'm also asking you some deep, fundamental questions, like *Whose me am I being?* because I want you to see with absolute clarity who you are and to have the strength and certainty to be that person consistently, every day.

Being authentic is the only way to feel fulfilled.

Delphine Rive

The most important things for me [about being an inspiring leader] ... are two things. One, is being yourself as a leader. I think, quite a lot, you have leaders who put on personas and they're not really who they are in their normal life, or life outside work.... And the second thing is, I think I'm someone who really lives by principles and values.

Authentic *Why*

As a leader and even as you lead yourself, you need to be constantly asking, 'Why should I follow myself?' If you have a strong enough *Why* you'll have the answer to that question. If that *Why* shapes all you do – if you are authentic with it – then you have an *Authentic Why*.

Remember how I said in Chapter 2 that people really aren't interested in what you do or even how you do it? People are interested in *why* you do what you do. They want to understand your motives and what you are trying to achieve. But they need to believe in you and they need to believe in your *Why*. The two are inextricably linked.

> What do you think would happen with the people you lead if they knew that part of **your** *Why* was to inspire **them**? What if they knew that you were committed to developing them and helping them find happiness and fulfilment?

In my experience, this is where many organisations struggle. They develop a vision and a mission and a purpose which sound good and are beautifully crafted but the people don't really understand them. They are seen as a badge – a requirement from the marketing department ("Right. We've got that done." *Tick*). They go up on the website and are stuck on the wall (if the budget will stretch to it, they become a screen saver and a mouse mat). For a little while, people memorise them – by rote as we did in school – then they are forgotten.

Because the leadership doesn't live according to that vision and mission and purpose, they aren't authentic. And if they aren't authentic, people won't follow.

So, make your *Why* authentic. Breathe life into it. Inspire it! If people know your *Why,* they will be inspired to follow you, they'll be inspired to know more. You might even want to think of yourself as your own brand. Why do you exist? What are you here to do?

I invite you to be really curious. Every time you walk into a room, ask yourself *Who has the biggest Why in the room?* Find people who have a strong *Why*, then listen and ask questions and learn from them. What do they stand for? What are they passionate about? Why do they do what they do?

The search for authenticity

The process of understanding your true self is not an easy one. We are all used to a world where we hide and present a front to the world which we think other people want to see. We feel insecure and vulnerable. We struggle to fit in and to be seen in a particular way (which is odd since, as I mentioned in Chapter 2, we don't all see things in the same way).

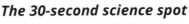

The 30-second science spot

The need to fit isn't a recent phenomenon – it is primal. Humans are tribal animals – we live in communities and hunt in packs. If, at the dawn of man, you were rejected from the *pack* your very life was at risk. So the idea of rejection provokes a fear response.

This is a massive challenge – one we see at its most emotionally extreme in puberty. That is where a sense of an independent self is becoming very clear but it is also in conflict with the desire to be liked by peer groups. More often than not that true self is eroded and parts of it are chipped and broken. As we move into adult life our character is distorted and can become lost. And, because everyone around you seems so together and secure in their lives, you feel even more of an outsider. It can feel incredibly lonely.

Let me tell you what we all have in common.

All those other people are struggling to fit in too. They also want to be part of the pack and fear being an outcast. They put on a front and pretend to be what everyone else (including you) want them to be.

We *all* have these fears: the need to fit, the need to be liked, the need to be right.

We *all* have doubts and uncertainties and we hit challenges which shake our faith in ourselves and those around us.

Can I show you a different way of looking at this, though?

Watch the video called 'Your Self Worth' at inspirators.me

If we don't acknowledge this, we become victim to the consequences of self-doubt. We will never be as capable as we are truly able to become.

Movie Time

In *Independence Day* we see this most clearly in the character of Russell Casse. Casse was a Vietnam War veteran. What he saw there, the conflict of the war coming up against his own values, caused such stress in his mind that he has become lost to himself. He loses himself in alcohol and delusions and even those he most loves are embarrassed to be around him. He is the epitome of the lost soul.

So, if you are finding yourself backing away from the idea of understanding your inner core – your true genius – know that you are not alone. When we started this Inspirator's journey together, I warned you it wouldn't be easy.

As you ask yourself the deep questions I will be guiding you through in this chapter and elsewhere in the book you will start to recognise uncomfortable truths about yourself. There will be things you have done which you aren't proud of and which you hide from the world. You may find that you will need to make radical and painful shifts in your life.

At the same time, there will be great rewards. You will understand yourself in a way you never have before. You will feel fulfilled in your life because you know, whatever you do, you are being authentic. Authenticity is what it all comes down to. You, writing your own future as the author of your own life.

Tony Taylor

I base my mantra on the fact of trust and transparency. Trust and transparency. I also like the word integrity, but it doesn't work quite so well (TIT), so trust and transparency with a bit of humour.

... It makes a big difference, people become less anxious, they see someone who's in control, and organised.

The search for one's true self can take a lifetime. Or, it can come to you in an instant of realisation. Be patient, and keep working on it – it will come.

What do you stand for?

The start of this search for one's true self, starts with one simple question:

What do you stand for?

Do you know? Have you ever even considered the question?

Me? I stand for fairness, kindness, humour, perspective and creativity. These are the values which, if they show up in my day, mean that I end the day feeling good about how things have gone and what I have achieved – even if the day didn't go 100% to plan.

I know what I stand for and I stand for it every day. I didn't always. I too went on a journey to understand myself and learn my true self and it wasn't easy.

> Ask yourself the same question.
> What do I stand for?
> And then consider how you currently express that in your life.
> You may realise that what you stand for and how you currently act aren't fully aligned; but that is the purpose of the exercise.
> For example, if one of those core values (or virtues, if you prefer) is honesty and yet, when someone asks your opinion, you tell white lies to spare their feelings, it will create an inner conflict. You aren't being true to yourself. You aren't doing them any favours either, in the long run, (although there are ways of telling your life partner that they 'look terrible in that shirt.' You don't have to be blunt to be yourself!)

As you look at your personal values, you may come to realise that they don't align with the values of the organisation you work for – but don't look at the values written on posters and in marketing materials for this - not every company actually lives according to its espoused values. What they do and say and how they ask you and others to act may bring you into conflict with your inner genius. That will lead you to deeper questions such as *Why am I working here?* That might be a significant and important question to ask – a leap forward in your own development – or it may be frightening. It will probably be both.

Either way, the question must be asked. If your values don't match those of your employer, are you able to be yourself? And are you able to bring your best self to help them achieve their goals?

Being yourself in the company of others is massively challenging. We all have to adapt to the circumstances we live and work in.

'Fun' is one of my personal virtues but, clearly, I'm not going to crack jokes and play the fool when I'm coaching someone on a painful and difficult topic. My true self steps back to accommodate the situation and what is appropriate in the moment.

The key is to make conscious decisions based on your virtues and to be clear on the decision you are making in the moment. Otherwise you are just *going with the flow* and not being yourself at all.

At every point in every day, it is about being yourself.

- Being yourself as a leader.
- Being yourself as part of your family.
- Being yourself as part of an organisation or as a business owner.
- Being yourself as a member of your community.

That is what it is to be an Inspirator: to stand for your own values and retain your individuality while adapting to the circumstances of the world around you.

 ### Movie Time

Sometimes the circumstances of the world around you will test you and what you stand for. Captain Hiller, the fighter pilot in *Independence Day* (played by Will Smith), is, at the start, the most secure in his own character. When, however, El Toro, the military base where he is stationed, is wiped out by the invading aliens – along with the bulk of the military forces of which he is a part – he starts to question himself. These challenges come to us all. Even Julius Levinson admits to his son, "I haven't spoken to God since your mother died." It is not that we face challenges that matters – what matters is how we deal with them.

Every one of us has challenges and when we do, (and sometimes when we don't), the duck rises up. It is always there, holding us back, causing us to doubt ourselves, to worry, to fear and to hesitate. You have to recognise that, in listening to the duck and taking the path of least resistance, you are backing away from your true self. Do you follow the duck or the genius?

Movie time

We see it in our movie. When Bill Pullman's President first appears, he is criticised by the media for being weak because he hasn't stuck to his promises. Here, then, is another character struggling with his identity. He was a fighter pilot and now he is beginning to flounder in the world of politics. For him, the opportunity to return to his previous role – to an identity which he recognises – is too great to resist.

All of these films talk to us. We watch them and it awakens a part of us which we can relate to. We connect with the hero, we sympathise and feel emotion. Then, when the film is over, we 'go back to sleep.' Your role is to wake up that hero in you, take the lead on your own journey and help others to do the same.

The journey you are on in your life is **your** movie. Would others want to watch it? Would you?

Are you playing it small?

Are you being guided by the duck in your life? And, if you are, are you living up to your true potential? What does that mean for how you live your life? Are you frustrated, unfulfilled or discontented with life? Is it possible that you are playing it small and, somewhere in your innermost thoughts, you know it?

It takes huge courage to be true to your virtues every day, especially if you haven't been living that way up to now. To quote Lao Tzu: *He who conquers himself, is mighty.*

The alternative, however, is to carry on as you have been doing. To give in to the more transactional way of leading – the dark side of leadership as mentioned in the introduction.

These are the leaders who are caught in a cocoon of self-absorption. They are desperate to fit in and seek recognition for their actions – often taking credit for the work of their teams. They are always seeking to improve and get better results by looking for everyone else to change. When things aren't going right, it is the fault of those around them.

These behaviours do not need to be obvious or extreme but tend to be quite subtle. The *dark side* I refer to isn't an evil force like we see in *Star Wars* or in the shape of the invading aliens in *Independence Day* who come to invade the world. This *dark side* is the result of giving in to fear and doubt and not being true to who you really are. This *dark side* shows up in a fear of mistakes or in thinking you aren't good enough or worrying what others might think. And, as a result, these people lack the confidence to allow others the freedom to be themselves either. It feels too risky for members of the team to act outside the limits of their own thinking.

The evidence of the *dark side* being in play is in the way that leader is viewed by those around him and the results they get.

As an example, let me tell you a story which I really like, that I heard once during a presentation.

Story Time

There was once a rowing race on the Thames. Two teams of coxed 8s were competing against one another. I don't know how much you know about rowing but the role of cox is critical. Their job is to steer the boat but also to inspire the team of rowers and to pace the race so they win.

In the teams in my example – let's call them Team A and Team B – the cox of team A was an Inspirator. The cox in team B was not.

Team A won over and over again when these two teams competed.

The cox in Team B would always shrug and say, "You've got a stronger team – your oarsmen are fitter." Then he'd go back to their boathouse and push his oarsmen to train harder and longer so they could beat Team A.

One day, however, a very wise old rowing coach made a suggestion to both teams.

"Why don't you swap coxes?'" he said. "Then let's see who wins."

Cox B was delighted and jumped at the suggestion. "It will be good to work with the top people for once," he said to himself.

Cox A felt a real wrench at leaving his team – they were a tight team and always trained and worked out race tactics together. He was willing to try it however, and, after some words of encouragement to his old team, went to work with Team B. He spent time getting to know his new oarsmen and trained and discussed race tactics with them. They were a bit surprised – Cox B had never done it like this – but they soon found they liked this new way of working.

Sunday came and it was race day. And who do you suppose won the race?

Team B – of course. It wasn't the team who was fittest and strongest – in fact both teams were well trained and at their peak. It was down to the way they were being led.

Cox A saw himself as part of the team and involved his oarsmen and gave them the chance to offer opinions. He wasn't afraid to hear different views and even to try new things. Cox B saw his role as 'being in charge' and thus directed the team as his own judgement told him. He didn't seek ideas from his oarsmen because he didn't want to open himself up to the idea of not being perfect.

Love your imperfections

I'm going to let you in on a secret. Nobody is perfect!

I'm certainly not. I have flaws and I make mistakes and I hit challenges in my life which make me doubt or take me off course.

So, if all these things happen to me too, why should you listen to anything I have to say? What makes *me* qualified to tell *you* what to do?

Precisely because I am *not* perfect and because I see that and accept it as part of who I am.

It isn't a question of **not** having imperfections which makes the difference between an Inspirator and the rest. It is what you **do** with your imperfections.

Let me ask you – when you think of some imperfection or error in your recent past, what is the voice in your head saying? Is it a duck – telling you how you are a fool for making that mistake, beating you up for not having done or said something different, telling you this is proof that you should just quit and stop pretending that you are worthy of being an Inspirator?

And how much time do you spend listening to the duck and buying in to what it is saying?

There is an alternative, however. Remember what I said earlier about you being a genius? That inner light which we all have? It is this which can show you the way. Because, you see, every one of your imperfections is an opportunity to *get better*. This is your chance to grow and improve.

It is a mistake to assume that learning is only something you can do in a classroom. I'm sure many of you have attended 'leadership training'. Similarly, there are lots of books on leadership – but the pages of a book can only give you so much.

There are other ways to learn too.

Jon Sellins

Wembley has been open 10 years and operates pretty well. I've only come here because I know it can be better. There are still things we can do better and the team know that. We can be a better venue. We can look after people better. We can deliver a better service. We can be safer. We're in a good place, but we can do better and that's why I came here.

The 30-second science spot

The first way we learn, in infancy, is by looking at what other people are doing and mimicking them. So look around you at other leaders – both those in your own direct sphere and those you have come across in the wider world. Ask yourself what they do which is inspiring and consider how to apply that in your own life and way of operating. Where you can, ask them questions to see if you can learn even more. What are their virtues? What do they stand for? How do their virtues show up in the way they move through the world?

Reading, education and observation all have their place but they are all external to you. It is another way of looking to the outside world for an answer. The answer is within you, though. Every time you go on a course or read a book or spend time with a mentor, say to yourself, "How do I *apply* this to my life?"

Be ever alert to how the information you are gathering can be used to understand your imperfections, to find ways to adapt and grow and evolve into an Inspirator. Try things, see how they work, reflect objectively on what went well and what you can do differently another time.

Seek out challenges to test yourself.

Relish mistakes for what they teach you.

Love your imperfections for the insights they give you into your relationship with yourself.

In all these situations and in others, ask yourself, "What can I learn from this? What does it tell me about myself? How can I get better?"

Build a clear view of what you do well, what works for you and for others and where you need to improve.

Perfectly imperfect

Nobody is perfect. Agreed?

At the same time, having a knowledge of your higher self – of knowing who you are and what you stand for – and striving to be that true self every day *is* a form of perfection. Strive for that perfection and accept that you will struggle and you will fall and forgive yourself when that happens. Never give up on your mission to becoming perfectly yourself.

That sense of selfhood is known by another term – Ipseity

Glyn House

There's a really good, simple model of loyalty that I read a long time ago. [Professor Royce in 1908 described] a triangle of loyalty. At the bottom is loyalty to the individual. Then in the middle is loyalty to a team, but to get real loyalty … if you can get people loyal behind a set of values [at the top of the triangle], that's really good.

It was Delphine Rive who first introduced the term *Ipesity* to me. If you listen to her interview, you'll hear us discuss how she came across it.

The word itself comes from the Latin *'Ipse'* which means 'self.' *Ipseity*, then means 'selfhood' or 'personal identity.' It means being yourself in everything you so.

Be taught by your team – Inspire other people

What if your role as a leader is to bring out the best in other people by being authentic? In a world full of so much fakery and posturing, people need something real to believe in and an inspirational leader to follow. Authenticity is a rare commodity and people crave it. Can you see how being an Inspirator is to be yourself?

If you are clear about what you stand for and express that in everything you do and say, then your team will know where they stand too.

Absolute consistency to your principles will also free others from fear. If they know what to expect, there is nothing to fear. And, in seeing you living your principles every day, you can also guide and encourage them to understand what they stand for too. They will start to find their own Ipseity.

In her interview, Delphine Rive mentioned a leader who inspired her, who had a great ability to read people and to understand their wants and needs – and then to do all he could to meet those needs for others.

A good place to start understanding this will be to ask your team what kind of leader they want. Simply put, ask them how they like to be led. Discuss with them the leaders they've had in the past (or across history) who inspired them and what it was about them that made the difference.

Be prepared to be taught by your team and encourage them to learn as well. Use the coaching questions throughout this book, especially, "What have you learned, what have you achieved, what are you going to do with it?" And develop a culture of reflection and learning in those around you.

But, first and foremost **keep your promises.** If you make a commitment to yourself or your team, invite the team to hold you accountable – and then never put them in a position where they need to call on that, by delivering ahead of the promise you made. This is an absolute fundamental for them to have confidence in you – and for you to have confidence in yourself.

Deep work

The key tool to have in being yourself isn't really a tool. It is a definition of who you are. We've mentioned it a few times in this chapter already – your virtues.

Don't get too hung up on the word by the way.

> *Virtue* has, like many words, been distorted in its meaning to be thought of as an overly pious stance. All it really means, when you look at its origins, is *'higher character.'*
>
> If you prefer to call them values, or personal morals or principles, then that's fine. What is most important is that you work to define them.

 What are the things you hold most dear? What matters to you above all things? What do you stand for?

There are ways to draw out these virtues – and one is to use a technique I first came across when reading Stephen Covey's *Seven Habits of Highly Effective People.*

Write your Eulogy

Imagine that you are at your funeral and friends, family and work colleagues are all there. Which of your qualities do you want them to describe in the eulogy? Do you want to be lauded for your fairness? Or your energy for life? Or your creativity? Or something else?

Once you've written your eulogy, discuss it with other people. Tell your parents, your children, your partner or your friends what legacy you want to leave behind. What you stand for is something you should be talking about. We all should be talking about this stuff. It's important!

Another way to tap into your inner self and start to understand these virtues is to use meditation. Take the time to stop and breathe and reflect on who you are, right this moment.

What's your story?

The coaching questions in this chapter are deeply reflective. They are questions you should be asking yourself every day. As we reflect on ourselves and on our past, they lead to actions in the future. Reflect on the goals you have set yourself and why you want to be an Inspirator – as I guided you in the first few chapters – as you work your way through these.

Coaching questions
1. How will the world be better with me in it?
2. What are my unique skills, talents and powers?
3. Who am I at my best?
4. Who must I fearlessly become?
5. What do I stand for?

And finally...

> You will never have a greater or lesser dominion than that over yourself...the height of a man's success is gauged by his self-mastery; the depth of his failure by his self-abandonment. ...And this law is the expression of eternal justice. He who cannot establish dominion over himself will have no dominion over others.
> **Leonardo da Vinci**

Knowing who you are and being true to that is a significant challenge for us all. It is something that we have been pursuing for centuries and, as the world becomes more advanced, the answers seem further away than ever. The search is a worthy one, however, as da Vinci knew in the 15th century.

As you read this chapter, however, you may feel it doesn't really make sense. It may well not. You may need to read this chapter again and it may still not make sense.

By continuing to work on yourself, as guided in the other chapters and by continuing to ask yourself the coaching questions provided, you will find that, eventually, you will begin to understand.

When you do, you will know what it is to be an Inspirator.

Hitting the Plateau

When it all gets a bit mundane.

They may not be the most sophisticated people but they do know how to divide and $20 million isn't shit when you split it between them. Second of all, these people don't dream about being rich. They dream about being able to watch their kids swim in a pool without worrying that they'll have to have a hysterectomy at the age of twenty ... Or have their spine deteriorate ... I want you to think real hard about what your spine is worth ... Then you take out your calculator and you multiply that number by a hundred. Anything less than that is a waste of our time.

Erin Brockovich

In this chapter, we will explore

- willpower – the queen of virtues
- grit – when the going gets tough
- hope – to believe in the future
- character – and what it takes to build yours
- what it really means to be a hero
- tools to help boost your willpower and grit.

⚠ WARNING!

This is going to be really boring!

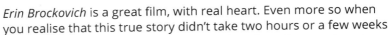

> ### *Movie time*
>
> *Erin Brockovich* is a great film, with real heart. Even more so when you realise that this true story didn't take two hours or a few weeks to reach a resolution, it took over *3 years*. It was a long hard journey to get adequate compensation for Hinkley, polluted by the nearby power plant, and there were plenty of times when the team felt they had hit a standstill.
>
> During that time the team representing the people affected by pollution were given several offers to settle. It would have been easy and must have been really tempting to accept. Erin and her family were threatened, all the costs of the case were being borne by the firm, everyone was working ridiculous hours, relationships suffered... Taking that $20million offer would have made life so much easier. Especially when it felt as if progress wasn't being made.
>
> But they stuck at it, kept going and, eventually, won the largest settlement in history for the people of Hinckley.
>
> And after they won, what did they then do?
>
> They started work on another investigation into a similar pollution case.
>
> Did Erin feel like keeping going? Did she feel like going again?
>
> Almost certainly not. But she had, and still has, a strong W*hy* which keeps her going.

If you have been applying my coaching from the previous chapters are you seeing some results? Are members of your team starting to see the change in you and are they stepping up too? Do you look in the mirror and see the Inspirator in you? Have you started to get a bit fitter and healthier and feel better in yourself?

Whatever the results, there are two things I want you to do now.

1. Celebrate the victories. You are doing great things and you deserve to recognise that.
2. Ask yourself – now what needs to be done?

Let me ask you a question. When do you imagine that the journey to becoming an Inspirator is at its end? When will you be able to say, 'I've made it?' When will you be able to stop working on this and move on to other things?

Are you at that point? Did it all feel really exciting and new when you read the first few chapters. Did you get fired up and get some results? Did you manage to overcome some obstacles and feel the sense of achievement? And has all that excitement faded and now, it just feels like a chore? Has it, in short, become a bit... well... mundane? Are you wondering when it will be over?

Not everything in life is as we want it. We may have goals and dreams and ambitions and then be disappointed. Day to day life can seem mundane and, frankly, a bit boring. Everything which is easy to do is easy not to do.

If that is how you view life you are living on *Someday Isle.* So many people live their lives saying "Some day, I'll quit the job and start my own business" or "Some day, I'll fit into that size 6 dress" or "Some day, I'll be happy." *Someday Isle* is a pretty crowded place.

When they are fired up with excitement for some new goal, they work hard. Then they hit obstacles or even achieve some of the goals. They stop doing what they had been doing and before you know it, they are stranded on the island.

Leadership is like that for many people. Don't let it be for you!

Leadership is seen by some as a 'sexy position' that you enjoy just like a trophy, but it's not. It's pretty unsexy. It's multidimensional. It's challenging. It requires an attitude of optimism and possibility and a set of rituals that need your total dedication.

If, having seen some success, you now stop – as you have always done in the past – you won't just stop moving forwards. You will go **backwards** because everyone around you will be moving forwards.

Or, are you thinking "This is progress, I'm happy with where I am. Now I can stop focusing on me and do other things?"

The problem is escalating all the time. Human beings have an incredible habit of being uncomfortable but getting 'comfortable at being uncomfortable.' They are content with 'good enough.' When progress is slow or doing the work seems like too much effort, they go back to the status quo, doing what is comfortable to them. They go back to default settings.

Can you think of cases where this has happened to you or you've seen it happen to others?

Just think about any diet you've ever been on, for example. You count the calories, or the points, you eat the eggs and grapefruit, you *beast it* down at the gym. You lose weight. Hurrah. Success. "Now I can eat pizza again!"

It is so much easier to go back to what we have done in the past rather than face the fear of being lost or out of our depth. This is why having a Mastermind Alliance around you is so vital – to support you when it feels uncomfortable so you don't go backwards.

What we are going to look at in this chapter are some invisible forces, that if addressed and built upon, can have a massive impact on taking you forward.

So what are these forces?

• Willpower
• Grit
• Hope
• Character

Just to warn you, at the end of this chapter, I'm going to ask you, which one of those four you think is the most important for your own development but also in regards to the success of an organisation. You can think about this as we go along.

The Queen of Virtues

What if you had unlimited willpower? What would you get done? What difference would it make to your life?

Remember how I said in Chapter 5 that an Inspirator has to **apply** their knowledge – be someone who takes action? Can you see how important it is to have the willpower to apply yourself?

Willpower is the science of self-control. It has been shown to out-predict IQ. Of all the qualities I've ever seen in any human being, the people who show most willpower have the greatest success in life and in business.

> There are many definitions of **willpower** which is a relatively modern word, meaning, as you might expect, *'having power over your decisions.'* The one I particularly like is:
> *The ability to do what needs to be done **even when you don't feel like it.***
> Willpower is the engine to achieve our goals, even when it is hard, even when you are under pressure, even when you aren't making progress, even when it is boring.

Willpower is a superpower – it is more important than intelligence and skills. If you have the willpower, you will stick at things and make them happen. You will find a way.

When you hit a plateau, this is when you **most** need willpower, because that is what will keep you going until life gets interesting again. It is not when you hit a major obstacle (after all, most of us step up and are our best when circumstances around us are at their worst). It is not when things are going well and we are feeling fired up by what we are doing. It is when we feel like we aren't making progress but there is no good reason for it.

Mmmmm – Marshmallows!

The 30-second science spot

One of the most incredible studies I ever came across was the 'Marshmallow experiment' of the 60s and 70s conducted by Walter Mischel at Stanford University. Preschool children (aged around 4) were taken into a room individually, shown a marshmallow and told by a teacher, "I have to leave the room for a little while. You can have this marshmallow if you want it, but, when I come back, if you haven't eaten it, I'll give you another one so you'll have two." The teacher would leave for 15 minutes, while the child was observed to see what they did. Some ate it at once, some waited the full 15 minutes and got the reward. Some would try to resist and then give in. Some even pretended that they had been promised the second marshmallow *regardless* of them having eaten the first. A whole range of responses were seen. It was a fascinating study into self-control and how much it was an inherent ability.

The most fascinating thing about the study, however, was what happened afterwards. The children who took part in the study were followed up some years later. Those who had shown more self-control were doing better in school, irrespective of their IQ. This prompted the researchers to follow those children for many years. The results were startling. The ones who showed greater self-control were less likely to have criminal records, be in broken relationships, and less likely to be in debt. It just went to show the power of willpower[1].

 Now, let me ask you a question. Imagine yourself at 4 years old. If you had been a subject of the marshmallow[2] experiment, what would you have done? Would you have eaten it straightaway? Would you have waited a while, felt like the marshmallow was talking to you and eventually eaten it? Or would you have had the willpower to have waited for the teacher to come back?

The leaders in the field of Willpower research, Roy Baumeister and John Tierney, have made it their life's work to understand what affects self-control and what can be done to improve it.

Recharging your Batteries.

Is willpower something that people are born with? Possibly. Can it be learned? Definitely.

 Take a look at your phone. How much charge is there left in the battery? Is it full? Half full? Nearly empty? Even if you haven't been using it much, has it been running down over the day?

The most important thing to understand about Willpower is that it isn't a fixed factor in your life. Sometimes you have it, sometimes you don't. Willpower drains the more you use it – just like the battery on your smartphone. So, as you use it, you end up with less and less and you only have a finite amount. How we live our lives and how we deal with stress affects our willpower.

 What drains you the most? Become aware of when your willpower is at its highest and at its lowest.

---

[1] This experiment has been repeated more recently using modern testing methods and, while it shows that there is still significance in the levels of willpower on future outcomes, other factors also need to be taken into consideration. There is always more to be learned.
[2] If you don't like marshmallows, imagine it was a piece of chocolate, a slice of cake or a piece of cheese. The idea is that it is something you like.

You use willpower in everything you do – every decision you take uses willpower. The more taxing and demanding the decisions, the more your willpower drains. Every time you call on your willpower to control yourself, your reserves are used up. So, if you have ever wondered how it is that you can manage a whole range of difficult people at work and then go home and shout at your son because they accidentally dropped a plate, here is your reason.

Every distraction going on around you, every time you are trying to concentrate and keep being interrupted, every time you have a battle with yourself to start working on that report that really needs to be written or to go for a run or to not eat that second slice of cake, is draining your willpower away. This is so seldom thought about. The impact of procrastination, indecision, distraction, lack of focus and even the duck, isn't just on the task in hand but on everything else you need to get done that day, that week, that month…

There are a number of factors which have been shown to improve our self-control. There's a catch, however. Most of the things you need to do to cultivate your willpower *require* willpower to get yourself to do them.

For example, sleep is vital for recharging your willpower battery. How hard do you find it to get to bed on time and to turn off digital devices so you get at least eight hours of quality sleep?

Exercise, too, can give your willpower a boost. Is it easy to make yourself go to the gym?

And this is why we need to look at what we can do every single day to help ourselves and the people in our business to have an optimal amount of willpower.

So, what are the top things you can do to boost your willpower?

- Don't go hungry – low levels of glucose in the brain will lead to poor decisions and more impulsive behaviours (especially, of course, in the decisions you make about food). Alcohol too can disrupt the glucose levels in the brain (which is why a kebab seems such a good idea after a few pints when you wouldn't dream of eating one when sober).
- Get plenty of sleep – the research is quite clear that a poor night of sleep has a massive impact on willpower. It also pays to be aware of times when you know you are tired and try to minimise the impact on your self-control. For example, can you reschedule the meeting where you have to be on your A-game and not lose your temper?
- Move more – this reduces stress, itself a drain on willpower, and also gives the willpower battery a top-up.
- Make it easy to exercise willpower – give yourself less opportunities to resist. The most obvious example of this is to lay out your gym kit the night before, so that you get up and are ready to work out without having to make any other decisions.
- Do one thing at a time – put yourself in a distraction-free state so you can focus and don't try to multi-task and juggle things.
- Practice delayed gratification – say to yourself "I could eat that slice of cake, but I'll have it later," to build up your ability to use willpower. And maybe you'll only resist for ten minutes today, but tomorrow you might make it to 15 minutes, and then 20 and…. You get the idea.

- Make it hard to do things that aren't helping you – if you know you want to avoid browsing the internet in the last hour before bed, for example, set up a timer on your broadband so it shuts off an hour before bedtime.

If you don't believe me, then try an experiment. Spend today eating junk food, stay up late, drink a bunch of alcohol and spend hours playing mindless games on your phone. See how your willpower is tomorrow. How has your willpower been in the past when you've been 'on the razzle' or made a poor decision?

How are you feeling right now? Are you feeling resistance to the idea of having to make these changes in your life to improve your willpower? Are you thinking you are 'too busy' to do these things?

In my experience, when you feel resistance to things which will improve your life, it is usually a sign that you need to do them.

Failing to recognise this is failing to take the lead – in your life and for others.

When the going gets tough....

... the tough stick at it. They have grit.

Grit is staying power. The word is first recorded in the context of 'not giving up' (as opposed to its original meaning of 'specks of dirt or gravel') in 18th century America. It is the ability to keep going when things get hard or boring. Think of it as being like Willpower, squared.

There is a science of grit, with some amazing work that has been done by Professor Angela Duckworth – showing that it revolves around having passion and perseverance.

Professor Duckworth's work includes a way of measuring your levels of grit. We have included the link in <u>inspirators.me</u> so you can find out just how gritty you are.

Gritty people will keep going, even when things are difficult. They'll keep chasing something, and realising that the chase is just as important as the capture. When they find themselves on a plateau, they continue to work on themselves, knowing that the best is yet to come. They know that the things they do every day will, eventually, lead to results.

Just to be clear, it's not that gritty people don't have negative thoughts. They still think, "This is boring, I really can't see the point of this," or, "This isn't really that important. I'll do it tomorrow" or, "I'm not making progress, I might as well just give up." The difference is that they recognise those thoughts, and when they catch themselves, they don't act on the impulse. They get gritty.

 What do you do when you are bored, or feel you aren't making progress? Do you have a talent for being gritty? Can you use it to master the mundane and survive the plateau?

Celebrate doing the 'boring things' and making small, incremental steps.

Effort Squared

How important is 'effort' in the science of grit? Does it matter whether you give 100% in everything you do?

One of the key points that Professor Duckworth makes in her book is that effort counts twice.

 Story Time
Let's take the case of Emma. Emma has a talent for computer programming. She puts in a lot of effort and develops her programming skill. Then, she takes that skill, puts in a lot of effort and this leads to achievement.

Achievement = Effort x Skill, where Skill= Effort x Talent.

So, what does it take to get more effort out of someone?

As I've pointed out a few times through the book, it is important to ask yourself, "What do people want?"

People want to feel they are a part of something. People want to be on a winning team.

 Story Time
President John F Kennedy paid a visit to NASA in 1962 and, as he was walking around, he stopped to talk to one of the janitors, who was sweeping the floor.
"What do you do?" Kennedy asked.
The cleaner, with a broom in his hand, replied, "Mr President, I'm putting a man on the moon."
He knew the part that he was playing, even though sweeping floors might seem quite menial to many. He knew the importance of keeping NASA clean so that others could do their jobs in order to put a man on the moon.

This is a significant goal for organisations. If you can make everyone aware of the big picture and see the part that they're playing in making that picture happen then you create the environment for passion and persistence to grow. You get a gritty community.

It isn't easy. For so many of the organisations I've worked in, very few people know what the mission statement of the business is, let alone being able to see exactly where the company is going.

Why, why, why, why, why?

I know I keep repeating this, but it's all about the *Why*. We get to see the best of people when they have a big *Why*.

Patti Dobrowolski

You envision the future state, but the way that your brain works is it creates a snapshot, like a picture of it in your mind. So if you have a picture for your team, and you're talking to it; and you're speaking to it; and you say, "Now where are you in this picture?" Then suddenly, like, "I understand. Oh, I'm the person on the forklift. I'm the person who is connecting to that person. So no matter how far down the line I am, then I know what my role is."

> ### Movie Time
> In the film *Erin Brockovich*, her *Why* was massive. She could see a terrible situation. People's lives were at risk, and her *Why*, if you could measure it, was so big that there was nothing that was going to stop her. Even though there were obstacles along the way, her *Why?* was so big it was a powerful force which kept her going and believing that there was a positive outcome in the future.

This is where it's good to talk about hope.

Hope IS a strategy

Having hope is another of the invisible forces for dealing with life on the plateau.

> **Hope** is from the Old English work *hopian* which means to have hope (or trust) in God's word. By the 13th century it also became used to mean 'to wish for' or 'desire' (something).
> The definition I like best though, is 'seeing the future and believing it is possible.'

Hope is most likely to flag when things get a bit dull. We have drawn on reserves in dark times and we have seen successes. *Now what? Is this mundane way of living all that is left?*

For me, the word 'hope' is a bit woolly. "I hope things turn out for the best." "Am I going to succeed? I hope so." It gets used in the same way as many use 'I'll try', in a soft and deprecating way.

When you think of hope as 'belief' and make it tangible, it takes on new meaning.

> Where do you have hope in your life? What is the future you see that you believe will happen?

The science of hope – and there is one – is, in simple terms, about believing that your future is better than where you are right now. There's nothing wrong with where you are right now, of course, but hope makes you excited about the future.

How NOT to have hope

Have you ever had a fantasy? A daydream about a future which you'd love to see happen?

If I won £1million...

One day I'm going to quit this job and sail round the world...

If I was free to do what I wanted, I'd move to France and live like a hermit...

We all do it – and it would be easy to confuse this with hope, especially if you are wishing for this thing so much it is your only plan. This, however, is **not** hope. It is fantasy. The difference is that people who fantasise about a perfect future very rarely take action.

Visualising the future in this way can create a feeling of calmness, rather than the activation energy needed to go out there and make the future happen. The other name for it is 'day-dreaming' and it is a dream – a nice place to be, but you are half-asleep.

Have you ever talked yourself out of things?

There is no point in buying a lottery ticket – the odds are tiny...

I can't leave my job – I have to pay the mortgage...

I couldn't live in France – I don't even speak French...

I'm sure you have. I know I have. This is the antidote to hope – to *dwell*, thinking about all of the problems and all of the things that could go wrong and to talk yourself out of it.

The 30-second science spot

At some point in our evolution we developed the capacity to create mental representations of ourselves and the world around us. We saw ourselves as time travellers moving through time. Much of this came about because we had to survive – so we learned to anticipate all that could go wrong. Life was about making it to the end of the day in one piece.

Now, in our more evolved state, we have the opportunity to do more than survive – we can thrive. It is time to do great things, and to use those mental representations to build hope and drive us forwards.

Hope is where you can see where things are going and you are aware of the obstacles that are coming. You believe you have the ability to deal with what's going to happen and you're prepared to take multiple pathways to get what it is that you want.

At the very start of this book I told you that your future is unwritten and you have the power to change. This is something I believe absolutely. We all have a future that is unwritten, that we want to move towards and we all have the power to go out and do something about it. What I'm really saying is that you are the author in your own life. You hold the pen and can shape yourself to be the very best version of yourself.

How we bring that to life is to tap into something else that I've already mentioned in this book, which is about your identity. Do you identify with the Inspirator that you want to become?

The 30-second science spot

In a recent series of experiments carried out at Harvard, people were put into an fMRI machine to look at their brain activity when given certain stimuli. They were first asked to imagine themselves and then to think of a stranger or an actor, in each case looking at the way the brain is stimulated.

Then they were asked to image themselves in the future. For the majority of people, the brain activity was similar to that of being asked to think of a stranger. Most people think of their future self in the third-person and don't really identify with them. Those who do identify with their future self are more prepared to do the work and invest in their long-term future.

When you identify with the person that you're going to become, it makes it a lot easier to move your life forwards in a powerful direction.

It's really important to rethink the way that you think about the future, because, while planning and visualising where you want to go are essential components, these alone don't drive us to take action. The key word here is to **connect** every day; to connect and commit to where you're going. To see the future and believe in it. To have hope.

One of the best people I know to show you how to generate hope is my colleague, Patti Dobrowolski, who specialises in helping people unlock the creative part of their brain to build visual representations of where they are going go, so you can see it clearly. The interview with Patti goes into this in more detail and is well worth watching.

Lucy Mellins

I know that the best teams are on the whole ... when people really know and understand each other, then you get the best work out of people. I think [it gives] a level of continuity and cohesiveness, and also just people genuinely... being happy to walk through the door in the morning.

Chipping away at the marble

It takes real character to show up every day in the face of the mundane and keep doing what you do every day. As a leader, your role is to develop **your** character so that others are inspired to develop theirs.

The word **character** is the oldest of our four forces. It comes from the Greek *kharakter*, meaning 'engraved mark' or more properly, 'an instrument for marking.' We'd call it a chisel. The *kharax*, which is the root of the word, may even predate Greek – it is a very old word indeed. Even in Greek times, it was used to mean 'a defining feature.'

I love that **character** and **chisel** come from the same word. It is a brilliant way of looking at it because we build character by chipping away the things we do not need.

 ### The 30-second history spot

One of the most famous and most revered sculptures in the world is the statue of 'David' in Florence, created by Michelangelo. It started, as all sculpture does, as a huge block of marble and Michelangelo chiselled away at it, removing the unwanted stone and the imperfections, until he revealed the amazing figure beneath.

> *Every block of stone has a statue inside it and it is the task of the sculptor to discover it.*
>
> **Michelangelo di Lodovico Buonarroti Simoni**

Michelangelo could see the statue that he was going to create from the outset, even though he had to work tirelessly for many thousands of hours to reveal 'the angel in the marble'. It took him more than two years, without stopping, to create the masterpiece.

What's more, the block of marble he used had previously been rejected by other artists of the time because it had too many 'taroli', (imperfections), and had stood, neglected, for 25 years in the Duomo in Florence. It was waiting for an Inspirator.

This is what it is to build your character: to not be deterred by the imperfections and only see the beauty which lies beneath; to keep going, day after day, month after month, year after year, to reveal each part of the beautiful essence beneath.

This is part of the mindset that I have created with many of the people that I've worked with. They developed the mindset of a sculptor, working on themselves, every single day, little by little, accepting the dust and grime that working on themselves might generate, to seek out the inner essence of who they are.

This mindset isn't some sort of innate character trait that you either have or don't have, or based on DNA or fate or luck. It can be harvested. It can be grown.

Have you ever stopped to consider what are your unique character traits? If you chip away at the surface stuff – all the habits and imperfections and unhelpful beliefs you have acquired during your life – what remains at your core? Character is the essence of who you are.

Are you ready to start chiselling away at yourself – and at the habits that really get in your way – so you can bring your best self to the party every day?

If you want clarity on this, watch any of the Inspirator interviews we have made. They all talk about character and the continual work on themselves.

For me, character is all about virtues. What are the values you hold dear? What do you stand for? We spoke about this much more in Chapter 9.

Can you now see why it's really important to know your *Why* – why you're doing what you're doing? Then, you can become more aware of the meaning that you're giving to what you are doing and build the character that you need.

Oxygenate – Inspire other people

So, which comes first, of those four? What do you think – is willpower, grit, hope or character the most important force to take you forward?

For me, it's all about **hope.**

Hope comes first. The belief in what you're doing, where you're going, and to use that to help others develop willpower and grit and to work on their character. This is where coaching can play an incredible part.

What is the engine in any organisation? The people, right?

We all know that it's the people that drive a business forward. It's the people that you need when things are going off course. When things happen or difficulties occur, you want the people to take responsibility for getting you back on track.

Do you remember what I've said before about *what people want*? How they want to be a part of something and they want to grow? Seeing the potential in them, seeing what the future can hold for them and believing in them so they can believe in themselves is what they most need.

How do they feel about where they are? How do they feel about the company and where the company is going? What is it specifically they need to do in order for things to improve?

Knowing these things means that they will be there, ready to help, when it is needed.

Quite simply, hope is like oxygen. Without it, we don't survive. Our relationship with the future determines how we live today.

One of the most alarming statistics that I've ever come across relates to hope. In one particular study, it showed that leaders who are not capable of inspiring hope have engagement levels of 1%. Leaders who can inspire hope have engagement levels of 69%. It is shocking but it matches my own experiences.

In the 25 years I've spent working with organisations I have lost count of how many I've gone into that have an air of plateau. They have an air of boredom. They have an air of staleness, as if it's an organisation that is not really going anywhere at all. They have no hope.

What a lot of organisations don't realise is that, when they are at a plateau, when nothing much is really going on, there is a real danger of a downward spiral. In my experience, the plateau seems to breed a sense of entitlement and a belief in people that they should be getting more. Even hostile environments start to be created.

How do you build hope?

It's hard for organisations to build a sense of hope in people – especially if things haven't been going well for some time. Let's face it, it's hard enough for leaders to be hopeful because, in many cases, they've never been shown how, themselves.

 Just for a moment, stop and consider: what would it be like to have that alignment? To be in an organisation which was full of hope and where, even if things were on a plateau, everyone believed that the future was going to be amazing?

Your mission as an Inspirator, then, is to give people something to see and something to believe in. To help them attach emotion to that future.

This is why we go and watch films. We love to see something happen. We love to see the hero evolve and overcome the adversity. We need to help all of the people in your business see the hero's role that they have to play in making the business succeed.

Can it be done? Of course, as long as you can help them find their big *Why*. Give them vision and help them answer the question, *"What's in this for me?"* They have to believe. They have to believe in your vision of the future – which means they have to believe in you.

Drew Brown

We've started ... talking to teams. Not just management ... but ... people who clean bedrooms, people who work behind the bar, people who work in the kitchens ... to give them confidence that they can talk, they can be part of the business, they can shape the business, they have a voice and a view within the business, which I'm really passionate about.

... We've started to open the channels of communication. to get people to come and talk to us, which I think is really vital.

 Now do you see why being able to look in the mirror and believe in yourself is so important? If you don't believe in you, how can they?

Be the beacon of hope to support them on their plateau.

But what do I actually need to DO?

This is where the other three forces come in. You build hope by encouraging those you lead to work on themselves and, especially, to have willpower, grit and character.

Know that, after a big success, there will be a drop in willpower – it will have drained away with all that effort. What can you do to recharge it? Could you have an away day to reward the effort, celebrate success and recharge? Are you making sure everyone has the chance to rest and recuperate?

When things seem flat and stale, go back to the vision of the future and how they fit. Reconnect them with it, so they find the grit to keep going. Ask questions such as, 'What went well?', 'What needs Work?', 'Now what needs to be done?' to encourage the setting of a new goal and challenge.

Help them find out what their unique character strengths are, and align them in some way to what the company's are, then all of a sudden we can get the best out of people.

Deep work

Mindfulness – to boost your willpower

I've mentioned Mindfulness as a massively powerful tool. Most people know it as a technique for reducing stress but tapping into the parasympathetic nervous system has other benefits too. In particular, it has been shown to boost willpower. Ideally, do your mindfulness practice at the same time every day – don't leave it to chance so your willpower isn't tested.

My priming meditation also helps with hope and grit so here is the link again to download it.

Another mindfulness exercise you could do is to visualise your willpower like the power meter on your phone. Check in with the icon throughout the day to see when you need to give your willpower a boost.

Ideal self-exercise

This exercise is one which specifically helps to build willpower and grit. Start by thinking of yourself in the future – perhaps 5 years from now – if you have unlimited willpower and have been gritty in everything you do. How will you act? What sort of a person will you be?

Then, list all the positives of being that ideal version of you. How will you feel? What impact will it have on your health and fitness? And what impact will it have on those around you?

Finally, consider **not** taking action and using willpower to achieve your ideal self. What are the consequences of that? What will it feel like in that future of giving in to impulses or giving up when things got tough?

This is a very powerful exercise and the real power comes in doing it often to continue to inspire yourself to do what needs doing, whether you feel like it or not.

What's your story?

Just by being aware of how the four forces show up in your life can be massively powerful. Start every day by answering these questions in your journal.

Coaching questions
1. What drains my willpower?
2. What do I need grit for today?
3. Who is in my gritty community?
4. What do I need to chisel away from my external self to reveal my true character?
5. What is the future I believe in?

And finally...

> *Gentlemen, we will chase perfection. We will chase it relentlessly, knowing that we will never attain it. But along the way, we shall catch excellence.*
>
> ***Vince Lombardi Jnr***

Imagine walking into your organization and the energy is there. There's never a plateau. People are always looking to improve things. People are always looking for that pursuit of excellence. Why? Because people want to be a part of something. People want to win.

11:  Flourishing

Who you are and how you shine.

Amelie has a strange feeling of absolute harmony. It's a perfect moment. A soft light, a scent in the air, the quiet murmur of the city. A surge of love, an urge to help mankind overcomes her.

Amelie

In this chapter, we will explore
- how to create a culture which brings out the best in people
- what it means to create a flourishing culture
- why motivation doesn't work
- the tool developed by the leading thinker in flourishing.

Movie Time

Amelie is a French language film (with English subtitles), with a wonderful message. As always, you don't *need* to watch it but it is worth it if you do, because Amelie is an Inspirator.

Amelie sees wonder in everything. This sense of curiosity and interest came out of the challenge of a loveless upbringing. Her neurotic mother died when she was young. Her unemotional father feared for her safety so much he didn't want her to leave the house. So Amelie retreats into her imagination.

Then a chance discovery of an old tin box sets her on a mission to find its owner and that shows her how she can help others. She does it in a completely selfless way without seeking recognition or reward. This is what leadership truly is.

She helps others to flourish and, in doing so – in becoming an Inspirator - she learns to flourish in her own life.

So far in this book, we've been looking at the true meaning of what it takes for you to be an Inspirator – someone who wants to follow yourself and is so much of an example that other people want to follow you too; to be truly authentic; to become psychologically stable so that you can deal with anything that comes along because you're being true to yourself. This is something that you can only do for yourself by going on the journey to develop your self-worth.

 When do you get the best out of people? What can you, as an Inspirator, do to help and support others through the process of change?

From my experience, true change happens when those who lead take full responsibility for driving a change in themselves. First and foremost, they **are** the change – an example to themselves. Then once they are the example, they are the example to others. That means they can be the example to you.

Go and take a look at some of the interviews I've made with Inspirators and see how they have worked on themselves to become inspiring. See for yourself how being inspiring is a choice.

So far in this book, I've shown how being an Inspirator is about creating more Inspirators. Even if an organisation exists to maximise shareholder value, it's quite clear that if the people in the organisation are being led by an inspirational leader, then those objectives are more likely to be achieved.

So now, in this chapter, I want to look more at being the leader of other people.

This could be with your family, your friends or other social groups but, most particularly, in organisations. I want us to explore what, specifically, that needs to look like.

Inspirators are the leaders of the future. I don't mean they are a new breed, to replace what has come before. I mean that they are committed to creating a *better* future. They are committed to helping people shine bright, to move away from the victim mentality and manage their duck so they can grow and be a part of something amazing. Together they are *building* the future. Their *Why* is to create a legacy for everyone in their circle of influence.

Chris Roebuck

For the first time, the chief executive of BlackRock Investing sent out a letter to all parties involved saying, 'We're not just going to be measuring financial performance, but we're also going to be measuring how much people are adding value to the community and society.'

This is an evolving science as, together, we start to understand more about how we genuinely get the best out of people. Even in the process of writing this book, my own understanding of what an Inspirator needs to know and do and be has grown and emerged.

It is evolving in the world of research too. More is known about this than ever through developments in science, neuroscience, psychology and positive thinking:

What does it actually take to get the best out of others?

And as Inspirators, how do we transfer to others all we have learned in the journey to get the best out of ourselves?

30-second history spot

How did jobs and corporations even come to exist?

For that we have to go back to the social and economic revolutions in agriculture and industry. Before that, in the mid 18th century, the vast majority of people were self-employed. They were self-sufficient farmers, they ran little shops, they made and mended things. Then came The Enclosures Act, taking land away from common use and into the hands of a few landowners. Then, later, the ideas of mass production and industry.

Over time, the balance shifted. A few people owned big businesses and everyone else had a job. In many cases, people took the jobs because they felt that they had to. They didn't have a choice because they needed to earn money. This state of affairs remained the same for, probably, 100 years. Most people worked for someone else. They were told what to do by a supervisor or manager and they did as instructed.

Leadership became a real buzz word in the nineties particularly in the US, because many businesses really needed help in order for them to survive. People thought that leadership was a manager with visionary capability who could magically empower people to get them to do what you wanted them to do.

As this has evolved, the expectation for leadership in the corporate world changed. It became about delivering a return on investment for investors. To a certain extent, many companies found this a successful formula. Leaders were those who looked at a business and asked, "How do we make more money?" Now, things have changed. We've come a long way.

For organisations to flourish they need every person working there to be committed to the business. They need to be at their best.

> ### *The 30-second science spot*
> If you want to know what a truly flourishing organisation looks like, take a look at termites.
>
> Termites are the perfect example of an organisation which flourishes through the power of a Mastermind Alliance. They work together as one, with their collective goal in mind as they do. They are constantly seeking ways to grow and thrive.
>
> Each termite has a role to play and is fully committed to fulfilling it. The leader of the community – the queen – is the hardest worker but not by watching over everyone else and instructing them. She trusts that the other termites will do their job so she gets on and does hers (laying eggs to produce more termites).
>
> If the termite community is under threat, every termite steps up and does what is needed to protect the community and the queen[1].
>
> What are termites doing that we don't? What do they focus on? What goals do they have?

So, how do we get the best out of people?

You are far enough into this book to know the answer to that already. None of it is rocket science.

It's actually common sense.

Of course, organisations must have goals, many of which are around achieving certain targets. To meet those targets there always needs to be a good strategy.

But what drives that strategy forward?

Quite simply, it's a great culture.

How we do things around here

There are so many definitions and models to define culture. From 'How we do things around here' to 'shared values and beliefs in an organisation' and pretty much anything in between[2].

---

[1] *Actually, the warrior termites are sent outside the colony and every exit is sealed so they have to kill off all invaders or die trying. Please don't adopt this approach in your organisation!!*

[2] *I found this one in my research. I don't know about you, but I'm not sure whether to laugh or cry!*
"Cultural management includes the planning, processing, monitoring, and controlling of management functions in an international and cross-cultural context. Cultural management addresses the minimization of cultural conflicts for an increased organisational efficiency considering manifestations of corporate and country culture." (IDI-Global)

The meaning of the word *culture* comes from the Latin verb *cultura*, the act of preparing the earth for crops.

I like this analogy of a leader being a farmer, preparing the crop, preparing the land for growth, preparing the organisation for growth. It gives some sense of the effort and, in particular, the time it takes to get to a point where you can reap the harvest. Culture is a slow and gradual process.

What's the best environment you've ever worked in? What was it about that culture that made it great?

A flourishing culture is one which makes people want to join your company and makes them want to stay. It is one in which they identify with the brand of the company, wanting to be a part of the it. Rather than brand loyalty being from your customers, you want it from your staff, first and foremost.

If this doesn't exist in your organisation then it is up to you, the leader, to cultivate it.

Glyn House

I became employment brand manager at Sainsbury's [employing] 165,000 people, and we were trying to work out why people would choose to work for Sainsbury's as opposed to choose to work for [anyone else].

This notion that we're turning on is that people choose the company as opposed to you choosing them.

 When you think about culture, how do you see it?
In my experience most people think about it in relation to the collective.
Culture is how groups of people interact – it is seen as a 'lump.'

Can I give you a different perspective? As your coach, that is, after all, what I am here for.

Culture starts with the individual. Every one of us has a culture within us. We have values and beliefs. We prefer to do things in a certain way. The way we interact with other people and how we relate to the world around us is all guided by this inner culture.

If you seek to grow a flourishing culture in an organisation can you see that you first need to grow a flourishing culture in each person within it to get the best out of them?

How do people tick?

This is the true role of an Inspirator. To be committed 100% to bringing out the best in people.

It is a mission to find out what makes people really tick and give them what they need. What they need is appreciation, kindness, love, respect, and help to grow. It's not just about being happy, it's about showing people how to flourish.

Many of us are victims of the culture that we exist in: we are afraid to speak out; we have been told to follow the process rather than rebel to find new and innovative solutions; we feel we have to fit in. But that can change and it's part of your role as an Inspirator – to change that culture in yourself and then manifest it in the other people around you.

It can take time but it's worth it, and it's essential in order to build world-class people in world-class organisations.

Just like growing plants, time, patience and attention are needed but it isn't *difficult*. If you are willing to make the daily steps to nurture those around you, the culture can start to grow itself in a positive way.

You will nurture a culture where people are more confident about giving their opinion rather than being frightened that they might lose their job or they might look stupid. This is where people and organisations go from just being ordinary to being extraordinary.

Story Time

I've had the opportunity to work with teams and to help them to flourish, but this hasn't always been in business.

In 1999, I worked with the Kent County Cricket Team, coached by New Zealand cricketer John Wright. I've always loved cricket. My first memories in life are watching my dad play. I know cricket is a bit like *Marmite* - you either love it or you hate it - but I grew up to love it and to play it to a fairly high level. You can imagine how excited I was when I got an opportunity to work with a high performing team.

I'll never forget my first introduction. I arrived in Canterbury when they were in the middle of a game. I met John and then went into the dressing room. It was a really uncomfortable environment. That day, the team wasn't performing very well, and when I walked into the room, I just didn't want to be there. The place was full of anger, frustration and fear.

Over the next two years, I worked closely with the team and especially with the coach. We spent many hours talking about people and the different types of personalities and what it really took to help people be their best.

I'll never forget a conversation where he explained to me that he likened being the coach of the team, the leader of the team, to being in the trenches in the First World War. He would imagine himself saying, "Right, come on guys, let's go. Over the top." Then he'd leap up and start running with a "Charge, let's go!" But he'd look back and everyone was still there because they were frightened to step up, move and go.

He explained the culture that existed and how he was working so hard to change it to one where people weren't scared, where people were prepared to move forwards into growth.

Over those two years, we created a culture where people were prepared to talk openly about their challenges, their insecurities, and about how they felt. The team's fortune changed and they became high-performing.

Continued on next page

In the process, John Wright became a better coach. He became a better leader and he ended up taking on the role of being the coach of the Indian cricket team, one of the greatest cricket teams of all time.

John became an inspiring leader because he developed his curiosity around creating a flourishing environment - one where people could be their best and perform at their best.

What eats strategy for breakfast?

The person who inspired me to write this book, Cosimo Turroturro, Director of Speakers Association asked me very early in our discussions, "What comes first?"

No, not the chicken or the egg. He wanted to know whether a good culture or a good strategy was more important in organisations.

I immediately answered there has to be a great culture and he agreed although, of course, you can't really have one without the other. For me, however, it's all about culture. And, from all of the work that I've done working with leaders in business, they all agree with me.

The journey of writing this book, however, has inspired me to realise that there is something **before** organisational culture – and that is the leader **within** the culture and their own internal culture.

Would it be okay if I give you a visual representation of how to see your business and the people that work in it?

Picture a target – the kind you see in Robin Hood films. A big round circle with rings, which an archer would fire an arrow into. That target is the organisation's goals.

The head of the arrow is the organisation's strategy. The shaft (the piece of wood that attaches itself into the head of the arrow) is the culture, the people who drive everything forward, and at the back, the feathers, (fletching), is **you** as the leader.

With an arrow, all the energy comes from the shaft. That's what drives the arrowhead forward and keeps it going so that it can cross the distance to the target. The fletching keeps the arrow on target. Without the fletching the arrow goes all over the place and your strategy never reaches its target.

This is how your business is functioning; how it is performing. You could have the greatest strategy in the world and have great SMART[3] goals but without people being onboard you're going to have issues.

 What would it be like if your business operated like this? If you were heading towards your goals, with a strong and clear strategy leading the way and all the energy and commitment of your people driving it forward? What if you were there to guide and correct the trajectory when you were blown off course?

---

[3] *Specific, Relevant, Measurable, Achievable, Timebound – an old acronym for how goals should be written.*

Can you see yourself as the fletching – not heavy or overbearing but light – ready to guide when you are needed?

And can you see the consequences if the shaft of the arrow is cracked or broken; if there are fractures or the separate fibres of the wood are working apart[4]? Minor problems can be corrected by the fletching but, in the end, it doesn't matter how great the fletching or how perfectly formed the arrowhead, there is no way the arrow will hit the target – or even cover the distance without an effective shaft.

The strong, energetic shaft that is culture takes work to create. People will align themselves to you if you give them a big enough reason. If you give them a big enough *Why?* and show them, by example, that you are authentic in who you are and what you do, they will drive your organisation to its goals. The old cornerstone of business was lifelong financial security – a stable, clearly designed role – but jobs for life don't exist anymore. People need something else to help them feel secure.

Are you ready, as an Inspirator, to wake up to the importance of helping people to flourish? To be aligned to the vision and purpose of the organisation, to see the target beyond the obstacles that are in the way? To overcome the resistance – internal and external – that they experience?

But, what does it take for an organisation to flourish?

Go to Work with a Flourish!

Flourishing is not the same as being happy, because happy is not a permanent state. We can flourish even when we feel unhappy – or angry or excited or frustrated or calm.

 ### *30-second science spot*
For many years the field of positive psychology focused on how to help people become happier – to experience *authentic happiness*. This was measured by how satisfied someone was - life satisfaction - and the goal was to increase that satisfaction.

It is a strange word, *satisfaction*. Do we just want people to be satisfied, rather than being driven to achieve more and to be the best that they can be?

How *satisfied* are people around the world right now? With depression being 10 times more likely than it was 50 years ago? With 800,000 people taking their own lives every year? With more people taking anti-depressants? With more people getting divorced?

Take a moment to reflect on those statistics. How must people be feeling about themselves?

People don't want to 'just have a job.' They don't want to settle. They want more. They want to flourish and be their best but that means they have to get uncomfortable and they are afraid. This is the elephant in the room – in **every** room. No one wants to talk about what it takes to get the best out of people.

Continued on next page

---

[4] *And yes, I know these days archers use carbon, aluminium or plastic but work with me here.*

Just like any model, it needed to be looked at and improved.

Some of the greatest work in this field has been done by Dr. Martin Seligman who is the forefather of positive psychology. He was very actively involved in authentic happiness and looking to measure it.

This is where one of the biggest changes came about, (creating positive psychology 2.0, if you will). Rather than measuring life satisfaction, he measured **well-being.**

This is where he came up with the acronym **PERMA.**

PERMA

P-E-R-M-A stands for **P**ositive emotion, **E**ngagement, **R**elationships, **M**eaning and **A**chievement. These are the key elements Seligman defines for people to be well.

PERMA is all about flourishing human beings and some of the work that has been done with this, especially in schools in Australia, is incredible. In helping students and teachers to develop PERMA, the results in all aspects of the schools' curriculum have been amazing.

Glyn House

I always say, 'I you want to be an exceptional organisation, you have to be an exception,' right? By definition. Because if you just benchmark yourself to everybody else, you're going to be like everybody else.

Movie Time

This is exactly what we see Amelie do in the film. Starting from one small quest, she finds meaning through giving joy to others. Instead of living in isolation, she builds relationships, achieves good outcomes for those whose lives she touches and is engaged in each small mission she embarks on. It is fun for her and, as a result of acting in PERMA for others, she recognises that she, too, has a right to flourish.

I believe that the organisations who really start to get their head around having PERMA in the workplace, are going to create incredible cultures.

Story Time

I never experienced this in the jobs I had in my early teens. I always felt that I couldn't be myself. I always felt on edge. I never felt I could really flourish. I never felt really valued. It was only when I was surrounded by inspirational people (coaches and mentors) that I started to see things differently and find PERMA in myself.

I've always been fascinated, though, by organisations where you walk in and you feel, "Wow, what a positive energy here. I can really be myself. I can learn, I can grow."

The Inspirator's challenge is to create an environment where this can happen.

Unpicking PERMA

High performing teams in high performing organisations are full of people who are flourishing. As an Inspirator, I encourage you to really take time to look at this acronym as we go through each letter of PERMA, and think to yourself, how could I flourish more? How, in doing so, can I be the example and help others to do the same?

P – Positive Emotions

People need to feel positive about what they are doing. This doesn't mean they have to be super-positive the whole time. A business full of Pollyannas might be a bit creepy.

Positive people relish the good times and, when things are not so good, believe that everything happens for a reason. They seek to learn from mistakes and are optimistic. They have hope (which we discussed in Chapter 10).

A positive mental attitude can be grown in some really simple ways. Expressing gratitude every day – for quite simple things – has been shown to massively improve mindset. Getting outside in the fresh air makes a difference too. Others which you can do come from asking better questions (Chapter 3). Encouraging people to celebrate the good things rather than just talking about the problems reminds them that it isn't all doom and gloom.

Inspiring people will have an impact so those around them are more positive. That impact is magnified when people feel engaged with what they are doing.

E – Engagement

Engagement comes when people are connected with what is going on around them and have some sense of autonomy. They become absorbed in what they are doing and enjoy it.

> ▌ *Pleasure in the job puts perfection in the work*

Do you know who said that? It wasn't Richard Branson or Steve Jobs or Winston Churchill. It was Aristotle, who lived around 350BC. So, although, new ideas are coming all the time, some of this common sense stuff, like the idea of engagement being beneficial, has been around for well over 2000 years.

And the biggest threat to engagement? Distraction!

This world of mobile phones and open office spaces where no one can think, can have a significant impact on our ability to flourish.

Alistair McAuley

Parenting is a brilliant test of leadership. I've got two daughters, aged 8 and 10, and we were recently up in the Lake District. It was horrendous weather and, although it was lashing rain, I wanted to get us out of the house. "Let's go out for a walk" I suggested.

"Why on earth would we want to go for a walk in this weather?"

A fair challenge! So I thought about it and said, "I'll tell you what, let's go out for a bike ride, and let's get seriously muddy. It'll be great fun!" All of a sudden they perked up and we went out and cycled 8 miles, creating a memory that will stick with us all for years.

So, take a look at those you lead and see how you can create an environment where they can engage with what they are doing. What will allow them to connect with their work? Even dull tasks can be more pleasurable if they have a purpose to them (that's where meaning comes in).

Helping people engage is not rocket science. Often the best way to help your team to engage more is to ask them, "What would make this more meaningful?"

R – Relationships

The multinational company, Virgin, did a study in which 40% of the respondents said their colleagues were the top reason they enjoyed their work. Two-thirds of them said it helped them to deal with stress. This is the power of relationships.

Human beings are social animals so we need to connect with other people and establish relationships.

Jim Rohn used to say that we are the average of the five people we spend most time with and I'm sure you can see the sense in that.

Take a moment or two to consider the five people **you** spend most time with. They might be a spouse, a friend, a work colleague. How do you act when you are around each one? How do they help you achieve your goals and support you in life? How would they react if you shared your innermost dreams? Would they come with you on your journey to becoming an Inspirator?

There is another aspect to relationships which cannot be ignored and that is the human desire to be liked. It is primal. We all have a need to be loved and, if we don't feel loved, it can manifest in pain. We fear being isolated from 'the pack' because, in primeval times, rejection would mean death.

What can you do to help your team feel more 'part of the pack'? They are all worried that they won't be liked – that they don't fit in. What would make a difference for them?

M – Meaning

Do you ever find yourself working on something and then stop and ask yourself *'Why am I doing this?'* Do you ever feel disconnected from the purpose of a task or unclear how your outputs will be used?

Knowing why we are doing things is so important in flourishing, both in terms of the tasks people are carrying out and also in themselves. We want to know why we are here and feel that what we are doing will make a difference.

In essence this is why we spent an entire chapter on the topic of *Why*. And is why we will spend another whole chapter (Chapter 12) on finding your purpose.

For now, though, just consider ways that you can help those around you find meaning in what they do every day so they can flourish and continue to grow.

A – Achievement

Who likes lists? Who just loves ticking things off their list? Who sometimes writes things onto their list **just** to tick them off?!

Humans just **love** to feel they are accomplishing things. It's addictive. Some will be big, collaborative projects, like the building of the new road bridge across the Firth of Forth but others can be tiny – like cleaning the kitchen.

We like to get things done.

And we like other people to **notice** that we are getting things done.

 How often do you acknowledge what people are achieving in your teams? How often do you tell them they are appreciated? How often do you notice the progress they are making?

Can you see how the five components of PERMA are interconnected? You can't just look at one in isolation. People enjoy what they are doing if those around them are positive and there are good relationships. They get engaged if they can see a meaning to what they are doing and know they will accomplish something in doing it.

Just imagine, for a moment, that you had PERMA into your organisation. What difference would it make?

PERMAnent state – Inspire other people

 Just imagine: what would it be like in your business if, every day, people asked themselves the question, "Am I committing everything I have to make myself better than I am right now, no matter how hard I have to work, no matter what I have to give up or how long it takes?"

Already in this book, we've asked: what does it take for people to be their best at work? What are people really looking for? We know that part of that is autonomy, mastery, purpose – people feeling that they have some form of autonomy over what's happening, they feel that they're getting better and they feel that they have a reason to be there.

We also know that effective leadership is about making people feel valued, making people feel heard, making people feel that they're a part of something much bigger than just themselves and they play an important role.

Quite simply, people want to be in an environment, in a culture, where they can be themselves, they can grow, they can be appreciated and they can flourish.

So how can you take PERMA to a completely different level in your organisation?

You can't make PERMA happen. You need to allow it to happen – by listening and finding out what is going on and then motivating others to own PERMA for themselves.

Let's get motivated!

Some of the greatest work on motivation has been done by Edward Deci and Richard M Ryan from the mid-1980s onward. Their work (such as their Self-Determination Theory) has been cited over 22,000 times in academic papers around the world, because quite clearly, it is brilliant! They really began to understand what it takes for someone to be motivated. It was from their work that Daniel Pink wrote *Drive,* the book that gives us the Autonomy, Mastery, Purpose model I've mentioned already. From that same original work, Lindsay McGregor and Neel Doshi developed a six-part model for motivation which they explore in their book *Primed to Perform* and which I want to touch on here.

Motivation isn't an old word – it is 19th century, emerging from the word '*motive*' and it means 'desire or willingness to do something,' or 'enthusiasm.'
It is a much-used word in business – I'm described as a 'motivational speaker', for example – and it is so often seen as an external force, something that is delivered to people, to make them want to do something they otherwise might resist.

This is extrinsic motivation.

Extrinsic motivation, coming from outside, is pressure. It may be emotional pressure, economic pressure, or inertia.

Emotional pressure is where people feel compelled to act because of the actions of others. An inspiring leader or motivational speaker will tap into emotions and build excitement and it will drive people forward.

 Have you ever been motivated this way? Have you been to a great training course or workshop, seen a great speaker, found yourself inspired by someone you work with? You've come away thinking "Yes! Let's do this!" Then, once the influence of that inspirational moment has faded, you go back to where you were before?
I'm sure you have, because everybody does some of the time.

Emotional pressure can be negatively driven too. Many people function from a place of disappointment or guilt or shame or fear. It is the only reason they do what they do. The work itself is not why they are doing the work. They do it because

- they are afraid to do what would really inspire them.
- it feels safe to not have to stretch themselves.
- they feel the need for prestige to boost their self-esteem.

Unfortunately, this is where so many people exist in life.

Economic pressure is even less effective. People come to work and stay in the job because they need the money. They're doing it for bonus or a regular salary. We know that money only motivates people so far (and it isn't far at all).

We think we want lots of money, of course. We live in a society where *what you have* seems to be important but all the evidence shows that people aren't really motivated by money.

 30- *second science spot*

A study was done on ways to motivate people to lose weight. Some were given coaching and shown how to enjoy the process while others were offered a reward of a large sum of money to lose weight.

Those who were offered the money lost more during the study. They got their money, felt happy and then put all the weight back on.

Those who had learned to enjoy the process lost weight more slowly during the study but carried on losing afterwards and many reached their ultimate goals.

Money does have the power to be a massive *demotivator* of course. I've seen endless performance-based pay schemes which give a lot of money to a few people (most of whom aren't that bothered about the bonus because they are motivated by other things). The rest of the team, who worked just as hard but aren't seen as a "top performer," get less bonus (or none) and think to themselves, "Well, that shows how little I'm valued. There's no point in knocking myself out day after day. I'll just do what it takes to stay out of trouble." Or, worse still, they leave – and you lose all their valuable skills and knowledge, as well as having to pay to recruit and train someone new.

The worst type of motivation, however, is inertia!

Now, I know what you are thinking. *Pete, isn't inertia about staying still?*

While the word **inertia** does derive from the Latin word *'iners'* which means inactive, the most familiar use of the word is in the world of physics and, in particular, in Sir Isaac Newton's First Law of Motion:

"...a power of resisting by which everybody ... endeavours to preserve its present state, whether it be of rest or of moving uniformly forward in a straight line."

Inertia is, in fact, resistance to change.

We, like everything in the physical universe, are motivated to stay the same. Our ancient ancestors knew that change represented threat, so it was safer to do what they had always done. We are no different today. We are motivated to avoid the unfamiliar and the uncomfortable and our brain is hardwired to resist any suggestion of doing something different.

This is what I've seen in so many organisations. Things are happening because they happened before. It isn't an inspiring place to be and, for most people, the job is drudgery. The motive for work is so distant from the work itself that most people have no idea how what they do has any benefit to the company, the customer or the wider world. They do what they do quite simply because they did it yesterday. People are slogging away because they can't think of a reason to leave. They just stay in the job because it's safe. Things are moving but they're not really going anywhere.

Every one of these extrinsic motivators can have an effect. People can feed off them but only for a short while.

I'm sorry if this all seems a bit 'doom and gloom.' If you are feeling that way, ask yourself, "What one thing could I do right now to make a difference?"

If you want a real change and for things to take a new direction which lasts, it needs to be something that comes from deep within.

The way to take PERMA to a completely different level is to help people become intrinsically motivated. Just as there are three levels of extrinsic motivation, there are also three levels of intrinsic motivation and these are **play, purpose, and potential.**

For people to be really connected to a flourishing environment, for people to be really connected to a culture, the first step is to help people play with what they're doing.

We want them to learn how to enjoy what they're doing. Countless studies show that when people enjoy the doing of things, they are much more connected. They are much more resourceful. The quality of their work goes up. If they come to work thinking, 'This is going to be great. I love what I do,' it shines through in the way they behave, how they treat other people and how willing they are to step up when needed.

Your goal as an Inspirator is to create a culture where people can play.

The second intrinsic motivator is purpose. When people can see the point to what they are doing, they'll do it even when they don't feel like it because they know the importance of getting something done, getting something finished. The next chapter is going to cover purpose in a lot more detail – how you find yours and how you help connect others to it.

Finally, we have potential. This is all about mastery, which we cover in the final chapter. People love to see that they are getting better at something.

We want people to be motivated for the right reasons and, as Inspirators, we need to create a state of PERMA through encouraging play, purpose and potential. The alternative is a place of inertia, where progress is made through emotional and economic pressure in ever increasing amounts. People do what they do for no great reason, 'it's just a job,' knowing deep down that it's not what they want.

People want to grow. People want to be the best that they can be.

Deep work

I could have talked about flourishing far earlier in the book. If we had, you might have liked the concepts and seen it as a 'magic bullet' to your organisational and leadership challenges. Knowing what you know now, however, means you will appreciate the work that needs to be done and understand it better. If you re-read the book, you will probably appreciate it even more.

Creating a flourishing culture is a gradual process and the greatest tool you can ever use is to be yourself – to be the example. There are, however, some useful ways to understand the culture within you and your people a little better and to get an idea of where they are coming from.

Seligman's Signature Strengths survey

I am not usually a fan of online assessments but the Signature Strength Finder developed by Martin Seligman and Christopher Peterson is something that I do recommend. It is research based, which means that every person who completes the survey is contributing to the academic understanding of positive psychology. We've included a link to this at inspirators.me

It asks you to rate how much you identify with a number of behaviours and gives you a ranked list of 24 strengths – values if you will. The results don't give you an 'answer' to your personal values, but knowing them can give you insights into what is important for you.

Inviting those you lead, or those in your Mastermind Alliance, or members of your family to also take the test and share the results can lead to a really enlightening conversation.

How do you feel

One of the things my coach always used to ask me was, "How do you feel about where you are?"

Simple question? Perhaps – but one which is really important and seldom asked.
Yet, how we feel affects everything.
As a leader, how much does how you feel impact those around you? People will pick up on how you feel and how interested you are in their feelings. If people in your organisation do not feel valued, do not feel important, if they feel stressed, if they feel anxious, then not only is that going to affect the people around them. It can affect their families. It can also affect your customers.

What's your story?

As always, take a few moments to consider the answer to the questions below and note in your journal the answer you get.

Also keep them in mind as you move through the world from now on. Start to see where the elements of PERMA show up for you right now and consider what changes you might want to make.

Use them with others as well, to help them see how they too can flourish.

Coaching questions

1. What are your top virtues and how do they show up in the world?
2. What in your life can you really engage with? When do you lose track of time?
3. What social interactions mean the most to you?
4. What percentage of what you do in work and life has a clear connection to your Why?
5. List things you have achieved in your life – big and small.

And finally...

> *The secret to happiness is freedom and the secret to freedom is courage*
> ### *Thucydides*

Even 2500 years ago, when Greek historian Thucydides was writing, the connection between happiness and strength was known. The journey you are on to become an Inspirator – with all the challenges and difficulties – will, ultimately, give you happiness.

You will be more positive and absorbed, have stronger relationships, know why you are doing what you do and celebrate the achievements.

It isn't easy though – you know that.

Finding True Purpose

What am I here for?

God says we need to love our enemies. It' hard to do. But it can start by tellin' the truth. No one had ever asked me what it feel like to be me. Once I told the truth about that, I felt free. And I got to thinking about all the people I know. And the things I seen and done. My boy Trelaw always said we gonna have a writer in the family one day. I guess it's gonna be me.

Aibileen Clark – The Help

In this chapter, we will explore
- how the meaning of your life is the meaning that you give it
- what is meant by purpose
- the power of self-belief
- the tool to find your ikigai – what makes you want to get out of bed.

WARNING!

Tumbleweed ahead

So here we are at the final chapter. How do you feel?

Can you see where you are on the journey in your own story? Is the journey almost at an end? Now you've been through the highs and lows and done the deep work, do you look in the mirror and see someone you want to follow smiling back at you?

What next?

As your coach, every page of this book has been guiding and preparing you for this moment. To wake you up and understand what really needs to be done. To get you ready for the journey of your life.

The journey to discover the *meaning of your life*.

There are some big questions we can ask ourselves in this chapter. *Why am I here?* is one of them[1].

> When in your life have you asked yourself what is the meaning of your life? What are you here to *do*?
> Is it possible that you've only ever asked that question when you've been struggling? In my experience, that is the only time people ask questions like '*What is the point to my life?*'

There are many answers to this question, from the purely biological '*to propagate our species*' upwards. Perhaps you see yourself as being here to care for your family or to do a good job at work. Or do you believe there is a higher reason for your existence?

I believe that everyone has a purpose – to be working towards an aim or intention. I believe that everyone has the chance to be working towards something which fulfils and inspires them. What's more, in all the work I've done – with Olympic athletes, with top business leaders, with the members of my coaching groups and with those who work at all levels in organisations – I have seen one simple truth; that everyone has a burning desire to live a purposeful life, to find meaning to their existence and to discover something that they can connect to.

I didn't always believe this. It is something that I have come to believe from the years I've spent working on myself and from working with inspiring people.

---

[1] *Which, incidentally, is one of the most Googled questions ever! If you are feeling curious, try finding out what some of the others are.*

People know there's more to life than school, education, marriage and retirement. What separates them from you is that you now know what needs to be done to find and fulfil yours.

> ### Movie Time
> *The Help* is a film all about purpose. Our hero, Skeeter's, purpose unfolds as we watch the film. She sets out determined to become a journalist but, as she starts on her mission, she realises a deeper meaning to what she is doing. She becomes committed to telling the truth about lives in the American South in the 1960s – to wake up the world to how 'the help' is integral to the family and yet, not included.
>
> In doing so, she inspires others to think differently. By the end of the film, Aibileen Clark, one of the maids that Skeeter interviews, has found her purpose too – and it is time for her to end her journey as an adjunct to the lives of others, and to start a different one.

I've mentioned purpose a few times in the book, usually in passing. How did you feel? I have rather assumed that you know your purpose and then moved on.

That's because 'purpose' is such a huge topic. For the duration of this book, your purpose was to be an Inspirator – to be the best version of yourself and someone that others want to follow. It has been enough.

As you start to grasp what that means, have you started to understand that being an Inspirator isn't the purpose – it is the means for you to achieve **your** purpose?

Having come this far, is your mind starting to open up to a new idea of living your true purpose; of being really authentic; of being something **beyond** an Inspirator?

To move on to the next goal after a success needs a higher purpose. Not just a goal for the goal's sake but for a greater reason.

Just as, at the start of this book, you may have wanted to resist the journey, now we are starting a new journey – to a new country. If you feel resistance, that is perfectly normal.

But let me just ask you, if that is how you are feeling: Have you come this far only to come this far?

'But I don't know what my purpose is!'

> ### Story Time
> As a keynote speaker, I do talks on a wide variety of topics but there is one which can bring any room to a dead stop – and that is purpose. If I ask people, "What's the meaning of your life?", the energy drops and it goes very quiet. It's rather like one of those Spaghetti Westerns, where the streets clear as the gunslinger walks into town. All you can see is dust and the occasional tumbleweed rolling across the scene.

'What are you here to do? How will the world be better because you are here? Who must you become?'

These are questions that people don't put much thought into.

The society we live in encourages people just to be like everybody else, so to seek out true purpose and fulfilment is frowned upon. I've seen it over and over again in the organisations I'm asked to work with.

Yet, we know that there can be a deep-seated uncomfortableness that exists when people are being just like everybody else. They know deep down they're not being who they're truly capable of being. They do what is expected of them but, all the time, they can be thinking to themselves, 'Is this all there is? There must be more to life than this.'

Have you ever felt that way? Or had conversations with those around you who are feeling like that?

It's not only that we live in a society that doesn't embrace people living their life's purpose, it's also the fact that people may not believe; in themselves, in their future or in anybody else. They may not even be willing to talk about it.

 Imagine asking someone, *What are you passionate about*?
How would you feel, asking that question? What reaction do you think you'd get from asking it?

Imagine taking a bird's-eye view of how we live our life and all the people around us. What would we see? Might we see why there is a lot of suffering in the world? How many people would we see going to work without seeing a bigger picture – just going through the motions to get through every single day.

 ### Movie Time
When Skeeter is interviewing Aibileen she asks, "Did you always know you would be a maid?"

"Yes," replies Aibileen, because it was what her mother had done and because her grandmother had been a house slave. She cannot conceive of any other way of living.

Not, that is, until Skeeter starts asking her questions about it.

This is another form of institutional blindness. Organisations don't understand the importance of explaining – and reinforcing – the reason why people do what they do and where the business is going. The people who work there, simply don't see any other way of thinking.

We are *teleological beings* – which means we are goal-oriented. We like having something to aim for. And there is a simple equation which no one ever thinks to mention to explain purpose in the simplest of ways.

Purpose = Goals x *Why*

Purpose is the driving force

What if the purpose of your life was to leave an imprint – to make an impact on the world? What if the purpose of your life was to help others to do the same? What if the purpose of your life was to get better every single day – a crescendo, building up and building up to the end of your time? And what if your purpose as a leader was to take everyone on that same journey of getting better every day?

It's hard to find a more powerful driver than a powerful purpose. The most effective and most powerful people in the world are the people that have a purpose that's driving them forwards.

Think now of some of the most inspirational people across history. What was their purpose, how clear was it and how consistently did they pursue it? Can you think of an Inspirator who *didn't* have a purpose?

 I invite you to think about what feeds your soul. We know what feeds our body, we know what feeds our mind but what about feeding your soul? This is your purpose – what are you here to do?

Can you connect with this? Can you, then, become the most curious leader on earth to think about all the people around you? What are *they* here to do? What are *their* hidden talents? And could you help them to discover that, connect to it and manifest it?

Purpose is the starting point of all achievement. As your coach, my challenge to you as you are reading this book, is to ask you to connect to what your purpose is.

Note: One of the things people who have yet to define their purpose often say to me is that they don't really know what is meant by purpose – let alone know what their own is. As we go through this section I'm going to share with you several different metaphors for purpose – some mine, some from other people. Not all of them will resonate – maybe none of them will – or perhaps each will add an extra element of perspective until you have a full understanding. Be open and curious to each one and see how it adds to your understanding but if something doesn't 'float your boat' then don't worry about it. Move on and let the idea drift. Who knows, it might make sense at a later date.

What is purpose?

Purpose – a life's purpose – can be anything. It can be huge (*to inspire 100m people to be better than their best every single day*) or it can be closer to home (*to be the best parent possible and inspire your children to live happy, healthy lives*). Whatever it is, once you know it, it will fire you up to go through any challenge and face any obstacles.

One of the best explanations I've ever come across of the importance of having a purpose came from motivational speaker and leader, Jim Rohn.

Here's a philosophy that helped change my life.
It's not what happens that determines your life's future. It's what you do about what happens.
All of us are in a little sailboat, and it's not the blowing of the wind that determines your destination. It's the set of the sail.... The same wind blows on us all.
The difference in where you arrive in one year, three years, five years, the difference in arrival is not the blowing of the wind, but the set of the sail.

If you don't have a purpose for life and you're not aiming towards something, then the wind will just blow you off course.

Remember the arrow analogy from Chapter 11? Can you see how the leader (the fletching, remember) guides everyone against the winds of change and challenge to meet the organisation's purpose?

Movie Time

Skeeter and her friends were all raised in the same way. Their white families had maids, who raised them. The families were all wealthy and surrounded by the idea of getting married and having babies and to hire their own maids as being the way to live life.

Skeeter, however, wanted to write and she set her sail in a different direction. They were all blown by the same wind but she ended up in college and, ultimately, in New York.

Your purpose fires you up and keeps you going when things get tough.

Purpose originates from two separate words. The '-pose' half goes right back into Ancient Greek meaning (strangely) *'to pause, stop, or cease'* with the 'pur-' part coming from Latin, meaning 'forth.' By the time the words met in early French, 'pause, stop, cease' had become 'to put' and **Purpose** meant *'to put forth'* which, by 13th century became an aim or intention.

As the meaning emerged, though, there was a definite intention that a purpose was something to be declared and shared with the world.

There are plenty of definitions of the word to be found, of course, but the one I particularly like is 'a stable and generalised intention to accomplish both a meaningful goal to the self and of consequence to the world and beyond the self.'

Read that a few times and let it sink in.
Do you have an intention to accomplish a meaningful goal? Is it meaningful for you? Is it of consequence for the wider world?

If it helps you, start to think of your purpose like the GPS in your car. I love using the app called *Waze* because I plug in my destination and it will take me to it. *Waze* looks ahead, though, and sees where there's traffic and it will change the direction to keep me moving. I will always be moving towards my final destination even though, sometimes, I might have to go backwards or sideways.

I know where I'm going. Purpose is my internal GPS system.

How to find your purpose

In Chapter 1 I shared with you my own coach's view that there are seven perspectives – up, down, left, right, front, back, within. Bear that in mind as I share some of the techniques you can use to identify and refine your purpose.

Iki... what, now?

If people in organisations aren't fired up by their purpose and don't know where they are going, all they are doing is waiting until they retire.

Did you know, however, that retirement isn't a natural phenomenon?

The 30-second history spot

Our ancient ancestors didn't stop working when they hit 65. Even our more recent ancestors didn't. Most people didn't live much beyond 40 and, if they did, they kept working until infirmity made that impossible. At that point, the family would care for them in their old age.

Retirement – stopping work at a specific age – was created by us because it was necessary. In the year 1881, there were too many people in the job market in Germany and not enough jobs for young people. Fearful that the young unemployed might try to overthrow the government, Chancellor Bismarck decided to implement a state pension.

The average life expectancy at the time was 67 so Bismarck set the age of retirement as 65. People worked for 50 years and then had two years to enjoy the fruits of their labour. This created a gap in the job market and gave work to those who might have risen up and caused trouble.

Of course, the idea of a state-funded retirement isn't as certain these days and the age being set is getting later and later. Personal pension plans and other forms of long-term investment, however, are there to ensure the time when we can stop work and relax. For many, this is their greatest ambition.

Would it be okay if I gave you something else to aim for? Something with a more inspiring aim than *stopping doing what I'm doing now?* Another way of moving through the world?

The Japanese are great examples of this. In Okinawa, an island in Japan, there is no such word as retirement. The people who live there have the longest life expectancy in the world. The difference? They have something called an Ikigai.

> **Ikigai** is, of course, Japanese, made up of two words *iki* (生き) which means 'life' or 'alive' and *kai* (甲斐) meaning 'result' or 'benefit.' So Ikigai is your 'reason for living'.
>
> In Okinawa, the people describe an Ikigai as 'the reason you get out of bed each morning.'

No wonder life expectancy is so high there. They all have something to move towards, a burning desire, which lights them up. It doesn't matter whether it's to see their grandchildren go to school, or get married, or to create something wonderful, or to make a difference in the community that they live in. They all have an Ikigai.

 Just imagine for one moment what your life would be like if, when you woke each morning, you had an exciting, real and inspiring reason to get out of bed and get the day started. How would that change things for you? What impact would it have on those around you? And how you took care of your health? And the work you did?

Ikigai is our tool for this chapter, so we'll explain how you can develop your own Ikigai a little later.

Follow the leader

Do you remember playing this game when you were a kid? It's a bit like 'Simon says' but designed for outdoors. Whoever was the leader would walk around the playing field or along the streets and everyone else had to follow them. So, if the leader climbed over a fence, everyone else climbed over the fence too. If the leader jumped up and down on the spot, everyone else had to jump up and down on the spot too. It was simple stuff, but we all loved it.

Why am I telling you this? Because that is what I invite you to do too.

One of the things I learned at an early age, especially from watching my father, was to ask questions of people to find out what they were really about. He was always interested in who they were, who they'd been and who they were becoming. I really encourage you to do the same.

I encourage you to listen to some of the interviews with our Inspirators and pay particular attention to what their purpose is. I didn't always ask the question of what their purpose was so they might not describe it in specific words, but as you listen to them, ask yourself, "Where is this person coming from?"

Simon Cook

I do believe that your purpose becomes why you get out of bed in the morning. Everybody gets out of bed for a reason, most people don't know what that reason is.

> **Movie Time**
>
> The setting for *The Help* is 1963. This was an incredibly import-
> ant year in US history. It was the year that Martin Luther King led
> peaceful protests in Alabama and the march on Washington where he made
> the iconic 'I have a dream' speech. It was also the year that John F Kennedy was
> assassinated in Texas.
>
> Both of these events, while not a part of the main plot, are featured in the film.

Look at great figures in history and the leaders of today and ask yourself, "What was driving them? What was their charge? What was their purpose?

What drove John F Kennedy to become the 35th US President, to form the US Peace Corps or to aspire to put men on the moon?

What about Martin Luther King? How did he set his sail to keep him on course when the wind that was blowing was for racial segregation?

But don't stop there. Pick the leaders who inspire you.

What was Mahatma Gandhi's purpose? He became the most important part of the Indian Independence Movement against colonial rule. What was it that was driving him?

What drove Abraham Lincoln, the 16th President of the United States? Why was he committed to ending slavery by making the Proclamation of Emancipation?

Even dictators such as Adolf Hitler, who was responsible for one of the greatest military expansions the world has ever seen, had a purpose. What was it?

What about Nelson Mandela, the first South African president elected via democratic elections? He was the main player in the anti-apartheid movement, and even though he was in prison for 30 years, when released continued to take massive action. Why?

There are so many examples: Julius Caesar, your mum, Queen Elizabeth I, that teacher at school, Winston Churchill, your best friend, Margaret Thatcher, a work colleague... Be curious and always ask: what was their purpose? What was their driving force?

Purpose wasn't everything of course. Some had to be a brilliant strategist. Most needed to be determined. Some had to be focused. Others needed optimism. Each required a range of different characteristics but, ultimately, what saw them through was a massive purpose.

What's my purpose?

I know this might all be feeling a bit heavy by now but let's just take a step back. Think of purpose as just being an aim or an intention which you can work on. To help explain this, would it be okay to share my purpose with you right now? As I do, think about how this might have been driving me forward in the writing of this book and in the way I have shared ideas with you in its pages.

My purpose is to inspire people to be better than their best every single day but not just to achieve personal goals. I want to inspire them in their home life, with their health and with their well-being. I want to inspire them to be the best that they can be so they can inspire others to do the same. It's what gets me up every single day.

I strive to inspire people to breathe life into what they do: breathe life, breathe love, breathe passion....

It's what gives my soul oxygen.

My mission then, is to inspire leaders to find within themselves what they need to be the very best that they can be. In doing that, they can go on to inspire others. That's why I believe leadership is the most valuable commodity on earth. I don't have time to doubt that belief and, if I do, I just re-engage and reconnect to what I'm doing and why I'm doing it.

Having a Vision

When I am connecting to my purpose every day, the question I like to ask myself and ask of others is, *"How do you see yourself?"*

This is why the work I do with Patti Dobrowolski has been so powerful for organisations and the people within them. By drawing pictures, they start to see a future that compels them to move forwards and they see the part they have to play.

To clarify the vision, right now, as I'm writing this book, I'm looking up on the wall, looking at the exercise I've done with Patti. In our leadership work together, I've defined the three bold acts that I need to take every single day: to commit to my purpose, to connect to my purpose and to love my purpose. They help me to choose love not fear, and to keep going no matter what.

Vision expands all of the horizons. This is how we can slowly start to build the most important element to supporting a powerful purpose, and that is **belief.**

Believe it!

What do you believe about leadership? What makes a great leader? What does it take?

When you look at some of the great leaders, such as Martin Luther King and Gandhi, they seem to have unwavering belief in something.

But did they? Did they move without doubt and hesitation? Or did they move forward **despite** fear, worry and doubt?

This is what great leaders, pioneers and visionaries do. Take Elon Musk as a contemporary example. He sees the world as it must be. When he was interviewed recently about the development of one of his cars, he thought that it might not work. That didn't stop him, though, because he thought at the time, 'this is too important not to give it a go.'

Musk is 100% authentic. When he has shared some of his ideas, the audience has laughed because they thought they were ridiculous. Musk doesn't. He's very driven towards making the world a better place. He never listened to his duck saying, "Oh, well. That's just silly." He believes that the ideas he comes up with are worth exploring even if they aren't successful. He believes in who he is and what he does.

This is the power of belief. Belief is a state of habit, of mind, in which trust or confidence is placed in some person or thing.

Do you believe?

This is where things start to get really interesting. I challenge you that the decisions you make today, and the ones you make in the future, are based on the same level of belief in yourself as Musk has in himself. Everything you do from now on should be shaped by your vision of the impact that you want to have in the world.

This is where we need to develop even more curiosity about the things that we believe, and where these beliefs come from.

Where do beliefs come from, Mummy?

Sometimes we have core beliefs, which are our deepest convictions. What is fascinating to me, as I've mentioned already in this book, is we naturally get to see the best in people when they're driven away from things, when catastrophes are upon us. It is then that core beliefs often show up. *People are more important than money* for example. *There is an answer for everything.* That's one of mine. *Everything happens for a reason.* I believe that too – and it is one that I see show up quite often.

When we aren't in a crisis, though, people often don't pay any attention to what they believe. They do what they have to do but, when they aren't working towards something, they can become like zombies, often consuming, not contributing just 'doing the do' and not questioning why.

Then there are cultural beliefs, which are the things we've grown up hearing. *There are starving kids in the world so always eat what's on your plate.* Or *Children should be seen and not heard.* Even though deep down we know it's nonsense, we've gone along with it so we choose to believe in it. Once upon a time, though, it was never our belief.

Many of the beliefs we have, have been handed down to us. Are you afraid of something because your Mum or Dad was?

Other beliefs have been passed on to us through advertising. Do you really *Love or hate Marmite*? Surely there are people who don't care one way or another? And who dictates that *Once you pop, you can't stop?* Since when was that an excuse for over-eating?

Movie Time

In *The Help,* the film is set in a time when generations of beliefs are being questioned and challenged and it is painful. The world is full of fear – of the changes that are coming and what that might mean; of the consequences of following new beliefs; of the fear of being who we truly are because of what others might think.

We see this most clearly in Charlotte, Skeeter's mother. She dismissed the family's long-serving help because of one moment of embarrassment in front of people whose respect she desired.

Later, recognising what Skeeter has been a part of, in waking people up to the rights of the maids who were part of the family and yet not included, she says, "They say that courage sometimes skips a generation. Thank you for bringing it back to our family."

This constant exposure to external belief shapes who we are and how we see ourselves. There've been many times in my life where I've doubted myself or my abilities, 'What am I doing here?' 'Does this person believe in me?'

What was a massive game changer for me was when I truly decided to connect to my purpose to inspire people to be better than their best every single day.

See it to believe it

> *You don't manifest what you want, you manifest what you believe*
> **Oprah Winfrey**

Here, then, is a reality check for you. What do you believe? Do you believe that you're an Inspirator? What do you actually believe an Inspirator does? Whether you believe it or not isn't as important as noticing what you say to yourself when asked those questions.

When I ask, "Are you an Inspirator?" what do you hear? Do you hear a *Yeah, but* ... or a *I'm not worthy*... or *I'm not sure I've got what it takes...*

Many people do. It's both common and perfectly normal. All those things we've learned in the past inhibit us from allowing ourselves to believe.

 Story Time

When I was a boy, I subscribed to a magazine called *Look-In*. It came every week and was all about that week's TV and pop news. I loved it. In the end, however, I outgrew the magazine so I stopped subscribing.

We all subscribe to something but, in many cases, we carry on with our subscription long after we use it or need it. Plenty of us continue to get a magazine long after we've stopped reading it, or stay a member of the gym even though we never go.

The same can be said for beliefs. We subscribe to them because they serve a purpose at the time but then we continue to use them long after they have ceased to serve us – they become 'limiting beliefs.'

And what's the antidote to limiting beliefs? A deep purpose that drives you forwards.

I invite you to take a look around you and become aware of how others feel lost and confused because they have bought a subscription to limiting beliefs. Is it any wonder that the world seems so messed up?

I encourage all of you to start looking at your beliefs as if they are something you've been paying a subscription to and to become curious. Be the detective in your own life and, with the beliefs that you have, ask yourself, *Is this 100% true? Where does this belief come from? Who would I be without this belief?* Rather than looking at your beliefs as right or wrong, just see them as an investment and ask yourself what is the cost of continuing to believe.

The power of belief

Story Time

This is a story that I don't often tell because my grandma told me not to talk about sex, money, religion or politics (a belief of hers which I have adopted, up to point). I feel that there's a point to this story that must be told though.

I was giving a talk once to a group of health and fitness professionals, and I wanted them to look at the beliefs that they had, because for most people in the fitness industry, they're not going to get very far. They work very long hours and there's only so much work they can do in a day. So I wanted to find out what they believed.

I asked them, "What is something that is 100% true?" People said things like, "The sun comes up every day", "I'm a man", "I'm a woman" and then someone said, "Jesus is the Son of God."

I paused for a moment and then asked him, "Is that true?" and he said, "Yes, unquestionably true."

I paused again – you can probably guess what my duck was up to by now.

I asked how many people in the room believed that Jesus was the son of God and, as you might expect, not everyone put their hands up.

I asked the man with the devout belief, "Are you saying that all of these people are wrong?"

He replied, "Yes."

I just said, "Okay, let's just move on. I respect your beliefs. Let's just move on," and I carried on.

After a few minutes, he announced to the room that what I was saying was blasphemy. The duck was having real fun with me now. *I'm going to lose the room if he doesn't stop. Why won't anybody else do something. Why can't he see that other people have other beliefs?*[2]

All I said, was, "Okay, well once again I respect what you believe but I'm not telling you what I believe. I'm just telling you, not everyone in this room agrees with what you believe."

He then told me that he could prove that Jesus was the son of God.

Well, I wasn't about to pass that up, so I said, "Okay, what's your proof?"

He said, "It's in the Bible."

I then asked the rest of the room, "Does everyone here believe that what is in the Bible is true?" And again, not everybody agreed with this man.

I asked my determined friend, "Are you saying that all these people are wrong?" And he replied, "Yes."

Continued on next page

---

[2] *And, because I am of a certain age, the very frivolous part of my brain was replaying the stoning scene from Monty Python's Life of Brian.*

> We had reached a point where the conversation really wasn't going any-where. This person clearly had a very, strong belief about something that was really important but he struggled with the fact that not everyone believed what he believed.
>
> I moved on once again and once again he interrupted me and, in the end, he was asked to leave the room and someone spoke to him outside.
>
> At the end of the session he came up to me and said, "Look, I'm really sorry about interrupting you, but Jesus *is* the Son of God."

The reason I tell you this story, of course, isn't to get into a debate about whether Jesus is or is not the son of God but just to show the power of belief. The influence it can have on people's lives is immense, especially if they feel that they are responsible for others or they feel they must be the best at everything or they feel they must be in control at all times.

 What do you believe with **absolute conviction?** What do you need to believe to take you forward in life and to be an Inspirator?

Question your beliefs and build ones that take you towards your purpose, but be-ware of forcing anyone else to have your beliefs.

Questioning purpose – Inspire other people

What if it were true that the purpose of your life is to grow, to get better and to leave a legacy? And what if it were true that the root of all people's suffering is the fact that they're not aware of that, they're not living it and they're just existing?

This is quite simply the difference that makes the difference. So let's stop for a minute and ask ourselves, "What do people want?"

Is it true that we all want the same thing? That we all want to be part of some-thing, we all want something to believe in, we want love and we want to make a difference?

What do *you* believe?

What if your role as an Inspirator is to coach people, to support people into believing in themselves much more, believing that they do make a difference, and they can be the difference that makes the difference? To have the faith in them-selves to follow their own purpose?

So, help them to see that certain things they've come to believe aren't true. In-vite them to see that see that that they can now let go of things they've subscribed to in the past.

What I mean by that is, it is our role is to help people find their own calling, their own life's purpose.

How do we find that out?

As I've already mentioned, by questioning.

What is it that will light people up? What is it that will make people come alive? What is it that will align people to the leader's vision, to the business' vision and ultimately the success of an organisation?

Can you believe that one day your organisation will be full of people who are inspired and purposeful? Do you believe you can start work on this right now? Can you show people how to connect to what they're here to do? Can you then show them that daily life in the work that they do is their opportunity to connect to their purpose? Then in every moment, moment to moment, they have the opportunity to live their lives on purpose.

Glyn House

I say to my team, '60% of it comes from you, 20% comes from me, and 20% comes from the organisation. We're going to put you on some courses. We're going to get you to read some books. We're going to expose you to some different thinking. I'm going to give you some feedback and maybe some counsel that I've learned, and 60% you're going to have to work out yourself.'

> More gold has been mined from the thoughts of men than has been taken from the earth.
>
> *Napoleon Hill*

Deep Work

Ikigai

Finding your Ikigai is not a simple and easy process but here is a tool which can help you think about it. First of all, write three lists:

1. What do I love to do?
2. What does the world need?
3. What am I good at?

Create a long list and don't try to fit them into any particular pattern. This is about free association and getting everything out of your head and onto the paper.

Then look at those three lists and map them out into three interconnecting circles:

In theory, your Ikigai is where those three circles overlap but, if it doesn't occur to you, then don't try to force it. It can take time to realise your purpose and, for many, it shows up when we least expect it and not where we are looking for it.

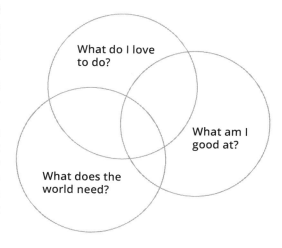

Repeat the exercise regularly and encourage those around you to do it too. It can be really powerful.

Message in a bottle

In Chapter 1, I asked you to consider what would be the message in a bottle which had washed up on the shore of your life. I invite you now to repeat that exercise:

Image you have found a bottle, washed up on the shore and it contains your one true message. If that was you, what might your one true message be?

What's your story?

There are many questions to help you find your purpose, but whether it comes to you in a moment of inspiration, or slowly dawns upon you over the course of many months, will be for you to discover.

It may be that, now, having completed this book out of a desire to be an Inspirator, you will want to repeat it, with the thought, instead, of finding your purpose.

Coaching questions
1. Who are you committed to becoming?
2. What would you do if you knew you couldn't fail?
3. What has driven you forward in the past?
4. What drives you forward now?

And finally...

> Learn to get in touch with the silence within yourself and know that everything in life has purpose. There are no mistakes, no coincidence; All events are blessings given to us to learn from.
>
> **Elisabeth Kübler-Ross**

This is a beautiful quotation from an eminent psychologist. Elisabeth Kübler-Ross is most famous for her 'change curve' which gets used and abused in so many organisations, but here you can see that she truly believes that life and purpose are interconnected.

Ultimately if you're going to take anything away from this chapter, it should be to decide what your purpose is at this moment in your life. This can change, of course, and it might be that your purpose needs many missions to achieve it and to help others to connect to it.

Whatever it is, always remember, you are who you are, you are important, you do make a difference.

Take a deep breath. You have done a great job in reading this book. Go and find a mirror and look at the person who stands there: someone who has gone on a journey and come out the other end.

My Dad, who passed away while I was writing this book, was a huge influence on my life. I've lost count of the number of times I heard him say, "If you are going to do a job, do it properly, or don't bother."

Deep down we all know if we have done a *proper job* of something and we know when we haven't. We don't need anyone else to tell us.

Smile.

Ask then: *What next?*

This isn't a book that you just read. This is a book that you apply. This is a book to put your heart and soul into and, when you do, you will not only become incredible, **you will become an Inspirator**.

But wait, there's more...

12½:

Mastery

Making success a habit.

You've been given a great gift, George; a chance to see what the world would be like without you.

Clarence – It's a Wonderful Life

In this chapter, we will explore
- persistence and consistency as the keys to mastery
- why it is so important to focus on the fundamentals
- mastering the mundane
- the tool to live your life by.

Movie Time

Of all the classic films to pick, *It's a Wonderful Life* is one of the best. It illustrates the themes of this chapter perfectly. Not because of the outcome – George Bailey's recognition of all he has – but because of where he has spent most of his life. If you haven't watched it, I do recommend that you take a few hours out of your busy life to do so.

George's focus has always been on the horizon – being an architect, travelling the world, leaving his home town of Bedford Falls, being wealthy – and never on the journey.

He is always looking at the destination as a place where happiness can be found.

Leadership is the same. As I've already said, so many people consider it as the destination and expect that, when they get that promotion, they can sit back and relax. "I've done it. I'm a leader. Job done."

Just like George.

And, just like George, I want you to recognise that leadership (and happiness) is not just about the destination. It is in the small steps you take every day to be the example.

We all know that success leaves clues. One of the things this book sets out to do is show you a different perspective of what great leadership really is. One component that shines throughout is how great leaders are always looking to get better. Inspirators have figured out that they need to grow. It's called *syntropy*. In order for us to do that, we have to go up against internal and external forces. That's why we always need to be at our best.

Recently, at a workshop that I gave to leaders, I started by asking the question, "Have you ever been outside and it's been cold or miserable or damp and you couldn't wait to get back inside? And when you came back inside you literally went, 'Ahhh' because it was comfortable and it was warm? It was a great place to be."

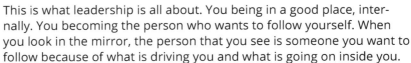

This is what leadership is all about. You being in a good place, internally. You becoming the person who wants to follow yourself. When you look in the mirror, the person that you see is someone you want to follow because of what is driving you and what is going on inside you.

It is saying, "Now what needs to be done?" when you look in the mirror and feel fear, worry or doubt.

Great leaders have rituals which ground them when things are challenging or they're busy or things don't go to plan. They understand that, sometimes, they are 'off being on.' They can look in the mirror and say, "I'm ready."

Their purpose inspires them to brave the cold and they have developed the skill of showing others how to do the same. Being an Inspirator is not just about you braving the cold but about helping others to do the same.

This is where the concept of mastery comes in.

Movie Time

Frank Capra's classic movie sees George finding love, a career and a loving family – everything many of us wish for.

For him it is a burden because he wanted something else for himself and he believes he isn't making a difference to the world.

Mastery is not a process. It's about staying on the path no matter what. We must master mastery.

Mastery is something which seems to be frowned upon today. Everyone wants everything **now** and people find it hard to work and to commit to something especially when there's external pressure on them. People sigh over their habits of smoking or eating sugar or lying on the couch binge-watching TV, but the idea of healthy habits are met with resistance and ridicule. For a leader, this is one of the greatest challenges that you will face in your journey to becoming an Inspirator.

You might have great intentions. You might be working on habits and rituals to bring your best self into the world each and every day and then, all of a sudden, when something happens that you didn't want to happen, everything falls apart.

This is my call to you as your coach. I want you to imagine me saying to you, "When the going gets tough, you should rely on something that brings you back to the path – so you can see where you are going with confidence and clarity. What you should be relying on is your rituals. Your daily practice."

Mastery is not an act. It's a habit. It's an example you set every single day.

This is where this chapter is going to hit home and why it is an extra chapter. It isn't a **part** of the journey. It is in **every part of the journey.**

This is about certain rituals and fundamentals. Some of those fundamentals are universal.

Movie Time

George Bailey gets to see a world without him. His brother is dead, his friend is a broken down drunk, his wife is a terrified spinster and his children don't exist. The entire community has suffered because George wasn't there.

His reward is the recognition of his place in the world and to realise that who he is, has made such an impact on the world.

Often, as we look for things outside of ourselves to make our world better and want other people to change, it is us who needs to change.

You have the power to change – remember that, way back in Chapter 2?

Is it okay if I make a prediction at this point? As we look at the universal fundamentals for your greatness, I predict that psychological reactance will come up – partly because everything we are talking about in this chapter is mundane, partly because no one likes being told what to do and partly because you're not perfect.

There is always going to be something that you need to work on and that sense of 'endlessness' can be discouraging. The rebel within you is nudging you to go back to what it familiar.

I mentioned before how I had the great fortune of working with some of the top golfers in the world over the years. One of the things that golfers really struggle with is not having perfection. They strive for perfection but when it's not there, they give themselves a really hard time. There's nothing wrong with striving for perfection but always understand that nothing is perfect. It sounds like a cliché, but all you can do is your best.

Every single day, you have the opportunity to do certain things, put certain things in place and then be able to reflect on *what went well and what needs work.* The hard truth about the journey to becoming an Inspirator is that it is not something that one can buy. Of course, you can buy a book to give you ideas, you can hire people who support you in this process, you can surround yourself with like-minded people who are all on the journey with you. Ultimately, though, it's down to what **you** do. You're the one who's going to bring your best self to the party.

Time to stand firm

Being an Inspirator is evolution. You have to evolve just as leadership has been evolving over the centuries. You must grow every day, as you chip away at all the different aspects of your life that it takes to inspire yourself.

In Chapter 2 we talked about the difference between us and animals as being how we make our decisions. They act on instinct and habit and it shapes their decisions. You can do the same, of course, but you can also decide to focus on being an Inspirator every single day.

If you do, you align yourself to growth. You align yourself to taking consistent action. And the more we act like the person that we want to be every day, the more we can expand into that person.

Being an Inspirator comes from applying 4Ps. **Purpose, Passion, Perseverance and Persistence**

> When you look at the word ***persistence*** it originates from the Latin, bringing together *'per'* – which means 'thoroughly' – and *'sistere'* meaning 'standing firm' or 'coming together.'
> Consistency has similar origins and therefore a similar meaning. It means 'to continue steadfastly.' In other words, keep going and never stop.

For so many people, this process of doing certain things each and every day might seem boring and monotonous, but it's much more than that. It's about consistency. It's about dedication. It's about growing. It's about setting an example. It's not about *hacking* at this – doing parts of it but not the whole – and then giving up after a while. It isn't about *dabbling* at this along with many other exciting programmes and getting nowhere as a result. It isn't about being *obsessive* about it – immersing yourself exclusively in this and forgetting about the rest of your life – then having to abandon it when some other aspect of life needs attention which can't be ignored.

It's about being an Inspirator and practicing.

If you make the commitment, you've got a really great chance of developing consistency in other people by being consistent yourself.

Humans have this incredible capacity to be consistent but we also have this incredible habit to get complacent when we see results. Then we get complacent with the things that we were being consistent at.

Simon Cook

If I was to put it into a music analogy, [a leader is] somebody that beats the drum and the rhythm of the music. What's the constant? What's the constant? For me, the constant is the purpose, why we do what we do.

Now is the time to remember, *The best is yet to come* and to go up a gear. That's where I want to help you really focus your attention around what you have committed yourself to doing.

> I once heard an expression, "Genius is not in the big actions, it is in the little things you do every day." I've mentioned *Genius* before as the inner light but light needs fuel to burn and habits, the little things you do every day, are the fuel that keeps your light burning.

It's all about rhythm. It is on that rhythm – those habits – that you build the strong foundations of your leadership. When you do, whatever the challenge, whatever new ordeal comes along, you will be ready for it.

> *If you plan on being anything less than capable of what you can be, then you'll be unhappy for the rest of your life.*
>
> **Abraham Maslow**

What else did Abraham Maslow say? He said that "What you can be, you must be," and he recognised that, right at the foundation of his hierarchy of needs, sit physiology and survival – in other words, health and wellbeing.

Focus on the Fundamentals

As a leader, you're in competition. Every single day, you're going out to perform. You are being looked at as the example, whether you like it or not.

I don't think this book would be complete without being really honest with you about how you take care of yourself. Is that okay with you?

The 30-second history spot

For many years, leaders of organisations have been known as the 'fat cats.' It stems from the times when people who were in position of power really were fat. They could sit back and they could afford to eat

Continued on next page

and drink to excess. Their obesity was a symbol of their success; of what they had, what they could eat, what they could do.

If we go back further, however, and look at the Greeks and Romans, they had a different approach. They dedicated themselves to improving their minds and produced may great scholars and philosophers. They prided themselves not just on their mental abilities, however, but also their physical and their emotional strengths.

What would you do if you had more energy – physically, mentally and emotionally? Taking care of health is about you becoming more energetic, having more activation energy and more willpower. It's about you connecting to yourself every day.

I invite you to listen to the interview that I did with one of the greatest nutritionists in the world, Dr. Robert Rakowski. He is the nutritionist to the Inspirators.

In the interview, he details what we call **The Magnificent Seven**.

Not a cowboy in sight!

The Magnificent Seven is a powerful strategy to help you get your health in check.

When most people think about health, they think about eating, moving, and possibly sleeping. These are extremely important but there's much more to it than that. As you will have guessed, there are seven things to consider.

Seven is a very powerful number. We see seven everywhere. Seven wonders of the ancient world, seven chakras of the body in yoga, the seven habits of highly effective people, seven spiritual laws of success, seven days in the week and now, the Magnificent Seven. It revolves around eating, drinking, thinking, moving, talking, sleeping, and pooing. These are clear indications of your health.

We have a very simple tool that you can use to track this and you'll find it at the end of the chapter. It is a circle that allows you to grade how you are performing every single day.

Take the time to listen to the podcast to understand it in more detail, and to read the overview in the tool, because the Magnificent Seven is your opportunity to use a very simple system and start to see patterns and to observe what is going on.

How are you performing with your health? Are you taking the lead? Do you have the energy you need every day to fulfil your purpose? Imagine for a moment that your body was a company. When we want to understand how a company is doing, we look at the books. If someone did an audit on your books now, what would they see?

If you want to know what great performance looks like then the Magnificent Seven is your way to find out.

And, as I've said before, if you experience psychological reactance, it is probably a sign that you need to do some work on these fundamentals. If you don't see how important your health is or think it doesn't need work, then you are kidding yourself. I strongly recommend that you seek out a coach or mentor who can help you. And re-read Chapter 8 to remind you of some of the consequences of ignoring your health.

You'll realise that, perhaps, if you didn't sleep well, it was because you were too stressed; or that you didn't go to the toilet because you didn't eat any fibre the day before. You start to see patterns. The Magnificent Seven gives you something to work on every day and I've seen countless people getting really, really good at this and transforming their life as a result.

Perfect Days

From all of the work that I've done with high-performing people, when you look at their habits, they leave nothing to chance. And, invariably, it's what they do in the morning to create their day that makes the difference.

They have rituals – the things they choose to do every single day. I want to make it as easy as possible for you to do the same. I want to help you build consistency and take you forward in daily small steps.

I'm getting you ready so you are more responsive when opportunities and difficulties come your way. This is how I suggest you do it.

In the personal development group that I coach, we have something called the *Mi365 Morning*. As the name suggests, it's a structure helping people map out what they do every morning. I want you to do the same. You're booking in time with yourself. If you only have half an hour, that's what you use. If you have an hour then use that. It is for you to decide how much time you want to invest in yourself.

By committing to a Mi365 morning you are stating clearly what you will do during this time, just like an appointment.

It isn't always easy. I know that many leaders have late nights when they are required to entertain people or catch up on work, but

Warren Rosenberg

My partner, Sarah, wakes up in the morning and the first thing she does is [say], 'I can feel, I can see, I can hear' and ... her cup's full and she's happy from the moment she wakes up. I've seen that consistently now for some time and to me, you can't ask for more than that.

I want you to 'discipline your discipline' and create time every single day to go to work on yourself.

As with any habit, it is essential to attach it to the idea of, 'This is where I want to go.' See the habits that you have every day as sending out little heat-seeking missiles that are locked on to where you want to go.

This is why the first hour or two of your day – every single day – should be about getting you in the right place mentally and physically; getting you aligned, getting you to commit – to recommit every morning – to where you're going.

Chris Roebuck

If we look at it from the purely financial perspective ... the bottom line on this is, if leaders do simple things day-to-day that inspire people to give their best, (which we know cost no money), [such as] showing you care, asking for ideas, showing people the big picture, it can put up to 10%, if not more, on the bottom line.

By starting the day right, you are setting yourself up for success. You are aiming for perfect days.

Of course, we both know that a day is seldom perfect. Nothing in life is. Think about an aircraft in flight. Perhaps 2% of the time it is exactly on course. The rest of the time it is heading somewhere slightly different and the pilot is making course corrections. In the same way, your days will never be perfect. Perhaps one or two days in 100 will be perfect. With strong habits and a focus on consistency, you'll be in a position to deal with the distractions that come up on the other 98 days.

Play the game

The best way to see this chapter is by seeing habits and rituals as a game. You're just playing a game. But as with any game, you need to understand why you are playing.

We play a game to win.

We want to have fun, of course, but if you start to see the game that you're playing – in your leadership and leading in the big three aspects of life – you begin to understand what it takes to win.

You're going to face opposition; your internal opposition as well as opposition from other people.

What you do in the mornings is a way of getting your mind right so you're ready to go out and play the game at the level that you need every single day. If it helps, think of it as your morning meeting – the morning meeting with yourself before the morning meeting with rest of your team.

Master the mundane – Inspire other people

If we are seeing habits as a game, ultimately you want the people around you to play for your team.

But why should they play for you? What is it that you're offering them? What is on the table?

People – all people – need to know where you are coming from. They need your consistency so they know you are a person of your word. In mastering your habits, they can see that you are demonstrating consistency in everything you do.

This is where we master the mundane because, let's face it, sticking to habits can be a bit dull. If you are getting up every morning, writing in your journal and meditating, you will soon be thinking, *I'm bored. Doing this every day is so tedious and I can't see the point.*

Remember what we said about psychological reactance in Chapter 3? This is one of the places where it is going to show up. Because, yes, daily rituals aren't exciting and can seem ordinary. They often don't deliver a result on the day you do them. Where they pay off is when you've done them for a few days or weeks or months. Then you look back, (one of the reasons you journal in the first place), and can see how you have improved and made progress.

Movie Time

George sees everything which is happening in his life as 'dull' and keeping him trapped. When he has to remain in Bedford Falls to manage the Savings and Loan business, all he sees is the mundanity of it.

With the change of perspective, seeing the outcomes of the life he leads, those daily habits then have a purpose and no longer seem so tedious.

It's about connecting to your perfect day every day and, even if things don't work out, it's about making a 100% commitment. Otherwise you leave a door open for other things to happen.

Let's say you are 90% committed to something. You'll use words such as, "I'll try…" or "If I can…" or "I'm cutting down…" When you do, you leave the door open for doubt and uncertainty.

Once you fully commit to something, you remove the doubts and hesitations because you know that you've made that commitment. And it shows in everything you do.

You become a person of your word. You will become a person who, when you commit to doing something, you do it. Those you lead will see that you are someone they can trust and will do what you say you are going to do – and you become the example to them.

Those around you see you improving and being more consistent. They see you getting healthier and having better relationships as well as getting more done at work. They see you tackling the things in your life that are in your way and committing to getting rid of them.

They see you being more consistent in how you interact with them too. Your intention to develop your people is an investment you make every day – not just for the life of a project or initiative or while you are reading this book.

This then, is the importance of setting goals but then working out the daily processes. By setting out the daily actions – the bold steps and also the really dull and boring ones – you move from your current reality to a desired reality and encourage other people to do the same thing.

Be the best you can be, moment-to-moment-to-moment, to be a shining example to others.

Deep work

We have given you a lot of tools throughout this book. Now there is only one more to introduce to you.

Magnificent 7

Remember, you are an Inspirator. You're performing every single day. You need indicators. You need markers. You need a strategy that gives you an overview of how you're performing every single day and making some small incremental changes will dramatically improve your life.

You can track how you have done against each of these on a daily basis and see what patterns emerge.

Magnificent 7

POO · EAT · DRINK · THINK · MOVE · TALK · SLEEP

Eat right

The facts is, most people don't eat particularly well these days. The number one cause of death in the world is malnutrition, due to people not getting enough nutrients from the food they eat. Some of the health challenges people face are going on behind the scenes and just by changing their diet, they can radically improve the symptoms or conditions they believed themselves 'stuck with.'

Can you, wherever possible, eat clean, predominantly green, and ideally, organic food? It's not about being obsessed. It's about being and doing the best that you can.

Drink right

Remember the proportion two-thirds. Two-thirds of the world is water and two-thirds of our body is water. Every cell in our body needs water. Most of us are actually dehydrated and we need to drink clean water and minimise everything else.[1] There are some crazy statistics coming from the US saying that 21% of calories come from the drinks that people are consuming. That mainly has to do with the massive amounts of sugars added to soft drinks and 'designer' coffees.

---

[1] *Unless, of course, you're drinking the world's healthiest tea and coffee – something that I recommend that all Inspirators switch to because of its incredible ingredient called Ganoderma, which is the most powerful super food on earth. If people want to find out more about that, visit inspirators.me so you can try these products and see the difference it makes to your life.*

Mental and physical performance can drop very quickly simply by not consuming enough water,

Think right

For me, this is probably the most important of the seven *Magnificents* because everything starts with a thought.

Poor thoughts lead to poor actions which lead to poor results. Good thoughts lead to good actions which lead to good results. Exceptional thoughts lead to exceptional actions which lead to exceptional results.

Our brains are the most nutrient-dependent, energy-dependent of the human organs and also the most vulnerable to toxicity and stress.

Emerging science is showing that our nervous system and our immune system really operate in tandem with each other. They influence one another.

Positive thoughts lead to positive emotions, which change our physiology and help our body to work better.

John Sellins

It's easy to go home and grab a glass of wine, which I undoubtedly do occasionally. You're just kind of masking issues. I've just found over the years having a fit body helps me ... clear my mind ... just running around the park for half an hour ... when you've had a rotten day. ...it just clears your mind.

I know I need my sleep. I don't like coming to work feeling physically under the weather ... I like to have a clear mind, feeling healthy, feeling refreshed; feeling relatively fit helps me do that.

Move right

Life is motion. We need to move – and I don't just mean exercising three times a week. Exercise sessions are great where you're working on your muscle tone, your muscle and joint flexibility and overall mobility.

Every single cell of your body is charged through movement, though. We need to move more. As Inspirators, we should be walking the floor and encouraging everyone to use their body for what their body is designed to do.

Sleep right

I'm sure I don't need to tell you that we live in a sleep-deprived world. How many hours did you get last night? And how rested do you feel right now?

There can be lots of reasons for poor sleep, but one of the biggest causes I see is that most of us are functioning on stress hormones rather than on rest and relaxation.

Talk right

Every cell of your body is talking to every other cell in your body. Life is about communication.

How you communicate with others is often a reflection of how you communicate with yourself. This is obviously related to how you're thinking but is also about what you say and the words that you use.

Listen to the interviews I've made with the Inspirators, they will use words which evoke positive emotions such as *excellent, fantastic, brilliant, awesome.*

What we say out loud is often a reflection of what is going on inside.

Poo right

Some people say you are what you eat. Some people say you are what you absorb. Others will say you are what you eliminate. What you eliminate – what comes out of your body – is a clear sign of how your body is working.

If you are struggling with issues with your digestion, then it can be to do with your neurological tone (your nervous system). If you're running on stress hormones, if you're not eating enough fibre, if you're not drinking enough water or if you're not getting enough sleep it can show up in how you eliminate. The whole system works as one.

What's your story?

We're going to come back to some coaching questions I have already introduced – because now I want you to make these questions a habit. Ask the first four questions every single morning and the other two every single evening.

Coaching questions

1. How will the world be better with me in it?
2. What are my unique skills, talents and superpowers?
3. Who am I at my best?
4. Who must I fearlessly become?
5. What went well today?
6. What needs work?

And finally...

> *If you are going to achieve excellence in big things, you develop the habit in little matters. Excellence is not an exception, it is a prevailing attitude.*
>
> **Colin Powell**

Colin Powell was an American military leader who served as a member of the Joint Chiefs of Staff and then became Secretary of State for Defense. He oversaw some of the most prominent American campaigns of the 1990s and 2000s.

If anyone knows about leadership, it has to be a military commander. They are asking people around them to risk their lives and, whatever you may believe about military discipline, bullying people into obedience really isn't effective. You have to be the example and Powell clearly knew that, to be able to do that, you have to build the habits that add up to excellence.

Where do we go from here?

The Inspirator's journey.

First of all, I want to thank you for coming on this journey with me.

As you know, this book was inspired by the work of Joseph Campbell and his *Hero's Journey*. We see it in nearly every film that you can ever think of. Someone is called to an adventure; they don't want to go; they get a mentor; they make the decision to step forward; they go to a place they've never been before; they face challenges; they get stronger; they form a mastermind-alliance; they take on the thing that once defeated them; they conquer it; they get stronger as a consequence; and finally, they return a better person.

 Do you ever wonder what happens after the film ends? What becomes of the hero when they have found themselves and achieved the task set to them in the film?

Are you ready for me to tell you what happens after your own journey ends? Do you want to know what comes next?

The life of a hero is one hero's journey after another. That is why there is a *Star Wars II* and *III* and more. That's why we keep revisiting *The Matrix*. That's why there are so many *Rocky* movies. The journey doesn't end and there is always more to learn and more to discover.

It is exactly the same for a leader. There is one leader's journey after another.

I invite you now to take all you have learned in this book and go out into the world to be the Inspirator. This is your next leader's journey.

The world needs more people to come alive and be fired up with inspiration to move forwards. I believe if you continue down this path you'll inspire more people to come on the journey with you. You'll leave a legacy on the earth – you'll leave a footprint long after you've gone. People will remember you.

This is my Driving Force

My purpose – my Ikigai – is to see the greatness in people and show them that greatness in themselves. In doing so, what we do and say on the outside matches what we do on the inside. We become shining lights, we become examples so other people want to follow us, but most importantly we want to follow ourselves.

As a leader, especially of people in organisations, part of your role is to bring out the greatness in you, so you can bring it out in others.

Perhaps now, the leader in you is inspired to be your ideal self in all the key areas of your life, each and every day: your health, your family, your friends, your relationships and your work.

Finding your mission

Part of this process has been about helping you discover your mission and purpose in life for, as businessman and philanthropist W. Clement Stone said,

> When you discover your mission, you will free its demand. It will fill you with enthusiasm as a burning desire to get to work on it.

As you feel the demand of your own mission and get to work on it, you will become the person you are capable of being.

I firmly believe that the turmoil many people experience inside themselves is because they're not being who they're capable of being. I recently heard someone say, "Hell is coming to the end of your life and meeting the person you could have been."

Are you ready to become the person you are meant to be? To look into the mirror and see an Inspirator smiling back?

It won't always be easy. I told you previously how my coach, Rafael, was so real, so transparent, so present, that I could see my reflection in myself. And I often didn't like what I saw. I saw parts of myself that I would hide away. What I've learned to do on my own leader's journey is to face up to those parts of me and do something about it.

Personally, I am absolutely committed to being the best person I can be and I challenge you to continue your own journey too. If I can help or assist you in any way, I'd be more than happy to do that.

Just visit inspirators.me, if you haven't already, where you can interact with other Inspirators. Here you can share where you're going, what's important to you, and how we can help you. You'll be surrounded by other leaders, as you continue this leader's journey on to the next one.

I mentioned Arambhashura in Chapter 2 a concept that has been around in ancient Indian Sanskrit for thousands of years, about being a hero in the beginning. It is as true now as it ever was that people start things with heroic determination, only for that desire to fade away after a few days or weeks of starting. You've seen it through to the end of this part of this journey and I salute you.

Ancient Intelligence

Now is the time for me to salute the greatness in you. *Namaskar* to you, as you continue on this journey.

There's an ancient Sanskrit word, **Namaskar,** which means *'to salute the greatness that lies within us.'* We have to salute the greatness of ourselves and others and seek to bring it out each and every single day. This is how we evolve.

As your coach, I salute the greatness in you. Whether you decide to use your greatness for the greater good is entirely up to you.

In a world that is full of artificial intelligence, it's the **ancient** intelligence that I want to remind you of in the summary of this book. Ancient intelligence has many things that Inspirators of the time said and are still relevant today.

I am sure there are many examples of this which you find personally helpful. Would it be okay if I share with you now, a few which mean the most to me?

> If anything is worth doing, do it with all your heart.
> **Buddha**

> If you bring forwards what's inside you, what you bring forth will save you. If you don't bring it forwards it will destroy you.
> **Jesus**

Perhaps here is where I should also be saluting the Romans, who believed that everyone had a genius inside them. So yes, I salute the genius inside you which has inspired you to move forwards in a positive direction, and to become the leader that you were born to be. It is the guiding voice that has helped you turn the pages, complete the exercises, do many things as you've been going through this process that perhaps you didn't want to do. Maybe it has helped you tell someone that you love them; maybe it gave you the realisation that there are certain things that you want to stop doing; maybe it has shown you how to face yourself in the mirror.

The greatest project, the greatest piece of work we will ever work on, is the piece of work on ourselves. We get to do it every day, chipping away, just like Michelangelo seeking out the statue of David in a huge and imperfect block of marble.

 Story Time

David, one of the Bible's early heroes, was himself on a hero's journey. As a boy, he had been anointed to be the next king but, not ready, he remained a shepherd until he was forced to face his destiny. It was David who took on the giant Goliath when not a single soldier in the army would. All he had was a sling and a rock, and, with them, he defeated his vast enemy.

I believe David represents the greatness in all of us, to take on the things that scare us. Just like Michelangelo chipping away at the marble, however, we have to chip away, every single day, to become who we're truly capable of becoming.

Competition

There's no question that when we surround ourselves with like-minded people, we end up vibrating at a different frequency.

If you're the leaders of many people, I believe it's absolutely essential that you surround yourself with others – those whom you aspire to become.

I invite you to enter into competition with these people.

Competition is a word that some people look at negatively (winners and losers – all about beating the other guy into submission), but for me it is a great concept.

I can think of a few people I am in competition with: my coach Rafael; health expert and nutritionist, Dr. Bob Rakowski, who is a massive part of the work that we do in helping people with their health; and Patti Dobrowolski, who creates a vision of the future that people and organisations can really identify with. These are people I'm in competition with.

What I mean by that is I get up every day to compete, to be like them. I don't seek to *be* them (I don't want to be anyone else!) but to learn from what they do to be a better version of me.

What this is all about is you being the very best that you can possibly be and becoming an athlete of your own life.

> The word *'athlete'* is a Greek word. It means *'competing and striving for a prize.'* If you're a sports person it's pretty evident what prize you're competing for. For leaders we're competing every day. And the prize is to be your own authentic self.

I invite you to really think about the prize of becoming the very best version of yourself.

I invite you to imagine meeting that better version of you in the future and seeing what you would see, hearing what you would hear, feeling what you would feel like to get to know this person. Because ultimately what is the prize?

The prize of the Inspirator is to be the person that you want to follow. The genius inside you will guide you forwards to make positive steps every single day and become someone who inspires others to do the same. As you become an example, others will follow your example.

Inspirator Equation

I want to leave you with one last tool to use. I mentioned in Chapter 4 the psychologist Piers Steel's Motivation Equation, but I'd like to take this to another level.

$$\text{The best } \textbf{you} \text{ ever} = \frac{(V^i \, | \, A)}{DIN_{st}} \equiv \text{An Inspirator}$$

Where:

V = Vision. The vision that you're aspiring to is the ideal you (that is the 'i' above the V – *Vision to the power of your ideal self*). The dot above the i that you see in the Inspirators logo represents what you are here to do. Being able to visualise the best you, the ideal version of you and your purpose is a key factor in being an Inspirator.

I = Immersion. You have to immerse yourself in your development. It's just like learning a language. The best way to learn a language isn't at school. To learn it fast and fluently, the best way is to live in the country and immerse yourself in it. Likewise, immerse yourself in your own personal and professional development. Make time available to you, so every day you're working on yourself.

A = Action. Recognise the action that needs to be taken, whether it's exercising, meditating, spending time with the people that you love or something else. Remember that knowledge doesn't bring results – it is applying that knowledge that makes the difference.

D = Distraction. Recognising when you're being distracted, personally or professionally, when you're going down a road that is a place you don't need to be.

I = Impulsivity. Here is where you are led astray and make poor choices rather than exercising willpower and focusing on what's really important.

N_{st} = Negative Self Talk. We all know it, either as a duck or a chimp or something else. This is the voice within you which tells you you're not good enough or can't achieve your goals or don't deserve the recognition and rewards for your efforts.

The goal, or course, is to drive up the factors at the top (VIA) and reduce the ones at the bottom (DIN) in order for you to be the best Inspirator you can possibly be.

Incidentally, *Via* is Latin for a road or route. This is the road to being an Inspirator, as we drive down the *din* in our lives.

Now as we bring everything together in this book, you must decide what is truly important in your life and create the time for you to grow, to develop and get better.

Let me say that again: To grow, to develop and get better.

And Finally...

You have a potential to fulfil. At birth, I believe, a seed was planted and it has assertiveness and it wants to grow and express itself. That's what you must do.

But wait! Not what you **must** do, (you might *must*-urbate, or you might *should* on yourself).

This is what you **get** to do. You **get** to be your best; you **get** to make a difference; you **get** to be an Inspirator.

What is the symbol that you will be left with? What is the theme of the rest of your life?

Life is one big adventure. Life is one leader's journey after another.

Acknowledgements

There are many people I would like to acknowledge in the writing of this book.

The first is my wife, Hannah Bradley-Cohen. The unconditional support that she gives me is ridiculous and I must be the luckiest person on the planet. She knows my mission is to inspire people all over the world and she understands the significance of this book. I appreciate her and I love her with all my heart.

There's nothing better than a great idea. The idea for this book came from Cosimo Turroturro of Speakers Associates (https://www.speakersassociates.com/). I am truly grateful to him because writing this book has impacted my life massively. In writing it I've really seen what it takes to be inspired and inspire others. There has never been a more important time for people to be inspired about who they are and what they're doing. Leadership is the most valuable commodity on this earth. Thank you Cosimo.

I want to say a massive thank you to Cate Caruth who has worked tirelessly on putting this book together in such a way that I'm really proud of it. Cate, your creative input and words flow through this book. Thank you for believing in me and getting my voice out there on this important subject. You are an Inspirator.

An extra special thanks to two incredible people, Mr Brian Johnson from Optimize and the incredible Dr. Bob Rakowski.

I want to acknowledge all of the leaders I personally coached and interviewed as part of the creation of the book:

Alistair McAuley, Delphine Rive, Glyn House, Richard Curen, Chris Roebuck, Neal Stephens, Patti Dobrowolski, Tony Taylor, Warren Rosenberg, Lucy Melling, Jon Sellins, Simon Cook, Chris Warburton and Drew Brown.

Your willingness to share your leaders' journey was greatly appreciated.

I also want to give a special acknowledgment to Joseph Campbell. His work around The Hero's Journey was a major source of inspiration to create what we call The Leader Journey.

Lastly, I want to acknowledge **you** for picking up this book and deciding to become the leader that you want to follow. I acknowledge you and I'm here to support you.

Join the Inspirators

You will find the full interviews with these, and other, Inspirators at: inspirators.me

Here you will also be able to apply to become a part of my Inspirators Community, a place where like-minded leaders in business and in life can come together to share their journey and support one another.

To create a free account, enter promotional code: INSPIRATOR-FREE at inspirators.me.

Get coached by Pete Cohen

As well as working with leaders in the top organisations around the world, Pete also coaches ordinary people from all walks of life via his unique Mi365 coaching community.

Mi365 is the most powerful and inspirational opportunity to create the life you want. The aim is to give everyone, regardless of their situation, access to world-class coaching.

Life coaching can be expensive, often requires travelling and you having to fit it into your life. Mi365 gives you the opportunity to decide when and where we will dedicate your time to get the greatest results that you want. It is incredibly flexible and you can work at your own pace.

Founded in 2015, this is the number one opportunity in the world right now for everyday people to get world-class coaching in the palm of their hands.

To find out more visit mi365elite.me

Further reading and watching

The films featured in this book

Star Wars (1997 – 2019). Dir: George Lucas. LucasFilms

Mary Poppins (1964). Dir: Robert Stevenson. Walt Disney Pictures

The Matrix (1999). Dir: Lana Wachowski, Lilly Wachowski. Warner Bros., Village Roadshow Pictures, Silver Pictures

The Sound of Music (1965). Dir: Robert Wise. Argyle Enterprises, Inc.

The Lord of the Rings (2001). Dir: Peter Jackson. WingNut Films, The Saul Zaentz Company

The Silence of the Lambs (1991). Dir: Jonathan Demme. Strong Heart/Demme Production

A League of Their Own (1992). Dir: Penny Marshall. Parkway Productions

The Darkest Hour (2017). Dir: Joe Wright. Perfect World Pictures, Working Title Films

Independence Day (1996). Dir: Roland Emmerich. Centropolis Entertainment

Erin Brockovich (2000). Dir: Steven Soderbergh. Jersey Films

Amelie (2001). Dir: Jean-Pierre Jeunet. Canal+, UGC-Fox

The Help (2011). Dir: Tate Taylor. Dreamworks Pictures et. al

It's a Wonderful Life (1964). Dir: Frank Capra. Liberty Films

Others books we recommend

The Hero with a Thousand Faces. Joseph Campbell. 1949. Pantheon Books

Start with Why. Simon Sinek. 2009. Portfolio

Think and Grow Rich. Napoleon Hill. 1937. The Ralston Society

Straight Line Leadership. Dusan Djukich. 2015. Corporate Reinvention and Associates

The Procrastination Equation: How to Stop Putting Things Off and Start Getting Stuff Done. Dr. Piers Steel. 2010. Pearson Life

The 5 Second Rule. Mel Robbins. 2017. Savio Republic

Getting Things Done. David Allen. 2001. Penguin

Fear Busting. Pete Cohen. 2011. Element

Shut the Duck Up. Pete Cohen. 2015. Filament Publishing

Forged in Crisis. Nancy Koehn. 2017. John Murray

The Seven Habits of Highly Effective People. Stephen R. Covey. 1989. Free Press

The Marshmallow Test. 2014. Walter Mischel. Corgi

Willpower: Rediscovering Our Greatest Strength. Roy F. Baumeister and John Tierney. 2012. Penguin

Grit. Angela Duckworth. 2016. Vermillion

Flourish. Martin Seligman. 2015. Nicholas Brealey Publishing

Drive: The surprising truth about what motivates us. Daniel H Pink. 2011. Canongate Books

Primed to Perform. Lindsay McGregor and Neel Dosh. 2015. HarperBusiness

Book Pete as a Keynote Speaker

Pete is one of the most sought-after inspirational keynote speakers.

> *The measure of success as a keynote speaker is not just relevance but impact. It's not just the immediate impact on the day, either, but the lasting impact of the days, weeks and even years afterwards. It's all about leaving an imprint and resonating with your entire audience. You create a buzz, people have had fun, they're inspired by fresh insights and new interactions and they can't wait to try them out for themselves.*
>
> *It is done by delivering surprising truths that encourage people to think and act differently. People don't change when we tell them what to do. People only really change when their perspective changes.*
>
> *I've been dedicated to supporting organisations and the people within them to flourish for over 20 years. As a professional keynote speaker and coach, I know exactly what holds people back. Most of us are caught up in our own heads. It's that noise, that interference going on behind the scenes and the self-defeating nature that the majority of people have learned, which holds them back.*
>
> *The fact is, there's a gap between where your business is and where you want it to be. That gap will be reduced significantly by having a more inspired workforce who have the tools and strategies to recognise and address the negative self-talk which blocks them. When they do, they are able to align themselves with the vision and the mission of the business.*

Pete offers quick, powerful interventions that can easily be applied and make a significant difference immediately.

From his in-depth research to create *The Inspirators: The Leader's Journey*, Pete is currently offering the following presentations:

Unlocking Potential: Mastering human behaviour in challenging times
- inspire people to align to the vision of the organisation.
- uncover the hidden power we all have to overcome obstacles and thrive in the modern workplace.
- tap into your talent to be your best every day.

Cultivating Leadership: Creating inspiring leaders in your business
- the new route map to becoming an Inspirator: a leader in a new age.
- become a leader who inspires others by being the example.
- understand how and why leaders are able to perform at a high level.

Resilience: How to have the mental strength to perform at your best
- the quality of your life comes down to the quality of your self-talk.
- cultivate emotional intelligence in yourself and others.
- develop the grit and determination needed to succeed.

Rethinking Wellness: Making 'corporate wellness' work
- make wellness a habit, rather than a short-lived project.
- simple coaching questions to tackle the vast majority of everyday stresses
- the power of coaching and how it compares to usual interventions for stress and mental health.

To find out more and enquire about bookings please visit www.petecohen.com